JUL 2 7 2018

2019
SUN SIGN
BOOK

D0974638

Forecasts by
Lesley Francis

Cover design by Kevin R. Brown
Editing by Andrea Neff
Interior illustration on page 19 by the Llewellyn Art Department
Shutterstock.com/54764008/© mart
Shutterstock.com/110290835/© Libellule
Shutterstock.com/122127973/© style_TTT

© 2018 by Llewellyn Publications
ISBN: 978-0-7387-4613-5
Llewellyn is a registered trademark of Llewellyn Worldwide Ltd.
2143 Wooddale Drive, Woodbury, MN 55125-2989
www.llewellyn.com
Printed in the United States of America

Contents

2018

SEPTEMBER
S	M	T	W	T	F	S
						1
2	3	4	5	6	7	8
9	10	11	12	13	14	15
16	17	18	19	20	21	22
23	24	25	26	27	28	29
30						

OCTOBER
S	M	T	W	T	F	S
	1	2	3	4	5	6
7	8	9	10	11	12	13
14	15	16	17	18	19	20
21	22	23	24	25	26	27
28	29	30	31			

NOVEMBER
S	M	T	W	T	F	S
				1	2	3
4	5	6	7	8	9	10
11	12	13	14	15	16	17
18	19	20	21	22	23	24
25	26	27	28	29	30	

DECEMBER
S	M	T	W	T	F	S
						1
2	3	4	5	6	7	8
9	10	11	12	13	14	15
16	17	18	19	20	21	22
23	24	25	26	27	28	29
30	31					

2019

JANUARY
S	M	T	W	T	F	S
		1	2	3	4	5
6	7	8	9	10	11	12
13	14	15	16	17	18	19
20	21	22	23	24	25	26
27	28	29	30	31		

FEBRUARY
S	M	T	W	T	F	S
					1	2
3	4	5	6	7	8	9
10	11	12	13	14	15	16
17	18	19	20	21	22	23
24	25	26	27	28		

MARCH
S	M	T	W	T	F	S
					1	2
3	4	5	6	7	8	9
10	11	12	13	14	15	16
17	18	19	20	21	22	23
24	25	26	27	28	29	30
31						

APRIL
S	M	T	W	T	F	S
	1	2	3	4	5	6
7	8	9	10	11	12	13
14	15	16	17	18	19	20
21	22	23	24	25	26	27
28	29	30				

MAY
S	M	T	W	T	F	S
			1	2	3	4
5	6	7	8	9	10	11
12	13	14	15	16	17	18
19	20	21	22	23	24	25
26	27	28	29	30	31	

JUNE
S	M	T	W	T	F	S
						1
2	3	4	5	6	7	8
9	10	11	12	13	14	15
16	17	18	19	20	21	22
23	24	25	26	27	28	29
30						

JULY
S	M	T	W	T	F	S
	1	2	3	4	5	6
7	8	9	10	11	12	13
14	15	16	17	18	19	20
21	22	23	24	25	26	27
28	29	30	31			

AUGUST
S	M	T	W	T	F	S
				1	2	3
4	5	6	7	8	9	10
11	12	13	14	15	16	17
18	19	20	21	22	23	24
25	26	27	28	29	30	31

SEPTEMBER
S	M	T	W	T	F	S
1	2	3	4	5	6	7
8	9	10	11	12	13	14
15	16	17	18	19	20	21
22	23	24	25	26	27	28
29	30					

OCTOBER
S	M	T	W	T	F	S
		1	2	3	4	5
6	7	8	9	10	11	12
13	14	15	16	17	18	19
20	21	22	23	24	25	26
27	28	29	30	31		

NOVEMBER
S	M	T	W	T	F	S
					1	2
3	4	5	6	7	8	9
10	11	12	13	14	15	16
17	18	19	20	21	22	23
24	25	26	27	28	29	30

DECEMBER
S	M	T	W	T	F	S
1	2	3	4	5	6	7
8	9	10	11	12	13	14
15	16	17	18	19	20	21
22	23	24	25	26	27	28
29	30	31				

2020

JANUARY
S	M	T	W	T	F	S
			1	2	3	4
5	6	7	8	9	10	11
12	13	14	15	16	17	18
19	20	21	22	23	24	25
26	27	28	29	30	31	

FEBRUARY
S	M	T	W	T	F	S
						1
2	3	4	5	6	7	8
9	10	11	12	13	14	15
16	17	18	19	20	21	22
23	24	25	26	27	28	29

MARCH
S	M	T	W	T	F	S
1	2	3	4	5	6	7
8	9	10	11	12	13	14
15	16	17	18	19	20	21
22	23	24	25	26	27	28
29	30	31				

APRIL
S	M	T	W	T	F	S
			1	2	3	4
5	6	7	8	9	10	11
12	13	14	15	16	17	18
19	20	21	22	23	24	25
26	27	28	29	30		

MAY
S	M	T	W	T	F	S
					1	2
3	4	5	6	7	8	9
10	11	12	13	14	15	16
17	18	19	20	21	22	23
24	25	26	27	28	29	30
31						

JUNE
S	M	T	W	T	F	S
	1	2	3	4	5	6
7	8	9	10	11	12	13
14	15	16	17	18	19	20
21	22	23	24	25	26	27
28	29	30				

JULY
S	M	T	W	T	F	S
			1	2	3	4
5	6	7	8	9	10	11
12	13	14	15	16	17	18
19	20	21	22	23	24	25
26	27	28	29	30	31	

AUGUST
S	M	T	W	T	F	S
						1
2	3	4	5	6	7	8
9	10	11	12	13	14	15
16	17	18	19	20	21	22
23	24	25	26	27	28	29
30	31					

Meet Lesley Francis

Lesley is a full-time practicing astrologer, intuitive, professional writer, teacher/facilitator, and speaker. She began her study of astrology in early 1974 while working as a journalist for Canada's fourth-largest newspaper and quickly found a lifelong passion, one that ultimately took her down a completely different path in the late 1990s after she left behind her 25-year career in journalism. This shift led to still more changes as Lesley developed both her psychic gifts and her very own intuitive tool, a deck of cards based in astrology.

Her monthly predictions graced *Llewellyn's Astrological Calendar*, the largest-selling calendar of its kind worldwide, for seven years, from 2012 to 2018, and she is a past contributor to other Llewellyn publications. Lesley has spoken at numerous astrological conferences, including NORWAC, SOTA, and the inaugural Canadian Astrology Conference in 2015.

Lesley can be reached through her website at www.lesleyfrancis.com.

How to Use This Book

by Kim Rogers-Gallagher

Hi there! Welcome to the 2019 edition of *Llewellyn's Sun Sign Book*. This book centers on Sun sign astrology—that is, the set of general attributes and characteristics that those of us born under each of the twelve particular Sun signs share. You'll find descriptions of your sign's qualities tucked into your sign's chapter, along with the type of behavior you tend to exhibit in different life situations—with regard to relationships, work situations, and the handling of money and possessions, for example. Oh, and there's a section that's dedicated to good old-fashioned fun, too, including what will bring you joy and how to make it happen.

There's a lot to be said for Sun sign astrology. First off, the Sun's sign at the time of your birth describes the qualities, talents, and traits you're here to study this time around. If you believe in reincarnation, think of it as declaring a celestial major for this lifetime. Sure, you'll learn other things along the way, but you've announced to one and all that you're primarily interested in mastering this one particular sign. Then, too, on a day when fiery, impulsive energies are making astrological headlines, if you're a fiery and/or impulsive sign yourself—like Aries or Aquarius, for example—it's easy to imagine how you'll take to the astrological weather a lot more easily than a practical, steady-handed sign like Taurus or Virgo.

Obviously, astrology comes in handy, for a variety of reasons. Getting to know your "natal" Sun sign (the sign the Sun was in when you were born) can most certainly give you the edge you need to ace the final and move on to the next celestial course level—or basically to succeed in life, and maybe even earn a few bonus points toward next semester. Using astrology on a daily basis nicely accelerates the process.

Now, there are eight other planets and one lovely Moon in our neck of the celestial woods, all of which also play into our personalities. The sign that was on the eastern horizon at the moment of your birth—otherwise known as your *Ascendant*, or *rising sign*—is another indicator of your personality traits. Honestly, there are all kinds of cosmic factors, so if it's an in-depth, personal analysis you're after, a professional astrologer is the only way to go—especially if you're curious about relationships, past lives, future trends, or even the right time to schedule an important life event. Professional astrologers calculate your birth chart—again, the "natal" chart—based on the date, place, and exact time of your birth—which allows for a far more personal and specific reading. In the meantime, however, in addition to reading up on your Sun sign, you can use the tables on pages 8 and 9 to find the sign of your Ascendant. (These tables, however, are approximate and tailored to those of us born in North America, so if the traits of your Ascendant don't sound familiar, check out the sign directly before or after.)

There are three sections to each sign chapter in this book. As I already mentioned, the first section describes personality traits, and while it's fun to read your own, don't forget to check out the other Sun signs. (Oh, and do feel free to mention any rather striking behavioral similarities to skeptics. It's great fun to watch a Scorpio's reaction when you tell them they're astrologically known as "the sexy sign," or a Gemini when you thank them for creating the concept of multitasking.)

The second section is entitled "The Year Ahead" for each sign. Through considering the movements of the outer planets (Uranus, Neptune, and Pluto), the eclipses, and any other outstanding celestial movements, this segment will provide you with the big picture of the year—or basically the broad strokes of what to expect, no matter who you are or where you are, collectively speaking.

The third section includes monthly forecasts, along with rewarding days and challenging days, basically a heads-up designed to alert you to potentially easy times as well as potentially tricky times.

At the end of every chapter you'll find an Action Table, providing general information about the best time to indulge in certain activities. Please note that these are only suggestions. Don't hold yourself back or rush into anything your intuition doesn't wholeheartedly agree with—and again, when in doubt, find yourself a professional.

Well, that's it. I hope that you enjoy this book, and that being aware of the astrological energies of 2019 helps you create a year full of fabulous memories!

Kim Rogers-Gallagher has written hundreds of articles and columns for magazines and online publications and has two books of her own, *Astrology for the Light Side of the Brain* and *Astrology for the Light Side of the Future*. She's a well-known speaker who's been part of the UAC faculty since 1996. Kim can be contacted at KRGPhoenix313@yahoo.com for fees regarding readings, classes, and lectures.

Ascendant Table

Your Sun Sign	Your Time of Birth						
	6–8 am	8–10 am	10 am–Noon	Noon–2 pm	2–4 pm	4–6 pm
Aries	Taurus	Gemini	Cancer	Leo	Virgo	Libra
Taurus	Gemini	Cancer	Leo	Virgo	Libra	Scorpio
Gemini	Cancer	Leo	Virgo	Libra	Scorpio	Sagittarius
Cancer	Leo	Virgo	Libra	Scorpio	Sagittarius	Capricorn
Leo	Virgo	Libra	Scorpio	Sagittarius	Capricorn	Aquarius
Virgo	Libra	Scorpio	Sagittarius	Capricorn	Aquarius	Pisces
Libra	Scorpio	Sagittarius	Capricorn	Aquarius	Pisces	Aries
Scorpio	Sagittarius	Capricorn	Aquarius	Pisces	Aries	Taurus
Sagittarius	Capricorn	Aquarius	Pisces	Aries	Taurus	Gemini
Capricorn	Aquarius	Pisces	Aries	Taurus	Gemini	Cancer
Aquarius	Pisces	Aries	Taurus	Gemini	Cancer	Leo
Pisces	Aries	Taurus	Gemini	Cancer	Leo	Virgo

Your Sun Sign	Your Time of Birth						
	6–8 pm	8–10 pm	10 pm–Midnight	Midnight–2 am	2–4 am	4–6 am	
Aries	Scorpio	Sagittarius	Capricorn	Aquarius	Pisces	Aries	
Taurus	Sagittarius	Capricorn	Aquarius	Pisces	Aries	Taurus	
Gemini	Capricorn	Aquarius	Pisces	Aries	Taurus	Gemini	
Cancer	Aquarius	Pisces	Aries	Taurus	Gemini	Cancer	
Leo	Pisces	Aries	Taurus	Gemini	Cancer	Leo	
Virgo	Aries	Taurus	Gemini	Cancer	Leo	Virgo	
Libra	Taurus	Gemini	Cancer	Leo	Virgo	Libra	
Scorpio	Gemini	Cancer	Leo	Virgo	Libra	Scorpio	
Sagittarius	Cancer	Leo	Virgo	Libra	Scorpio	Sagittarius	
Capricorn	Leo	Virgo	Libra	Scorpio	Sagittarius	Capricorn	
Aquarius	Virgo	Libra	Scorpio	Sagittarius	Capricorn	Aquarius	
Pisces	Libra	Scorpio	Sagittarius	Capricorn	Aquarius	Pisces	

How to use this table:　1. Find your Sun sign in the left column.
2. Find your approximate birth time in a vertical column.
3. Line up your Sun sign and birth time to find your Ascendant.

This table will give you an approximation of your Ascendant. If you feel that the sign listed as your Ascendant is incorrect, try the one either before or after the listed sign. It is difficult to determine your exact Ascendant without a complete natal chart.

Astrology Basics

Natal astrology is done by freeze-framing the solar system at the moment of your birth, from the perspective of your birth place. This creates a circular map that looks like a pie sliced into twelve pieces. It shows where every heavenly body we're capable of seeing was located when you arrived. Basically, it's your astrological tool kit, and it can't be replicated more than once in thousands of years. This is why we astrologers are so darn insistent about the need for you to either dig your birth certificate out of that box of ancient paperwork in the back of your closet or get a copy of it from the county clerk's office where you were born. Natal astrology, as interpreted by a professional astrologer, is done exactly and precisely for you and no one else. It shows your inherent traits, talents, and challenges. Comparing the planets' current positions to their positions in your birth chart allows astrologers to help you understand the celestial trends at work in your life—and most importantly, how you can put each astrological energy to a positive, productive use.

Let's take a look at the four main components of every astrology chart.

Planets

The planets represent the needs or urges we all experience once we hop off the Evolutionary Express and take up residence inside a human body. For example, the Sun is your urge to shine and be creative, the Moon is your need to express emotions, Mercury is in charge of how you communicate and navigate, and Venus is all about who and what you love—and more importantly, how you love.

Signs

The sign a planet occupies is like a costume or uniform. It describes how you'll go about acting on your needs and urges. If you have Venus in fiery, impulsive Aries, for example, and you're attracted to a complete stranger across the room, you won't wait for them to come to you. You'll walk over and introduce yourself the second the urge strikes you. Venus in intense, sexy Scorpio, however? Well, that's a different story. In this case, you'll keep looking at a prospective beloved until they finally give in, cross the room, and beg you to explain why you've been staring at them for the past couple of hours.

Houses

The houses represent the different sides of our personalities that emerge in different life situations. For example, think of how very different you act when you're with an authority figure as opposed to how you act with a lover or when you're with your BFF.

Aspects

The aspects describe the distance from one planet to another in a geometric angle. If you were born when Mercury was 90 degrees from Jupiter, for example, this aspect is called a square. Each unique angular relationship causes the planets involved to interact differently.

Meet the Planets

The planets represent energy sources. The Sun is our source of creativity, the Moon is our emotional warehouse, and Venus describes who and what we love and are attracted to—not to mention why and how we go about getting it and keeping it.

Sun

The Sun is the head honcho in your chart. It represents your life's mission—what will give you joy, keep you young, and never fail to arouse your curiosity. Oddly enough, you weren't born knowing the qualities of the sign the Sun was in when you were born. You're here to learn the traits, talents, and characteristics of the sign you chose—and rest assured, each of the twelve is its own marvelous adventure! Since the Sun is the Big Boss, all of the other planets, including the Moon, are the Sun's staff, all there to help the boss by helping you master your particular area of expertise. Back in the day, the words from a song in a recruitment commercial struck me as a perfect way to describe our Sun's quest: "Be all that you can be. Keep on reaching. Keep on growing. Find your future." The accompanying music was energizing, robust, and exciting, full of anticipation and eagerness. When you feel enthused, motivated, and stimulated, that's your Sun letting you know you're on the right path.

Moon

If you want to understand this lovely silver orb, go outside when the Moon is nice and full, find yourself a comfy perch, sit still, and have a nice, long look at her. The Moon inspires us to dream, wish, and sigh, to reminisce, ruminate, and remember. She's the Queen of Emotions, the astrological purveyor of feelings and reactions. In your natal chart, the condition of the Moon—that is, the sign and house she's in and the connections she makes with your other planets—shows how you'll deal with whatever life tosses your way—how you'll respond, how you'll cope, and how you'll pull it all together to move on after a crisis. She's where your instincts and hunches come from, and the source of every gut feeling and premonition. The Moon describes your childhood home, your relationship with your mother, your attitude toward childbearing and children in general, and what you're looking for in a home. She shows what makes you feel safe, warm, comfy, and loved. On a daily basis, the Moon describes the collective mood.

Mercury

Next time you pass by a flower shop, take a look at the FTD logo by the door. That fellow with the wings on his head and his feet is Mercury, the ancient Messenger of the Gods. He's always been a very busy guy. Back in the day, his job was to shuttle messages back and forth between the gods and goddesses and we mere mortals—obviously, no easy feat. Nowadays, however, Mercury is even busier. With computers, cell phones, social media, and perhaps even the occasional human-to-human interaction to keep track of—well, he must be just exhausted. In a nutshell, he's the astrological energy in charge of communication, navigation, and travel, so he's still nicely represented by that winged image. He's also the guy in charge of the five senses, so no matter what you're aware of right now, be it taste, touch, sound, smell, or sight—well, that's because Mercury is bringing it to you, live. At any rate, you'll hear about him most when someone mentions that Mercury is retrograde, but even though these periods have come to be blamed for all sorts of problems, there's really no cause for alarm. Mercury turns retrograde (or, basically, appears to move backwards from our perspective here on Earth) every three months for three weeks, giving us all a chance for a do-over—and who among us has never needed one of those?

Venus

So, if it's Mercury that makes you aware of your environment, who allows you to experience all kinds of sensory sensations via the five senses? Who's in charge of your preferences in each department? That delightful task falls under the jurisdiction of the lovely lady Venus, who describes the physical experiences that are the absolute best—in your book, anyway. That goes for the music and art you find most pleasing, the food and beverages you can't get enough of, and the scents you consider the sweetest of all—including the collar of the shirt your loved one recently wore. Touch, of course, is also a sense that can be quite delightful to experience. Think of how happy your fingers are when you're stroking your pet's fur, or the delicious feel of cool bed sheets when you slip between them after an especially tough day. Venus brings all those sensations together in one wonderful package, working her magic through love of the romantic kind, most memorably experienced through intimate physical interaction with an "other." Still, your preferences in any relationship also fall under Venus's job description.

Mars

Mars turns up the heat, amps up the energy, and gets your show on the road. Whenever you hear yourself grunt, growl, or grumble—or just make any old "rrrrr" sound in general—your natal Mars has just made an appearance. Adrenaline is his business and passion is his specialty. He's the ancient God of War—a hot-headed guy who's famous for having at it with his sword first and asking questions later. In the extreme, Mars is often in the neighborhood when violent events occur, and accidents, too. He's in charge of self-assertion, aggression, and pursuit, and one glance at his heavenly appearance explains why. He's The Red Planet, after all—and just think of all the expressions about anger and passion that include references to the color red or the element of fire: "Grrr!" "Seeing red." "Hot under the collar." "All fired up." "Hot and heavy." You get the idea. Mars is your own personal warrior. He describes how you'll react when you're threatened, excited, or angry.

Jupiter

Santa Claus. Luciano Pavarotti with a great big smile on his face as he belts out an amazing aria. Your favorite uncle who drinks too much, eats too much, and laughs far too loud—yet never fails to go well above and beyond the call of duty for you when you need him. They're all perfect examples of Jupiter, the King of the Gods, the giver of all things good, and the source of extravagance, generosity, excess, and benevolence in our little corner of the Universe. He and Venus are the heavens' two most popular planets—for obvious reasons. Venus makes us feel good. Jupiter makes us feel absolutely over-the-top excellent. In Jupiter's book, if one is good, it only stands to reason that two would be better, and following that logic, ten would be just outstanding. His favorite words are "too," "many," and "much." Expansions, increases, and enlargements—or basically, just the whole concept of growth—are all his doing. Now, unbeknownst to this merry old fellow, there really is such a thing as too much of a good thing—but let's not pop his goodhearted bubble. Wherever Jupiter is in your chart, you'll be prone to go overboard, take it to the limit, and push the envelope as far as you possibly can. Sure, you might get a bit out of control every now and then, but if envelopes weren't ever pushed, we'd never know the joys of optimism, generosity, or sudden, contagious bursts of laughter.

Saturn

Jupiter expands. Saturn contracts. Jupiter encourages growth. Saturn, on the other hand, uses those rings he's so famous for to restrict growth. His favorite word is "no," but he's also very fond of "wait," "stop," and "don't even think about it." He's ultra-realistic and quite pessimistic, a cautious, careful curmudgeon who guards and protects you by not allowing you to move too quickly or act too recklessly. He insists on preparation and doesn't take kindly when we blow off responsibilities and duties. As you can imagine, Saturn is not nearly as popular as Venus and Jupiter, mainly because none of us like to be told we can't do what we want to do when we want to do it. Still, without someone who acted out his part when you were too young to know better, you might have dashed across the street without stopping to check for traffic first, and—well, you get the point. Saturn encourages frugality, moderation, thoughtfulness, and self-restraint, all necessary habits to learn if you want to play nice with the other grown-ups. He's also quite fond of building things, which necessarily starts with solid foundations and structures that are built to last.

Uranus

Say hello to Mr. Unpredictable himself, the heavens' wild card—to say the very least. He's the kind of guy who claims responsibility for lightning strikes, be they literal or symbolic. Winning the lottery, love at first sight, accidents, and anything seemingly coincidental that strikes you as oddly well-timed are all examples of Uranus's handiwork. He's a rebellious, headstrong energy, so wherever he is in your chart, you'll be defiant, headstrong, and quite unwilling to play by the rules, which he thinks of as merely annoying suggestions that far too many humans adhere to. Uranus is here to inspire you to be yourself—exactly as you are, with no explanations and no apologies whatsoever. He motivates you to develop qualities such as independence, ingenuity, and individuality—and with this guy in the neighborhood, if anyone or anything gets in the way, you'll 86 them. Period. Buh-bye now. The good news is that when you allow this freedom-loving energy to guide you, you discover something new and exciting about yourself on a daily basis—at least. The tough but entirely doable part is keeping him reined in tightly enough to earn your daily bread and form lasting relationships with like-minded others.

Neptune

Neptune is the uncontested Mistress of Disguise and Illusion in the solar system, beautifully evidenced by the fact that this ultra-feminine energy has been masquerading as a male god for as long as gods and goddesses have been around. Just take a look at the qualities she bestows: compassion, spirituality, intuition, wistfulness, and nostalgia. Basically, whenever your subconscious whispers, it's in Neptune's voice. She activates your antennae and sends you subtle, invisible, and yet highly powerful messages about everyone you cross paths with, no matter how fleeting the encounter. I often picture her as Glinda the Good Witch from *The Wizard of Oz*, who rode around in a pink bubble, singing happy little songs and casting wonderful, helpful spells. Think "enchantment"—oh, and "glamour," too, which, by the way, was the old-time term for a magical spell cast upon someone to change their appearance. Nowadays, glamour is often thought of as a rather idealized and often artificial type of beauty brought about by cosmetics and airbrushing, but Neptune is still in charge, and her magic still works. When this energy is wrongfully used, deceptions, delusions and fraud can result—and since she's so fond of ditching reality, it's easy to become a bit too fond of escape hatches like drugs and alcohol. Still, Neptune inspires romance, nostalgia, and sentimentality, and she's quite fond of dreams and fantasies, too—and what would life be like without all of that?

Pluto

Picture all the gods and goddesses in the heavens above us living happily in a huge mansion in the clouds. Then imagine that Pluto's place is at the bottom of the cellar stairs, and on the cellar door (which is in the kitchen, of course) a sign reads "Keep out. Working on Darwin Awards." That's where Pluto would live—and that's the attitude he'd have. He's in charge of unseen cycles—life, death, and rebirth. Obviously, he's not an emotional kind of guy. Whatever Pluto initiates really has to happen. He's dark, deep, and mysterious—and inevitable. So yes, Darth Vader does come to mind, if for no other reason than because of James Earl Jones's amazing, compelling voice. Still, this intense, penetrating, and oh-so-thorough energy has a lot more to offer. Pluto's in charge of all those categories we humans aren't fond of—like death and decay, for example—but on the less drastic side, he also inspires recycling, repurposing, and reusing. In your chart, Pluto represents a place where you'll be ready to go big or go home, where investing all or nothing is a given. When a crisis comes up—when you need to be totally committed and totally authentic to who you really are to get through it—that's when you'll meet your Pluto. Power struggles and mind games, however—well, you can also expect those pesky types of things wherever Pluto is located.

A Word about Retrogrades

"Retrograde" sounds like a bad thing, but I'm here to tell you that it isn't. In a nutshell, retrograde means that from our perspective here on Earth, a planet appears to be moving in reverse. Of course, planets don't ever actually back up, but the energy of retrograde planets is often held back, delayed, or hindered in some way. For example, when Mercury—the ruler of communication and navigation—appears to be retrograde, it's tough to get from point A to point B without a snafu, and it's equally hard to get a straight answer. Things just don't seem to go as planned. But it only makes sense. Since Mercury is the planet in charge of conversation and movement, when he's moving backward—well, imagine driving a car that only had reverse. Yep. It wouldn't be easy. Still, if that's all you had to work with, you'd eventually find a way to get where you wanted to go. That's how all retrograde energies work. If you have retrograde planets in your natal chart, don't rush them. These energies may need a bit more time to function well for you than other natal planets, but if you're patient, talk about having an edge! You'll know these planets inside and out. On a collective basis, think of the time when a planet moves retrograde as a chance for a celestial do-over.

Signs of the Zodiac

The sign a planet is "wearing" really says it all. It's the costume an actor wears that helps them act out the role they're playing. It's the style, manner, or approach you'll use in each life department—whether you're being creative on a canvas, gushing over a new lover, or applying for a management position. Each of the signs belongs to an element, a quality, and a gender, as follows.

Elements

The four elements—fire, earth, air, and water—describe a sign's aims. Fire signs are spiritual, impulsive energies. Earth signs are tightly connected to the material plane. Air signs are cerebral, intellectual creatures, and water signs rule the emotional side of life.

Qualities

The three qualities—cardinal, fixed, and mutable—describe a sign's energy. Cardinal signs are tailor-made for beginnings. Fixed energies are solid, just as they sound, and are quite determined to finish what they start. Mutable energies are flexible and accommodating but can also be scattered or unstable.

Genders

The genders—masculine and feminine—describe whether the energy attracts (feminine) or pursues (masculine) what it wants.

The Twelve Signs

Here's a quick rundown of the twelve zodiac signs.

Aries

Aries planets are hotheads. They're built from go-getter cardinal energy and fast-acting fire. Needless to say, Aries energy is impatient, energetic, and oh-so-willing to try anything once.

Taurus

Taurus planets are aptly represented by the symbol of the bull. They're earth creatures, very tightly connected to the material plane, and fixed—which means they're pretty much immovable when they don't want to act.

Sequence	Sign	Glyph	Ruling Planet	Symbol
1	Aries	♈	Mars	Ram
2	Taurus	♉	Venus	Bull
3	Gemini	♊	Mercury	Twins
4	Cancer	♋	Moon	Crab
5	Leo	♌	Sun	Lion
6	Virgo	♍	Mercury	Virgin
7	Libra	♎	Venus	Scales
8	Scorpio	♏	Pluto	Scorpion
9	Sagittarius	♐	Jupiter	Archer
10	Capricorn	♑	Saturn	Goat
11	Aquarius	♒	Uranus	Water Bearer
12	Pisces	♓	Neptune	Fish

Gemini

As an intellectual air sign that's mutable and interested in anything new, Gemini energy is eternally curious—and quite easily distracted. Gemini planets live in the moment and are expert multitaskers.

Cancer

Cancer is a water sign that runs on its emotions, and since it's also part of the cardinal family, it's packed with the kind of start-up energy that's perfect for raising a family and building a home.

Leo

This determined, fixed sign is part of the fire family. As fires go, think of Leo planets as bonfires of energy—and just try to tear your eyes away. Leo's symbol is the lion, and it's no accident. Leo planets care very much about their familial pride—and about their personal pride.

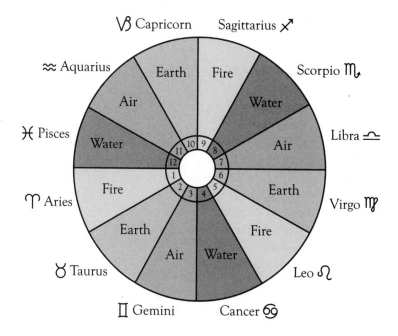

Virgo

Virgo is mutable and therefore easily able to switch channels when necessary. It's part of the earth family and connected to the material world (like Taurus). Virgo energy loves to work, organize, and sort, but most of all, to fix what's broken.

Libra

This communicative air sign runs on high. It's cardinal, so when it comes to making connections, Libra is second to none. Libra planets are people pleasers and the honorary cruise directors of the zodiac, and are as charming and accommodating as the day is long.

Scorpio

Scorpio is of the water element and a highly emotional creature. Scorpio energy is fixed, too, so feelings are tough to shake and obsessions are easy to come by. Planets in this sign are devoted and determined and can be absolutely relentless.

Sagittarius

Sagittarius has all the fire of Aries and Leo but, due to its mutable nature, tends to be distracted, spreading its energy among projects and interests. Think of Sagittarius energy as a series of red-hot brushfires, firing up and dying down and firing up again in a new location.

Capricorn

As the third earth sign, Capricorn is concerned with reality and practicality, complete with all the rules and regulations it takes to build and maintain a life here on Planet Number Three. Capricorn energy takes charge and assumes responsibility quite easily.

Aquarius

The last of the three communicative air signs, Aquarius prefers mingling and interacting with a group via friendships. Freedom-loving Aquarius energy won't be restricted—not for long, anyway—and is willing to return the favor, in any and all relationships.

Pisces

Watery Pisces runs on its emotions—and even more so on its intuition, which is second to none. This mutable, flexible sign is aptly represented by the constant fluctuating movements of its symbol, the two fish.

Aspects

Astrological aspects describe the relationships between planets and important points in a horoscope chart. Basically, they're the mathematical angles that measure the distance between two or more planets. Planets in square aspect are 90 degrees apart, planets in opposition are 180 degrees apart, and so forth. Each of these aspect relationships seems to link energies in a very different way. For example, if two planets are in square aspect, think of what you know about "squaring off," and you'll understand exactly how they're interacting. Think of aspects as a way of describing the type of conversation going on between celestial bodies.

Here's a brief description of the five major aspects.

Conjunction

When two planets are within a few degrees of each other, they're joined at the hip. The conjunction is often called the aspect of "fusion," since the energies involved always act together.

Sextile

Planets in sextile are linked by a 60-degree angle, creating an exciting, stimulating astrological "conversation." These planets encourage, arouse, and excite each other.

Square

The square aspect is created by linking energies in a 90-degree angle—which tends to be testy and sometimes irritating but always action-oriented.

Trine

The trine is the "lazy" aspect. When planets are in this 120-degree angle, they get along so well that they often aren't motivated to do much. Trines make things easy—too easy, at times—but they're also known for being quite lucky.

Opposition

Oppositions exist between planets that are literally opposite one another. Think about seesaws and playing tug-of-war, and you'll understand how these energies get along. Sure, it can be a power struggle at times, but balance is the key.

2019 at a Glance

The major theme in 2019 involves Saturn and Pluto. For the second consecutive year, they continue to inhabit the sign of Capricorn, inching ever closer to full-on contact next year. This is definitely not a union made in heaven. Each planet seeks personal empowerment, but for very different reasons. Saturn, especially in his very own Sun sign of Capricorn, is driven to manage and direct and even control what is going on so that he can put his personal stamp on things and feel the satisfaction that comes from that accomplishment. This means he is deeply committed to maintaining the status quo. After all, what benefit is there in building something and then letting it fall to wreck and ruin? This, of course, leads to direct conflict with the forces of nature and the constant reminder that nothing is permanent. Pluto, on the other hand, represents the complete opposite approach, that the only way to personal empowerment is through a total willingness to turn inward, dig deep, take everything you find, break it down, and transform it, and in doing so, reveal the true stuff of which you are made. That's the source of power—what lies within.

For more than twelve months, Saturn and Pluto have been eyeing each other, wondering who is going to emerge victorious. Because make no mistake, these two planets, who seek to express power in different ways, are on something of a collision course in your life unless you find a way to initiate a dialogue that honors the intention of each one. The first step is to understand that Saturn's nature is to shut down anything he doesn't find useful, while Pluto resents any attempt to control his efforts to get to the bottom of things. The next step to resolving this potential conflict is to find personal value in what each of them is initiating in your life. Then you can see how to use Saturn to harness and focus all the energy released by Pluto stripping away any inner detritus and transforming it. This is not just a desirable approach but a necessary one if you are to make the best possible use of their up-close-and-personal meeting in 2020.

While you are doing that, don't overlook the other big news of 2019: Uranus finally moves into Taurus on March 6 for his next seven-year cycle. Yes, you got a hint of what that might mean last year, but now it's time for the full story—and what a story it's likely to be. Uranus is a catalyst, always primed to remove anything from your life that no longer serves a purpose, while Taurus is a fixed earth sign whose innate nature is to preserve things, hold on to things, and nail things to the floor—not exactly a meeting of minds. It really is a case of the immovable object meets the irresistible force. So initially this is likely to be uncomfortable, to put it mildly. Since there is no way to predict with any certainty the exact details of how Uranus is going to turn things upside down, the best way to prepare is to accept that things are going to change in the area of your life you believe is the most safe and secure. There's no way of avoiding it, because change is inevitable. The gift in this is the opportunity to grow.

Finally, there is a very powerful trend toward working with the tangible and the feeling worlds. Saturn and Pluto are in Capricorn, Uranus is moving into Taurus, and Neptune is in Pisces, giving you an opportunity to access what they have to offer with a little more ease than usual because there is an essential harmony to how they interact. This leads to an abundance of opportunities, especially if you are an earth or water sign. If you are a fire or air sign, you need to work harder to tap into the benefits of this setup.

2019 SUN SIGN BOOK

Forecasts by
Lesley Francis

Aries

The Ram
March 21 to April 20

♈

Element: Fire	Glyph: Ram's head
Quality: Cardinal	Anatomy: Head, face, throat
Polarity: Yang/masculine	Colors: Red, white
Planetary Ruler: Mars	Animal: Ram
Meditation: I build on my strengths	Myths/Legends: Artemis, Jason and the Golden Fleece
Gemstone: Diamond	House: First
Power Stones: Bloodstone, carnelian, ruby	Opposite Sign: Libra
	Flower: Geranium
Key Phrase: I am	Keyword: Initiative

The Aries Personality

Strengths, Spiritual Purpose, and Challenges

Life isn't life if you are not ready to rush headlong into it, if you aren't in motion, if you aren't in action, if you aren't ready to start something. At the core of these strengths is the need to take a risk, any kind of risk. In fact, taking a risk is the same as breathing for you. Of course, there are many different ways to do that, but at the very center of your being is the push to put yourself out there. Without risk, you feel flat and out of focus because you are not fulfilling your spiritual purpose. This can lead to foolhardy behavior if life gets too predictable or you feel too confined. There must always be something to master, something to initiate. So you are constantly scanning the horizon, searching for the next adventure, ready to engage. The downside of this is you often rush away from things you've started before you really have the opportunity to experience them, leading to a vague sense of dissatisfaction percolating deep within. Recognize that always overcoming obstacles or trying to prove yourself can be exhausting. Too much adrenaline is just as depleting as not enough.

Use your gifts, chief among them your courage, your resilience, and your hunches, wisely and well. Know that you are always testing yourself, pushing yourself to new heights, and that sometimes you will fall down and go boom. Just don't forget that you have the greatest talent for picking yourself up and getting back in the game. After all, beginning again is the stuff of life for you. It's one of the reasons why you are always at the front of the line, ready for anything and everything. However, that capacity does not equate to you knowing all the answers, having all the answers, or being right 150 percent of the time.

Relationships

Your desire to be first and foremost is not always the best foundation for building intimacy and a sense of connection, making this one of the more difficult areas of life for you. Because you are so self-reliant and self-contained, you really don't understand what relationships are for, at least not healthy ones. Now this doesn't mean that you don't desire connection with others—you do. You just don't trust that desire because you fear you will lose your independence. The result is you often find yourself trying to take charge of others so you can keep them from trying to run your life.

First, you need to let go of the notion that being connected to others automatically leads to a power struggle. Communicate clearly what works for you without being pushy, bossy, or overbearing. This applies to all the relationships in your life, whether it's your partner, your children, your parents, your siblings, your friends, and even your acquaintances. Then ask them what they feel works for them, remembering to really listen to what they are saying. (After all, you do have a tendency to assume that what works for you will work for everyone.) Using an approach that is both open-minded and respectful creates real connectedness. It's a whole lot better than living in a constant state of believing that you have to fight for everything you want. That way you get to be truly present for the gift that only relationships can bring: seeing others and being seen by others at a heart level.

Career and Work

You definitely want to do something meaningful with your life. The challenge here is whose definition is being used: yours or someone else's? Well, it better be yours. So here's your list of requirements for job satisfaction. Freedom to come and go. Freedom to make independent decisions. Freedom to be a self-starter. Freedom to move around. Freedom to be self-determining (aka you don't want to ask someone's permission to go to the washroom). Freedom and opportunity to master many things. No doubt the list could be longer, but obviously there's a theme here. It's important that most of these desires be met. You really do best when you get to flex your reality and follow your instincts. This leads to the kinds of results that garner praise, raises, and advancement—all things that increase your self-esteem and confirm that you are number one. Your biggest challenge is to recognize that excellence in others doesn't cramp your style or dim your light. It just leads to a great environment in which to create and accomplish. This is especially important if you find yourself running your own business. Acting like you are the only one who has anything to offer leads to resentment and toxicity.

Money and Possessions

These are two things that are not primary motivating factors for you, in and of themselves. If they are the result of the risks you've taken and the things you've initiated, then they bring you a lot of pleasure and satisfaction. But generally speaking you are not inclined to see them as the sole reason for you doing something, nor do you really have a deep desire to accumulate stuff, unless it's connected to the things you love to do. However, having a lot of possessions doesn't make you any happier than not having them. Your biggest challenge in this arena is your capacity to forget to attend to the everyday details of life, like balancing your checkbook or going to the grocery store, which leads to overdrafts and an empty fridge—until you realize that these are things to be mastered like the rest of life, forcing you to make sure they are taken care of. After all, you can't have anyone accusing you of not doing the right thing.

The Light Side of Life

You like to play. It's as simple as that. Life without the space to have fun, to challenge yourself to try new things, is quite simply drudgery to you. Sometimes the challenge is that no one can keep up to you because you move from one thing to another with such speed. What lights you up is the desire to master something, to do something for the first time, to test yourself, to compete (if only with yourself)—all for the sheer joy of doing it, of feeling that rush of adrenaline coursing through your veins. When the adrenaline stops and the joy disappears, you move on, quickly and without a backward glance. You are truly engaged in the experience, and when you have had your fill, you let go. No hankering after what is gone. Just a willingness to live life to the fullest by always being ready to try something new.

Aries Keywords for 2019
Passion, purpose, planning

The Year Ahead for Aries

A perfect confluence of focus, determination, perseverance, and a deep drive to accomplish come together to make 2019 a year to remember. It won't be the most comfortable year you've ever had. With Pluto and Saturn challenging you in the areas of career, purpose, and satisfaction from the sign of Capricorn, you may feel like somebody turned out the lights and pushed you into the darkest hole you've ever experienced. This is a necessary journey from which you emerge with a new-found desire to use your strengths, talents, and abilities to go beyond what you know you are capable of to master what continues to elude you: the capacity to not just initiate something but to see it through to completion. This truth applies not just to your outer world but to your inner one as well. Self-awareness is not your first choice. Of course, you are aware of your body and what you desire, but you are not always interested in looking at the how or why of your life. At the root of this is your fear of being wrong. This year offers the chance to transmute the belief that you must never be wrong into an understanding that life is about more than being right or wrong. Its beauty lies in experience and what you choose to do with what happens, rather than whether you can put it in a nice, tidy little box that makes you look good.

Now, if all this sounds just a little bit too scary or ponderous for you, take a deep breath and dive in anyway. Use your innate ability to take risks and transform yourself from the ground up, from the inside out. Of course, there will be times when you wonder just who or what is running your life, because you are quite certain it isn't you. This is part and parcel of the transformative experience. You are the rattlesnake in the process of getting a new skin—the old one is coming off over your head and you can't see where you are going. This is Pluto at work. Of course, Saturn will want to control it. He's not particularly fond of things outside his purview (the third dimension), so keep him busy with plans, hard work, and concrete targets. This won't be difficult since opportunity comes knocking several times this year with a number of potential projects. Be choosy and take on only those that spark a deep interest in you. Otherwise you create such a conflict between trying to do too much and not doing enough. You need to keep busy in your outer world at the same time that you create inner space for that big shift that will alter your life in ways that will astound you. The year 2019 promises a complete overhaul of how you experience things, how you do things, how you feel things, and how you complete things.

Saturn

Saturn definitely pushes a number of Aries buttons in 2019. You find yourself struggling to overcome an overwhelming feeling that there is no end to the number of things you have to do, instead of the usual list of things you like to do. That's because there is a deep call to take your time and actually create a long-term plan that focuses on creating and accomplishing something of lasting value. In other words, what do your actions reap? After all, the initiating part of the equation, the getting started part, is rarely an issue for you. However, in 2019 there is a demand that you develop the capacity to sustain your efforts. And it won't be hard, because you discover that the fix you usually get from starting something and then quickly moving on is suddenly dissatisfying. You desire a more substantial outcome other than getting high on what you did in the last ten minutes. So take your innate desire for mastery and marry it to something that has deep significance. Or face the prospect of feeling like you dropped the ball—which isn't something that sits well with you. Saturn's message to you in 2019 is that failure is not an option. At least, not if you give up. Saturn offers perseverance and a quiet determination that, if you allow it, supports your impulsive, let's-get-it-started nature in ways that surprise you and please you. Embrace the opportunity to take a deep breath, then take a good look, develop a strategy, and, last but not least, follow through. What happens next takes your breath away and leaves you with a profound sense of satisfaction.

Uranus

There are some last-minute rumblings as Uranus gets ready to depart the sign of Aries for the last time on March 6, 2019. How much this affects your sense of who you are and how you express yourself in the world depends on whether or not you have been not only changing but growing as well. Now, as an Aries, movement is not an issue for you, but movement that you didn't initiate is a different story altogether. However, what you have learned over the last seven to eight years is that you cannot outrun the kind of disruption that Uranus brings, because he asks you to get rid of the deadwood in your life, to strip yourself of anything that is no longer healthy, and to wake up to new possibilities beyond the confines of your current reality. So the first two months of 2019 are about taking an inventory of where you are now compared to where you were in June 2010, when Uranus took his first tentative step into your sign. This is necessary so that, as Uranus enters the part of your world connected to all the things that you value, including yourself, you are a clearer, newer version of yourself, ready for the next phase of the rollercoaster ride that is Uranus. What he will be asking of you from now until 2026 is to be prepared to overhaul what you accumulate, whether it's teddy bears, retirement funds, people, or thoughts and beliefs. There is much that we think we own. But what truly do we possess? The next seven years will be about answering that question.

Neptune

It would be so much easier if Neptune announced his presence with a little more oomph and, well, something tangible. But the world of Neptune has little or nothing to do with that. He is the stuff of dreams (both day and night), imaginings, illusions and delusions, the world of all possibilities. Everything is wispy and ephemeral, which makes it difficult to pin down exactly what his influence is except to acknowledge that everything always seems on the verge of dissolving and/or disappearing, leaving us shaking our heads and pondering just what is real. Well, he is currently rummaging around in your unconscious. This leads you to wonder if anything ever actually happens or is it all just a mirage? The truth is some of what is emerging just might be inconsequential or it could be the harbinger of something truly magnificent. You just won't know unless you stand still and let all that Neptunian stuff wash over you and carry you along into uncharted waters. And, if you find this concept overwhelming, take up meditation, or go sit in a hot bath, close your eyes, and let your inner world swirl around in your consciousness. Neptune's job in your life right now is to take you to that place where you can strike up a conversation with the less obvious but nonetheless important parts of yourself that are the spark of imagination in your life. And remember, your strong sense of self is the only life preserver you need for this adventure.

Pluto

You've been in search of a deeper sense of purpose for what seems like forever (actually it's been about ten years) and, while on the search, you've been constantly bombarded by an ongoing sense of inadequacy that is quite foreign to your sense of self. That is what happens when Pluto challenges you from the sign of Capricorn. It is not enough to find that deeper sense of purpose; you must bare your soul while you are doing so—even if you only share that revelation with yourself. This process feels very much like undoing all that you are and all that you have been, because Pluto reaches so inexorably into the depths of your life and there seems to be no choice but to go along with it. Well, there is a choice. You can resist and find yourself in the most barren of places with nowhere to go, or you can embrace the unnerving invitation that is Pluto and run with it. Just not literally. After all, being in motion is your default position, and this requires internal shifting instead. Accept that this takes as long as it takes and 2019 promises to be a watershed year for connecting to what you desire next. Harness that to the invitation Saturn is extending and your capacity to take your rekindled passion for life to newer and better heights grows exponentially. There is no more successful combination than passion, purpose, and planning.

How Will This Year's Eclipses Affect You?

Eclipses signal intense periods that highlight major growth opportunities for us in the process of creating our lives. They are linked to the lunar phases—specifically the New and Full Moon—and involve the relationship between the Sun and the Moon and the Earth. A Solar Eclipse is a magnified New Moon, while a Lunar Eclipse is a magnified Full Moon. Eclipses unfold in cycles involving all twelve signs of the zodiac, and they occur in pairs, usually about two weeks apart.

In 2019 there are five eclipses, three solar (two in Capricorn and one in Cancer) and two lunar (one in Leo and one in Capricorn). The first Solar Eclipse arrives on January 5 and gives you a tremendous opportunity to tune in to the major growth theme of the year. Do you stick with tried-and-true results, or do you dig deeper into your core to find the raw material necessary to transmute long-standing emotional blockages into a brand-new outlook on life? To do this, you must take the energy of the Lunar Eclipse in Leo on January 21, with its focus on love and loyalty, creativity and fun, and use it to break down walls you have created to protect yourself. The push this year is to discover a new pathway to creating success in your life, and this out-of-sync Lunar Eclipse holds the key. Why is it out of sync? Well, eclipses occur in cycles that highlight pairs of signs: Aries/Libra, Taurus/Scorpio, Gemini/Sagittarius, Cancer/Capricorn, Leo/Aquarius, and Virgo/Pisces. This year the focus is primarily on Cancer/Capricorn, so an eclipse that is outside that pairing is by definition out of sync. Now this can make it an irritant or an opportunity.

For you, it is the latter because it occurs in one of your fellow fire signs. It's a powerful energy boost, something necessary for you as you start your trek through 2019, a year where the biggest challenges for you come from water and earth signs (Solar and Lunar Eclipses as well as Saturn and Pluto in Capricorn). You can harness this Lunar Eclipse as fuel to take on the challenges these Solar and Lunar Eclipses represent, including the two in July (solar on July 2 in Cancer, lunar on July 16 in Capricorn) and the final one of 2019 (solar on December 26). The reality is earth and water signs bog you down, so a year where you are pushed to grow in areas that can rob you of your usual buoyancy are immediately problematic for you. Most of the action and discomfort is connected to home, family, career, and reputation—your roots and your purpose. All are undergoing a rebuilding from the inside out, so you need to find a way to integrate the need to clear your inner emotional landscape of detritus without losing track of where your life is going in the outer world. The tendency at times is to focus on one while ignoring the other until a crisis occurs. This is probably not avoidable. The key is to maintain awareness so no matter what happens, you take your experiences and build something valuable with them.

Aries | January

Overall Theme

You are ready for fun and activity, so you won't get much rest and relaxation this month because your engine is on high as you enter 2019. Make a concerted effort to take a break from January 10 to the 12th or burnout will hit just as things really start to shake, rattle, and roll after January 20.

Relationships

Make sure you don't overextend yourself by making promises you can't keep, because there won't be enough hours in the day to show up for all the things you get invited to do. It's time for some discretion and prioritizing rather than operating on impulse. Otherwise you may find yourself in the doghouse with one or more of the important people in your life.

Career, Success, and Money

Unexpected opportunities manifest toward the end of January. Be prepared to grab them and run. A lot of hard work finally pays off, giving you a chance to plant new seeds. Keep discretionary spending to a minimum. Find other ways to express your enthusiasm and exuberance, unless you intend to invest in something that bears fruit for a long time.

Pitfalls and Potential Problems

There's a strong push to be more serious than you generally like to be. It starts January 1 and continues throughout the month, with Mercury, Saturn, and Pluto challenging you to be accountable. Pay attention or the Solar Eclipse on January 5 could set the stage for some unwelcome fallout.

Rewarding Days

12, 13, 25, 26

Challenging Days

5, 6, 19, 20

Aries | February

Overall Theme

Your energy remains in overdrive until February 14, when suddenly it feels like your engine is in reverse. Take advantage of the slowdown and recalibrate. Bouncing from one thing to another, as exhilarating as that might be, doesn't recharge your batteries. Eventually exhaustion sets in, a real possibility from February 6 to the 8th and again on February 24 and 25.

Relationships

Gone is the fun of last month, replaced by an overwhelming sense that everybody has a list of things you need to do. That's okay if it leads to some sense of personal accomplishment, but menial tasks are out of the question. This could lead to serious disagreements on February 4 and 5 and again on February 10 and 11. Take a deep breath and negotiate.

Career, Success, and Money

The shift that takes place when Mars enters Taurus on February 14 is so noticeable that it knocks you off balance until you realize that focus and planning are required if you want to take advantage of the opportunities that fell into your lap in January. Take concrete action and set the stage for the kind of visible results that lead to abundance.

Pitfalls and Potential Problems

The latter half of the month, with its emphasis on the elements of earth and water, leave you feeling stuck. With Mercury in Pisces, Venus in Capricorn (energizing the Saturn-Pluto combo once again), and Mars in Taurus, there's no dancing the light fantastic. Just stay the course.

Rewarding Days

4, 5, 9, 10, 26, 27

Challenging Days

14, 18, 19, 24, 25

Aries | March

Overall Theme

Things lighten up mentally on March 2, and that little bit of breathing room recharges your enthusiasm, a necessary thing before Uranus moves into Taurus on March 6 and everything starts to vibrate and intensify. Although you are happy that things are moving again, you are unprepared for the overwhelming sense that you are on the brink of disaster. Breathe.

Relationships

You've been more than a little tongue-tied (or is that lost?) when trying to communicate anything to anyone since February 10, when Mercury moved into Pisces. Well, buckle up. This state of affairs continues until April 17, when Mercury finally enters Aries after a retrograde period that begins on March 5 and ends on March 28. This is a good time for restraint and reflection as well as a few self-imposed timeouts.

Career, Success, and Money

Put your impatience on hold and remember that things are moving, even if you can't measure them on the scale that is intrinsic to you—which is somewhere between the speed of light and warp 10. It takes time to get everything in place, so trust the processes you initiated last month. Stop pushing, because that will only turn potential success into unrealized dreams.

Pitfalls and Potential Problems

Ignore the voice inside your head that urges you to escape the irritation and frustration plaguing you from March 5 onward by taking a risk—any kind of risk. With Mercury in Pisces retrograde, Venus in Aquarius, and Uranus newly in Taurus, the temptation is strong. Resist.

Rewarding Days

3, 14, 20, 21, 26, 27

Challenging Days

6, 7, 8, 9, 29

Aries | April

Overall Theme

You feel released from purgatory as Mars moves into Gemini. Your brain explodes with a multitude of ideas, but physically it still feels like life is happening in slow motion. Go inward and find the joy in small things, in things that touch you. It's the respite you need to move forward with renewed confidence and vigor.

Relationships

Everything feels fuzzy around the edges as Venus, the planet of connecting, moves into Pisces to join that retrograde Mercury. The message is clear: listen, be empathetic, and refrain from making pronouncements. It's a good time to realize you don't have all the answers and that being present for others is the best gift you can give.

Career, Success, and Money

You are so excited by all the possibilities exploding out of your mind that you can barely contain yourself. So don't. Record (either on a piece of paper or on a voice recorder) anything and everything that gets you excited. Somewhere in the midst of that chaos is a seed worth planting. You just can't see it right now.

Pitfalls and Potential Problems

Two messages emerge this month and they are at cross-purposes. The first is to hold down the fort and not stray too far from the known, and the second is to open up and let go, especially emotionally and spiritually. The first represses some profound changes trying to break free and happen, while the second offers a chance to harness that repressed energy in a life-affirming way.

Rewarding Days

4, 5, 13, 14

Challenging Days

2, 3, 22, 23

Aries | May

Overall Theme

Your idea of relaxation is not sitting idly by and watching the world around you. However, this is required on May 3, 7, and 8. Otherwise you fall victim to some mental impulses that, in the latter half of the month, make you shake your head at your foolhardiness. No matter what your head tells you to do, take a deep breath and sit down.

Relationships

Out-of-the-blue power struggles highlight a big focus on resources, both personal and shared. The underlying message is to take a look at what you value and stand your ground at the same time that you respect and acknowledge the choices of others. Remember, your reality is not the only one on the planet.

Career, Success, and Money

Just when you think it's clear sailing, life throws a number of curve balls that force you to reexamine the plans you put in place. Take heart. Consider this an opportunity to make some necessary adjustments. It might feel like you are careening toward a huge mess, but the unexpected challenges turn out to be blessings.

Pitfalls and Potential Problems

The answer to any bumps in the road you face is not to go faster, push harder, or throw caution to the wind. If something isn't working right now, let it percolate, and turn all your boundless energy toward the sheer pleasure of living and being. Not everything comes to fruition five minutes after you initiate contact.

Rewarding Days

1, 2, 11, 12

Challenging Days

17, 18, 22, 23

Aries | June

Overall Theme

Your usual get-up-and-go is either missing or on vacation. You aren't sure which. Added to this is an overwhelming sensitivity that leaves you wondering what happened to the fire in your belly. It hasn't disappeared; it just needs more fuel, something in short supply because you are running on empty.

Relationships

You are strangely quiet with the people in your world for much of June. It's more important to you to just hang out and be, rather than solve problems, direct traffic or prove you know all the answers. Of course, you are more than a little out of your comfort zone but the deep enjoyment and the even deeper connection that results is so satisfying.

Career, Success, and Money

The mellowness you are experiencing in other parts of your life extends into this area as well. Let it. It's time to take a break from micromanaging and trust that the things you set in motion will lead to success. There will be plenty of signs at the end of the month to confirm you are on the right path.

Pitfalls and Potential Problems

Inaction often equals an overwhelming case of the blues for you. Be aware that stillness is a quality that leads to the potential to trust yourself more deeply. It is definitely not the same thing as doing nothing. The month of June is the consummate testing ground for understanding the difference.

Rewarding Days

3, 7, 8, 25, 26

Challenging Days

5, 6, 12, 18, 19

Aries | July

Overall Theme

You start to feel your internal engine roar to life on July 1, yet you still feel bogged down. Take it easy on yourself by not pushing the start button over and over again until you are exhausted. Play, have fun, and let your need to be constantly in motion give way to a more focused application of your energy.

Relationships

Be wary of opening your mouth without first considering what you are going to say. It's truly a case of engage your brain before you engage your voice. Or else you are likely to say stuff that, while it may be true, is going to be hurtful, offensive, or disrespectful. Being rude is not the same as being direct. Find more diplomatic ways to share your thoughts.

Career, Success, and Money

There's only one question on your mind in July: Why am I not satisfied? And it won't have anything to do with what is going on in your external world. You are definitely on the road to redefining what success is to you. Is it mere accomplishment? Is it financial rewards? Is it something you can't identify? It's probably the latter.

Pitfalls and Potential Problems

The total Solar Eclipse on July 2 unleashes a wellspring of uncomfortable feelings that no amount of sentimentality can ease. It's time to go beyond the warm and fuzzy to a more complex definition of being connected that begins by seeking a deeper awareness of what you truly feel.

Rewarding Days

13, 14, 22, 28, 29

Challenging Days

2, 3, 4, 15, 16

Aries | August

Overall Theme
Life is happening at warp speed and you couldn't be happier, so there's no slowing you down for any reason. The source of this energy boost is a shift in your approach to life. The need for instant gratification is giving way to the recognition that you need experiences that result in a longer-lasting satisfaction.

Relationships
You are feeling all kinds of love and generosity as long as no one decides to stand in your way. You want what you want, when you want it. What's more, you believe you deserve it. Just remember, getting what you want isn't supposed to come at the expense of others. Being loving and generous doesn't include driving over others.

Career, Success, and Money
Every day feels like the best day you've had in a while. Life is easy and breezy and things are finally moving full speed ahead. And, as if by magic, nothing is getting in your way. Take a second look and you'll realize it's not magic but the result of marrying risk taking with good planning and determination.

Pitfalls and Potential Problems
Avoid running roughshod over the whole world. With Mars in Leo and then in Virgo, you want to be in the driver's seat 24/7/365, and that's impossible. What's more, it's not good leadership. Recognize that being a leader means giving others the space and the support to do what they do best, rather than doing it all yourself.

Rewarding Days
1, 9, 10, 14, 15

Challenging Days
18, 19, 20, 27

Aries | September

Overall Theme

Normally you are so confident in your ability to handle whatever happens that this internal nagging feeling that you aren't quite up to scratch throws you off balance and off course, raising your stress level into the stratosphere. Relax. No one is perfect. Not even you. And a little humility only makes you more attractive.

Relationships

Something strange is happening. You are easily offended by how others are treating you, leading you to amp up your need to be right in every circumstance. Much to your surprise, this doesn't alleviate your hurt feelings, nor does it change the dynamic between you and the rest of the world. Try sharing how you feel instead. It will only make you stronger.

Career, Success, and Money

Accept that this month requires a lot of hard work and recalibrating. Pay attention to all the details, no matter how trivial you think they are. Taking charge of your own destiny means being accountable for all aspects of it, not just the parts you like. This is a crucial month for creating long-term success.

Pitfalls and Potential Problems

Don't let the momentary feelings of irritation, frustration, and boredom while Mars is in Virgo derail any or all of the hard work you've done, both personally and professionally. This can only lead to confusion and a lack of direction, just when big success is within reach. Instead, take time to double-check each and every step you have taken in the last eight months. What you find pleases you.

Rewarding Days

7, 8, 24, 25

Challenging Days

10, 11, 16, 22, 23

Aries | October

Overall Theme
The desire to push things to the extreme without pausing to consider the long-term consequences is overpowering and, if not checked, leaves you overextended and overwhelmed. Listen to your body when it tells you to slow down and sit down, preferably outdoors in a quiet place.

Relationships
The best thing you can do this month is listen—to everyone and everything. This greatly improves the odds that you will end October on a high note in all your relationships, personal and professional, with a broader understanding and an abundance of insights about how others experience life. The wisdom gained definitely aids you in some unexpected ways before the end of the year.

Career, Success, and Money
Be cautious about any impulse to be extravagant, with your money, your time, or your energy. Whether you like it or not, there are limits, and this is a month when you do need to acknowledge that or you may end up in some very sticky situations, ones that no amount of take-charge bravado can easily remedy.

Pitfalls and Potential Problems
The biggest question this month is whether you stick to your old habits or create new pathways in your life that lead to a winning combination of deeper emotional satisfaction and powerful external success. It's no longer a case of either/or for you. Choosing one over the other, no matter which, creates imbalance and possible chaos.

Rewarding Days
2, 3, 5, 22, 23

Challenging Days
10, 11, 19, 20, 28

Aries | November

Overall Theme

Things remain fairly mellow, which in your world means you are going at three-quarter speed, until November 19, when Mars moves into Scorpio and all bets are off. No more middle ground for you. It's time for a game of all or nothing, so take a good look before you jump.

Relationships

You are definitely in the mood for fun and adventure, and you find you want to do it all by yourself. Make sure it's not a way to avoid any uncomfortable thoughts or feelings that keep burbling to the surface about the connections you have with others. Acknowledging what is going on inside you is the first step in sorting out some long-standing issues you have in how you relate to others.

Career, Success, and Money

The external world of work and accomplishment isn't really on your radar this month. Oh, you definitely take care of what demands your attention, however reluctantly. It's just that you are more in the mood to escape the expected and the mundane so you can feel the freedom that comes from ignoring anything you choose.

Pitfalls and Potential Problems

Your emotional intensity shocks you to the core, leading you to feel like you need to get out of your own skin. Take a deep breath and dive in. There is a wealth of creative inspiration and ideas just waiting to expand your life and offer you new territory to master.

Rewarding Days

4, 5, 26, 27

Challenging Days

1, 11, 12, 17, 18

Aries | December

Overall Theme

The nitty-gritty details of life take center stage, leaving you feeling a little too earthbound. Turn inward and find your own sense of joy and inspiration. You are so good at being self-reliant, so take that talent and use it to paint your life whatever color you fancy. It's so much better than getting bogged down, and, in addition, it offers a glimpse of what 2020 will bring.

Relationships

Take care of your commitments to others responsibly and you will find that things go a lot more smoothly. That includes saying no with grace and diplomacy. Being outraged that others are demanding you do what they want only creates more problems than it solves. Be clear and direct about your boundaries and save everyone from your indignation and irritation. They aren't necessary to make your point.

Career, Success, and Money

You are a whirlwind of energy and ambition, pushing yourself and others to get results. This works well for you as long as you are focused on a plan and not merely being bossy. If you avoid throwing your weight around, a lot gets accomplished, including creating the foundation for some long-term abundance.

Pitfalls and Potential Problems

The amount of energy coursing through your body needs an outlet, so make sure you are as physically active as you can be. Otherwise crankiness takes over and you create an inordinate amount of drama in your life that has the potential to impact your emotional well-being for months to come.

Rewarding Days

6, 7, 16, 17, 24

Challenging Days

9, 10, 11, 22

Aries Action Table

These dates reflect the best—but not the only—times for success and ease in these activities, according to your Sun sign.

	JAN	FEB	MAR	APR	MAY	JUN	JUL	AUG	SEP	OCT	NOV	DEC
Move		9, 10			1, 2		8, 9		28, 29			
Start a class	23			2, 3	6, 7				5, 6		13, 14	
Seek coaching/counseling		23, 24				12, 13		30, 31		12, 13		
Ask for a raise	15, 16		27, 28			1, 9			17, 18			17, 18
Get professional advice		19, 20					16, 17			28, 29		5, 6
Get a loan			9, 10		17, 18					15, 16		
New romance				13, 14		7, 8	4, 5	1, 2				
Vacation	30, 31			22, 23				10, 11			23, 24	28, 29

Taurus

The Bull
April 21 to May 21

ठ

Element: Earth	Glyph: Bull's head
Quality: Fixed	Anatomy: Throat, neck
Polarity: Yin/feminine	Color: Green
Planetary Ruler: Venus	Animal: Cattle
Meditation: I trust myself and others	Myths/Legends: Isis and Osiris, Ceridwen, Bull of Minos
Gemstone: Emerald	House: Second
Power Stones: Diamond, blue lace agate, rose quartz	Opposite Sign: Scorpio
	Flower: Violet
Key Phrase: I have	Keyword: Conservation

The Taurus Personality

Strengths, Spiritual Purpose, and Challenges

You are like the little sprout in spring that's just poked its head through the soil, searching for the sunshine, depending on its roots to nurture it, pushing through all obstacles to survive and to thrive. The urge to grow is strong, the determination and the will are without compare, the resourcefulness is deeply imbedded. All this is intrinsic to Taurus. The challenge is that the need to survive can overshadow the knowledge that, if anyone knows what to do to make things work, it's you. No one has quite the resources that you do to make something of life, nor do they have the perseverance. Once committed to a course of action, you do not rest until you have done what you set out to do. This makes you reliable and steadfast, practical and dependable.

However, in your quest to fulfill your spiritual purpose—determining value—you can and do get stuck. It's just part of the process, because how can you know if something is valuable if you don't hold on to it? So you commit yourself to what you've built, to what you've bought, to what you've created, to what you've accumulated. None of that is the source of your value. They are symbols of what you are capable of but not the source of who you are. Making that distinction is a big challenge for you, because you do find great security in external things. After all, like the sprout, if you don't conquer the outer world, you will die. Yet, if you look at the little sprout, you realize that it too will let go of whatever will keep it from thriving. Be open to this so you can nourish your life more effectively. Let go of your need for predictability. Keep only those things that truly nurture you. Take time to acknowledge all that you have accomplished. Know that the security you seek is within, and it's not built on anything in your outer world. It's built on a drive and determination that cannot be extinguished by anyone but you.

Relationships

Because Venus, the planet of love and desire, is the biggest influence in your life, you like people and you enjoy being around them. When it comes to love, you are steadfast and loyal, capable of commitment through thick and thin. Any promises you make to others you will keep, even if it means sacrificing yourself, because a promise is a promise is a promise. You require honesty and respect from anyone you invite into your world, and you offer the same in turn. Once you trust someone, it's hard for you to accept any form of betrayal or any awareness that tarnishes your commitment to them. You will hang on to partners, lovers, children, friends, or family long past the point it makes sense for you to do so. Not only do you have difficulty letting go, you also tend to exert ownership over those you love. This causes significant problems because love and ownership do not mix well. In truth, their energies are diametrically opposite, and it may take some time before you truly understand that. However, because you are always in it for the long haul, this can be worked out, provided you are willing to listen to the other person.

Career and Work

It's not in your nature to choose to do something that has no long-term value, that doesn't have tangible results. You definitely like to see the fruits of your labors, whether you work in finance, graphic arts, construction, medicine, running your own business, etc. What's more, what you choose to do must be seen as valuable, not just by you but by those close to you. You really aren't concerned with making a big, public splash as much as you wish to be acknowledged and respected by those in your immediate world. Hard work and being in it for the long haul definitely come naturally to you, and you are never happier than when you get to build something from the ground up, making sure it stands the test of time. A shoddy work ethic or a lack of commitment to excellence don't make any sense to you because you see everything you do as an extension of who you are.

Money and Possessions

Let's face it: you like stuff. It gives you a deep sense of security because it's a reminder of what you have accomplished and how hard you have worked. Your challenge is to remember that things don't guarantee security. However, that doesn't mean they are less valuable to you. In fact, that's not really why they are valuable at all. You need your environment to be pleasing because it really is like looking at the inner parts of yourself, which is, on a deeper level, why you become so attached to things. Everything you surround yourself with is hugely symbolic as well as highly stimulating because you are so visual and so tactile. It is so much more than ownership or comfort that motivates you. The same cannot be said for how you feel about money. This is where your need for security and your capacity to attach without question can get out of hand so that your image of yourself gets completely immersed in how much money you have or don't have. Easy enough to do in a world where money is often the sole arbiter of success. Remember, it's a resource, not the final judgment.

The Light Side of Life

You are a sensual person who delights in all things connected to the five senses. So when it's time to relax, your attention naturally goes to things that feel good, look good, smell good, etc.—in short, anything that makes the world around you more comfortable and enjoyable. You don't like anything discordant to find its way into your reality, whether it's music you don't like, people who are disrespectful, anyone who makes it their mission to change your mind, etc. You do enjoy letting your hair down once in a while, provided you are in good company, which equates to people you know and trust.

Taurus Keywords for 2019
Flexibility, courage, resourcefulness

The Year Ahead for Taurus

It's going to be a difficult year for you to predict anything with any certainty because the planets demanding your attention—Uranus, Saturn, Pluto, and Neptune—are a mixed bag of opportunity, stability, compulsiveness, and chaos. This is quite the combination and quite the dilemma for someone who not only likes steadiness and constancy above all else but gets entirely lost and knocked off balance by the slightest suggestion that what you have so diligently planned and executed just isn't going to work out the way you expected. You are a creature of expectations as well as desires, needs, and requirements. You simply cannot see how life can function without them. There has to be some meaningful starting point, something you can rely on to guide you through life. Well, get ready to redefine all the known quantities in your life as Uranus charges into your Sun sign on March 6 and life feels a little more electric than you might like. This triggers a desire to dig in (especially if you were born in the first part of Taurus) and find something solid to see you through the turmoil. (Those born in the latter part of Taurus will just have to wait their turn to get the full effect.)

The key here is to recognize that change (aka Uranus) is not going to stop knocking on your door, even if you barricade it with all your favorite ideas, beliefs, possessions, money, or anything else that you think is what keeps you safe. There really is no escape. The more you resist, the more likely it is that you will make things worse. This year signals an opportunity to step into the authenticity of who you are, which may require stripping away anything you've accumulated that no longer serves any purpose while actually creating an energetic drag on your life. Now, with Saturn in Capricorn encouraging you to believe that anything you have or have done should not be relinquished without a fight, Neptune asking you to look beyond the end of your own nose, and Pluto nudging you from the depths to find some real passion in your life and express it, you definitely feel you are in the middle of a war you didn't start. While that is true, that doesn't alter the fact that what keeps all things healthy is the capacity to grow. That's what you need to do.

Recognize that complacency—everything is fine just the way it is—is the forerunner of disconnecting from the vibrancy of life, with all its twists and turns. You are here to continually evaluate what matters to you through the medium of your life experience, not hang on to the last best thing you did, hold your breath, or resist anything and everything that doesn't match your carefully crafted picture of life. The security you think the outer world provides is transitory at best. Besides, you created it anyway by applying yourself with determination and hard work. You are truly the source of your own security. That is what the next seven years will demonstrate to you—if you are open to it. Otherwise, life promises to be extremely difficult until you realize you are being your own worst enemy.

Saturn

As 2019 opens up, life feels solid and grounded, and you can thank Saturn in Capricorn for that. He is, after all, the stabilizer, and he has brought some much-needed order (in your mind, anyway) to all the topsy-turvy energy that has been lurking in the back of your consciousness for longer than you care to remember (actually it's seven years). In fact, you may feel he has managed to keep anything that disturbs your equilibrium at bay permanently. Not so fast. He is a lot of things but Saturn is not a miracle worker, and he certainly doesn't have the capacity to stop the inevitable advance of change. Oh, he can definitely lull you into a false sense of security and convince you that nothing can upset your world. However, if experience has taught you anything, you know that isn't true. And, if you cling to that unrealistic hope, you are creating a perfect storm of upheaval, turbulence, and disorder in your own life. Accept that change is inevitable and use the growing sense of confidence that Saturn nurtured in you in 2018 and you can meet the demand for change and growth as it pushes open the door, crosses the threshold, and plants itself firmly in your life for the next seven years. Saturn's job now is to assist you in finding constructive ways to deal with the lack of certainty that comes with a major turning point in your life. Make no mistake: that is what is on the agenda. Turn to the knowledge that you can create security from within with little or nothing to go on except complete faith in yourself.

Uranus

If you think Saturn is your very best friend this year, you definitely feel Uranus is your enemy. In fact, you might be tempted to call him the Bogeyman because he symbolizes everything that makes you break out in a cold sweat. And that can be summed up in a single word: change—the one thing you resist with every fiber of your being. If you could immortalize everything in the moment you found it satisfying, you would. So it annoys you that nothing is set in stone, shaking you to the very core. Well, be prepared. The next seven years of your life will test everything you hold dear and then some. Now, before you assume this is some special torture cooked up just for you, remember change is inevitable for *everyone*. Yes, repeat that to yourself at least ten times. When you are done, take a look at your life and ask yourself what is truly necessary for you to be you. With any luck, you'll realize the only thing you really require is yourself, that everything you have you created, which means you have a profound capacity to take any set of resources and make something out of it. So stop nailing everything to the floor, get rid of the tunnel vision, and look around you. Life is full of opportunity, not disaster. With one proviso: you don't always have control over how opportunity shows up. That's Uranus. Inherent in every experience he triggers is the chance to grow beyond what you already know and create something new. It just requires that some things get blown to smithereens.

Neptune

With Uranus rattling around in your Sun sign, Neptune feels pretty innocuous and nonthreatening. In fact, you may choose to go and hide out in his world, where illusion is the escape hatch we use to convince ourselves that nothing is wrong. The first order of business for you is to get past the notion that, if your life is in turmoil, it must be the result of some mistake you made. No, if nature teaches us anything, it's that nothing is permanent. So before you go into convulsions at the mere thought, recognize that this truth is actually a liberation instead of a punishment. Then you can tap into the peace that Neptune offers, because he is the doorway to what lies beyond our fear of impermanence to the deeply felt yet unquantifiable sense of connection to the Divine. On a more practical note, Neptune can help you with that Uranian problem you feel is plaguing you by softening your need to hold things so rigidly in place, by helping you to look beyond the obvious, and by creating the space to let things go. Granted, this is a tall order of business, but you have a large chunk of time to work on it. Some strategies that might be helpful include taking time to sit in nature and observe the changing of the seasons. See how nature builds upon change. Take up yoga, start a dream journal, make friends with those whose point of view is very different from your own, or just dance.

Pluto

You might not have noticed Pluto as much in the last year because Saturn dominated the conversation in your world, at least on a conscious level. However, Pluto is much more at home in your subconscious, where he's definitely been making an impact for the past ten years, often in subtle ways that don't seem obvious until you discover, much to your surprise, that some integral part of how you view the world or what you stand for has shifted profoundly. With Saturn as Pluto's partner for the last year, there has been a push to use those shifts in some very practical and measurable ways, leading to some uncomfortable moments—for you, anyway—as you felt compelled to forcefully assert your point of view and challenge others to come clean and be accountable. This continues in 2019 with one noticeable difference: you are no longer embarrassed by yourself. Gone are the days when you were prepared to quietly go your own way, believing that your actions sufficed in signaling to the world what you valued. Not only do you need to speak up, but you are compelled to do so from somewhere deep inside you that you don't quite understand. Don't worry about it. Just go with it. What you find out about yourself in the world is a life-altering surprise.

How Will This Year's Eclipses Affect You?

Eclipses signal intense periods that highlight major growth opportunities for us in the process of creating our lives. They are linked to the lunar phases—specifically the New and Full Moon—and involve the relationship between the Sun and the Moon and the Earth. A Solar Eclipse is a magnified New Moon, while a Lunar Eclipse is a magnified Full Moon. Eclipses unfold in cycles involving all twelve signs of the zodiac, and they occur in pairs, usually about two weeks apart.

In 2019 there are five eclipses, three solar (two in Capricorn and one in Cancer) and two lunar (one in Leo and one in Capricorn). The first Solar Eclipse arrives on January 5 and immediately puts you on notice that sticking to old thought patterns and rigid attitudes leads to a sense of isolation that will only be amplified by the Lunar Eclipse in Leo on January 21. It truly is time to abandon any inclination that life must be taken care of properly, aka I must always do the right thing for the right reasons while following all the correct procedures. This is not what will bring you satisfaction. It never has, on a deeper level. Doing your duty doesn't recharge your batteries if you are simply following protocol rather than giving of yourself on a heart level.

There is a theme this year that asks you to consider what emotionally satisfies you, what your true responsibilities are (both to yourself and to others), and what the real definition of service is. Is it subservience or is it the true gifting of yourself, whether to people or to situations? At the heart of these eclipses (including the Solar Eclipse on July 2, the Lunar Eclipse on July 16, and the Solar Eclipse on December 26) is a call to redefine your priorities, emotionally, spiritually, intellectually and physically, to take stock of what fulfills you and expands your commitment to living life to the fullest, and to define what that really means. You can get so stuck in patterns and forget to get rid of the deadwood in your life because you think that if something was valuable to you once, it must still be valuable. However, life changes you and therefore changes the landscape. This year, the landscape that changes centers on using how you feel as a benchmark for what you are prepared to do in all areas of life. No more blindly following the path you once set. Instead, you seek to make yourself the heart of your life going forward. Step into this with grace and you will find that, whether you believe it or not, you need variety and excitement to flourish. No more need to continually prove yourself in any way, shape, or form. The prospect of building anew is far more satisfying than maintaining the status quo.

Taurus | January

Overall Theme

You feel restless and you aren't really sure why. All you really know is something isn't sitting right in your consciousness, leading to an inability to focus, an inability to get much done, and an inability to feel at home in your own skin. Definitely not a comfortable month. However, resistance is futile, because the only effect it will have is to amplify what already is a challenge.

Relationships

Exhausted from trying to keep everybody happy in the last thirty days, you strike out on your own for some much needed freedom from the concerns of others. It's almost as if someone shut off your capacity to hear anything from anyone. Oh, you can see people's mouths moving, but somehow the words are not penetrating that self-protective bubble you set up around yourself.

Career, Success, and Money

Much to your surprise, the only items on your agenda are less work, less worry, and less effort. You find yourself relying on past performance to carry you through a time when you apparently don't care. That's not really true. You are just preparing to recalibrate what you value in life by taking a step back from everything.

Pitfalls and Potential Problems

The Solar Eclipse on January 5 could trigger a huge guilt complex. Are you doing enough, being enough, caring enough? Avoid diving into this particular black hole, not only because it's exhausting and debilitating but also because it interferes with that gut feeling you have that you need to make some emotional changes in your life.

Rewarding Days

14, 15, 23, 24

Challenging Days

5, 6, 25, 26

Taurus | February

Overall Theme

Your energy stabilizes, making you happier and less overwhelmed. You don't fare well if everything keeps moving and changing before you can get a handle on what's happening. Well, this is the calm before the storm, so enjoy the sense of direction and determination that floods your being. You'll need it in March.

Relationships

You return to a more practical and stable approach to relationships, meaning you are once again your reliable, steadfast self. You pride yourself on being someone others can count on, and you have many opportunities this month to demonstrate that. A word of caution: you can support people, but rescuing them never works.

Career, Success, and Money

A lot of focus on what you are doing and why dominates your thinking for much of February. You find yourself asking a lot of questions about what you desire, not just about the practical aspects of your career but also about whether you are truly satisfied. Some new people crossing your path trigger a profound realization that you are searching for a completely new direction.

Pitfalls and Potential Problems

The deep sense of foreboding you feel in the pit of your stomach is a sign that you know the unexpected is just around the corner. And it is. But instead of allowing that feeling to consume you, recognize that you have the skills to deal with whatever happens. After all, this isn't the first time change has come knocking on your door.

Rewarding Days

11, 12, 23, 24

Challenging Days

8, 9, 21, 22

Taurus | March

Overall Theme

A major turning point looms on the horizon as Uranus crosses the threshold into your Sun sign for a seven-year stay. Granted you had a taste of this erratic energy in 2018, but that was just a whisper of things to come. Now it's time for the main event, and you are caught between the need to cast everything in concrete and the awareness that maybe your world needs a little shaking up.

Relationships

Well, the restlessness of January reappears and you suddenly find yourself being more than a little bit disagreeable. Not content with taking a break from others, you are in outright rebellion against anyone who tries to push you in one direction or another. It's not that you aren't listening, it's that you just don't see much value in what is being said.

Career, Success, and Money

Work presents a number of challenges, beginning with what you consider a lack of respect for your efforts and ending with outside people weighing in on things you think are none of their business. While you may be right, being combative won't solve either of those issues. Pat yourself on the back and back away from the interference.

Pitfalls and Potential Problems

Your equilibrium takes a big hit when Uranus moves into Taurus, leaving your sense of self bouncing around like a ping-pong ball and your belief that you can handle anything almost shattered. This uncertainty makes you hypersensitive about and hyper-vigilant to all incoming data. Use the Mercury retrograde period (March 5 to 28) to do some real soul-searching.

Rewarding Days

10, 11, 19, 20

Challenging Days

8, 9, 23, 24

Taurus | April

Overall Theme

Your stress level remains high as you question anything and everything. What's more, there don't seem to be any clear answers. You could cope quite nicely with this change, if only you knew what it was. Relax. Well, at least breathe. You can't solve anything holding your breath. All will be revealed in good time.

Relationships

Talking to people seems to be a waste of your time, so your dissatisfaction with others continues. Why? Because you don't feel anyone is listening to you. The truth is, those around you are a little freaked-out at you being freaked-out, so when you start sharing your inner turmoil, they just don't know what to do. Let them know you don't need them to do anything but be present.

Career, Success, and Money

With everything in a state of flux, you turn to the one thing that usually guarantees some stability: your work. But somehow, even that doesn't make you feel any better. In fact, it's downright stultifying. When, you wonder, did everything become so flat and uninteresting? Be careful. You may start spending money to inject a sense of security into your world.

Pitfalls and Potential Problems

You really aren't sure where to go or what to do. The push from Saturn tells you to get moving, get going, get something done. After all, you can't drop the ball now. Meanwhile, Uranus dares you to break down everything that's defined your life up to this point and begin anew. What's a self-respecting Taurus supposed to do? Examine your life and keep only what you truly value. This is a difficult process for you, but it has to be done.

Rewarding Days

6, 7, 15, 16

Challenging Days

4, 5, 18, 19, 20

Taurus | May

Overall Theme

The world doesn't feel quite as wobbly as it has recently, plus you don't feel as flat as a pancake. All this reenergizes you and allows you to stop spending so much time grabbing for anything that you can use as a flotation device to weather the hurricane you believe has enveloped your life. Instead, you turn your attention to rebuilding your sense of confidence in yourself.

Relationships

Life with others becomes less hazardous as your mood softens and you realize that it's far too easy to project onto others the dissatisfaction you essentially have with yourself. The root of this is your expectation that, if you are doing it right, nothing (whether external or internal) should ever rock the foundation of what you have built. Can you say unrealistic?

Career, Success, and Money

You make tremendous strides in finding a solution to the ennui you have accumulated in the last two months. The key is revisiting ideas, projects, and plans you had in the works before life seemed to turn upside down. You discover, quite happily, that they still galvanize you as much as they ever did. Soon, everything is percolating and you are rewarded with a deep sense of satisfaction.

Pitfalls and Potential Problems

Things motor along quite nicely and you encounter few bumps in the road. The opportunity here is to acknowledge all the fears stirred up by the constant inner push for change emerging from inside you. This is not a passing phase, so taking stock gives you the chance to get on board with the need for change.

Rewarding Days

4, 5, 13, 14

Challenging Days

15, 16, 17, 18

Taurus | June

Overall Theme

Having regained your equilibrium, you set aside your apprehension in favor of moving forward with a renewed sense that life still has much to offer you. As much as you are reluctant to acknowledge it, you are beginning to see that your life has become far too predictable, even for you. Now begins the process of climbing out of the rut you didn't realize you dug.

Relationships

You are the soul of discretion as you find yourself being everyone's confessor/counselor/chief support system. What you find out about yourself gives you a deeper sense of how much you truly have to offer others in the way of wisdom, compassion, and true understanding. This restores your faith in both yourself and others.

Career, Success, and Money

This month signals a time to reward yourself, whether that means going after a promotion or raise, taking a risk on an investment you've been pondering for some time, or buying yourself something special. And those are just three of a myriad of possibilities. Ask yourself what you deserve for being who you are and doing what you do. No matter the answer, do it.

Pitfalls and Potential Problems

Although you are more at peace with the reality that change is necessary, you need to be careful you don't convince yourself that you are 100 percent ready for what is bound to come next. None of us can ever be that prepared, no matter what we do. Accept that and you are free to tap into the huge reservoir of resources you consistently use to solve life's ups and downs.

Rewarding Days

9, 10, 23, 24

Challenging Days

5, 6, 18, 19

Taurus | July

Overall Theme

You are so sensitive that you want to crawl under a rock and wait for it to pass. It's not that you are unhappy. The truth is your circuits are on overload and you really do need to schedule a timeout because you feel it all intensely and unrelentingly. This is not your comfort zone, which only makes it more challenging.

Relationships

You can't walk into any room without tuning in to the prevailing emotional winds. This leaves you feeling like you need to defend yourself before you've even said hello. The solution is to consciously acknowledge where you are at before you walk through that door. That way you know what's yours and what's not. Remember, you are not responsible for how others feel or react.

Career, Success, and Money

Try not to say yes to everything that is asked of you. It only leads to resentment, as there is at least one person prepared to dump work on you that they not only are quite capable of doing but are responsible for. On the bright side, you are in line for some much-needed acknowledgment from a higher-up, which signals an important positive development in your career.

Pitfalls and Potential Problems

Both the Solar Eclipse (July 2) and the Lunar Eclipse (July 16) combined with a retrograde Mercury (July 7 to July 31) create a highly defensive attitude that promises to overwhelm you. Normally you are not prickly or easily offended. This month is the exception. Find ways to nurture yourself and count to ten before speaking.

Rewarding Days

6, 7, 25, 26

Challenging Days

1, 2, 23, 24

Taurus | August

Overall Theme
The desire to have fun takes precedence over everything else. Now, that doesn't equate to forgetting your responsibilities; it just means your number-one priority is making sure that what you do brings a smile to your face. You are truly in love with life and want to pack every moment full of as much pleasure as you can muster. Which happens to be a lot.

Relationships
Well, there isn't anyone you don't like this month, unless, of course, they are a bit of a sourpuss. You are definitely not open to complaints or harangues or grumbles of the inconsequential kind. For those who truly need support or a shoulder to cry on, you are all heart and compassion, so much so that you find yourself galvanized to give your time or money to something you deem worthwhile.

Career, Success, and Money
Expect some surprising developments in this area, especially around August 15. There could be a sudden shift in the hierarchy at work that leads to a potential promotion or an unexpected realization that the time has come to move on. This leads to stress and a loosening of the purse strings. Steer clear of buying for the sake of buying.

Pitfalls and Potential Problems
Be careful about throwing caution to the wind, which is an overwhelming temptation after all the months you've been coping with your life rocking and rolling. Enjoy the release of all those tensions; just avoid doing anything you will regret later. Relax. Have fun. Just don't jump off a cliff without a parachute.

Rewarding Days
1, 2, 22, 30, 31

Challenging Days
12, 13, 24, 25

Taurus | September

Overall Theme

You finally feel like you have a handle on all that pushy Uranian energy that's been forcing you to move forward whether it's what you want or not. Take advantage of your renewed confidence to truly engage with that energy. It's time to stop resisting, or you will crash and burn, if not this month, then soon. Take an inventory of your life and you will discover that there is much you would be happy to change.

Relationships

Remember to take time to connect with your partner, your family, and your friends. It's imperative because a number of important milestones occur this month and you may be missing in action, largely because work is taking up all the oxygen. First step: put it in your calendar. Second step: look at your calendar. Otherwise, you might end up disappointing someone very close to you.

Career, Success, and Money

A number of critical deadlines all converge, leaving you reeling from the amount of pressure it creates. Somehow you did this to yourself, and your head feels like it is going to explode. Forget that you overloaded your own plate, and ask for help. It won't hurt, and it will give you space to be a human being, not a human doing.

Pitfalls and Potential Problems

One of the things you did to cope with your fear of change was to overcommit yourself and take on too many things. You believed that if you kept busy, you could ride out the call for change and keep everything the way it was. This month you discover that was wishful thinking.

Rewarding Days

3, 4, 18, 19

Challenging Days

10, 11, 28, 29

Taurus | October

Overall Theme

Surprising revelations catch you unawares and shake your security to the core, making you wonder whether everything you believe has any actual value. Again you are confronted with the main message of Uranus in your Sun sign: take stock of what is important to you and be prepared to get rid of anything dragging you down.

Relationships

It feels like everyone in the world who has a problem has your phone number. And what they need help with seems so, well, small. All this leaves you wanting to scream, if only silently. You don't mind helping people or supporting them, but you aren't interested in rescuing or babysitting. The solution? Listen and be supportive, but don't fix anything. It's not your job, even if it's someone you love. Instead, tell them you trust they can find a solution (but only if you mean it).

Career, Success, and Money

You are mentally focused in a way that has eluded you since the beginning of 2019, and you are anxious to make use of it. New pathways worth exploring open up, as well as new opportunities for investment. Don't dismiss anyone who comes to you with a crazy idea with an awesome financial upside. It has great potential.

Pitfalls and Potential Problems

Your vaunted patience disappears in the onslaught of other people's concerns, problems, and crises, because no one seems to realize that not only do you have your own worries, but you are feeling really creative and you just want to run with it. So go all in on what you desire. That's much better than being cranky, rude, and resentful.

Rewarding Days

10, 11, 24, 25

Challenging Days

12, 13, 20, 21

Taurus | November

Overall Theme

You feel at war with everyone. Why can't you just get on with what is calling to you from within? After all, you've got important stuff to do, and yet the whole world seems to think you are on vacation. Why else would they assume you have nothing to do but take care of stuff that you, quite frankly, don't care about? The process of redefining your values has begun.

Relationships

Those closest to you are a little nonplussed at what they perceive to be your sudden desire for emancipation from everything and everyone in your life. You keep trying to assure them that is not the case. However, you aren't quite sure how to explain what is going on inside you because you haven't quite figured it out yourself. Instead of camouflaging your uncertainty, tell them. It will help.

Career, Success, and Money

There's a powerful focus this month on shared resources of all kinds, from money to time to ideas, and you find yourself conflicted about how much you are supposed to share and with whom, for how long, and for what purpose. The result is you won't commit without a clear idea of just what is being asked of you. Stick to your guns and don't let anyone guilt you. Your questions are perfectly reasonable.

Pitfalls and Potential Problems

Avoid being strident and abrasive. If you truly want people to hear you, try saying what you want to say out loud to yourself first. That way you get a sense of just how irritated and annoyed you are feeling, the result of Uranus poking away at you. Then you can get people's attention in a positive, more satisfying way.

Rewarding Days

20, 21, 29, 30

Challenging Days

11, 12, 16, 17

Taurus | December

Overall Theme

A sense of calm dominates much of the month, and not because life is calmer or easier or more stable. You are, and it comes from a sudden realization that you have a lot of tools in your tool kit that you can call on to see you through whatever life offers up. It's your desire to hold on that creates most of the problems.

Relationships

Gone is the need to separate yourself from everyone, and you are deeply relieved to return to a more reliable, steadfast state of affairs in your relationships. Enjoy it, but refrain from apologizing for being less than accommodating last month. Your job is to be true to yourself, not to be a doormat—as you will discover, beginning December 20, when you once again push back against people trying to run your life.

Career, Success, and Money

As the year winds down, you review not only what you have done in these areas but also the impact your actions created. Surprisingly, you don't find disaster, but rather a new appreciation for yourself and your resourcefulness. No matter what gets thrown at you, you find a way to make it work for you. Pat yourself on the back.

Pitfalls and Potential Problems

Feeling grounded and more centered is not a message that it's okay to go backward. You can't. But you can go inward and confront whatever is troubling you, which at this moment is the feeling that everything is okay—which seems antithetical to what you experienced this year. The truth is, things can be difficult and okay all at the same time.

Rewarding Days

8, 9, 30, 31

Challenging Days

6, 7, 11, 12

Taurus Action Table

These dates reflect the best—but not the only—times for success and ease in these activities, according to your Sun sign.

	JAN	FEB	MAR	APR	MAY	JUN	JUL	AUG	SEP	OCT	NOV	DEC
Move					10, 11			4, 5				
Start a class	15, 16									19, 20		
Seek coaching/ counseling			23, 24				25, 26			9, 10		
Ask for a raise		4, 5							12, 13		3, 4	
Get professional advice				6, 7				13, 14				3, 4
Get a loan			10, 11			15, 16					15, 16	
New romance		19, 20			26, 27		6, 7		3, 4			
Vacation	10, 11			24, 25								17, 18

Gemini

The Twins
May 22 to June 21

Ⅱ

Element: Air

Glyph: Pillars of duality, the Twins

Quality: Mutable

Anatomy: Shoulders, arms, hands, lungs, nervous system

Polarity: Yang/masculine

Colors: Bright colors, orange, yellow, magenta

Planetary Ruler: Mercury

Animals: Monkeys, talking birds, flying insects

Meditation: I explore my inner worlds

Myths/Legends: Peter Pan, Castor and Pollux

Gemstone: Tourmaline

House: Third

Power Stones: Ametrine, citrine, emerald, spectrolite, agate

Opposite Sign: Sagittarius

Flower: Lily of the valley

Key Phrase: I think

Keyword: Versatility

Money and Possessions

You really aren't one to consciously attach yourself to either money or possessions. The only value money has for you is in facilitating the life you want to live, making it easy for you to follow up on whatever catches your fancy. The same is true of things. That doesn't mean you can't accumulate money and/or possessions. Far from it. You often find yourself with more of both than you actually thought you desired. However, once you have them, you can be loath to let go. What kicks in is the feeling that if something somehow came to be yours, you should hang on to it, even if you aren't really sure why. This area of life can be ruled by your feelings, so you need to be cautious and use some discernment about what to do with the resources you accumulate. There is a happy medium between stinginess and wastefulness.

The Light Side of Life

It's hard to separate the light side of life from the rest of your life because you believe the potential for fun, amusement, and joy is always right there if only you know how to tap into it. This doesn't mean you lack a serious side, it just means that serious doesn't equal grim, severe, or foreboding for you. To make your point, you use satire as a perfect example of how humor can be used to illuminate difficult things. Laughter really is at the center of your being. The capacity to giggle or guffaw at what happens is truly your lifeline, and if you lose your sense of humor, it's a sign that you have lost touch with your core.

Gemini Keywords for 2019
Authenticity, determination, clarity

The Year Ahead for Gemini

The year 2019 promises to be a time when you make significant inroads in clearing out any self-defeating, self-imposed fears that you are never quite enough. This year demands that you finally define what that means to you, how that perception came to be so deeply lodged in your subconscious, and why you have rarely questioned that attitude. Oh, you've ignored it, glossed over it, and projected it onto others, simply because it made you feel inadequate. Yet you were afraid to confront it for fear it was actually true. Instead of using that lovely mind of yours to distract you, 2019 asks you to engage it full throttle by doing Mercurial things, beginning with writing down everything you believe about yourself without exception. This can be in sentences or groups of words or even single words. Once done, put the compilation away where you can't see it for at least a week (or whatever time frame feels right to you). Then take it out. Put all the words on sticky notes and attach them to a mirror. In that moment, you begin to see how difficult it can be to see yourself clearly. Next, remove all the beliefs that result from other people's input. How many sticky notes remain? This gives you an idea of how much of what you believe about yourself actually comes from within. Now that's just a start. Obviously this exercise can take you many more places.

Trust yourself to be your own guide in either continuing to use this exercise as a jumping-off point or finding other approaches that bear fruit. What you do and how you do it is up to you. The only thing that matters is reconnecting to the authentic you. After all, that is what 2019 is about—stripping away the false, the nonsensical, the rubbish, that you internalized as definitive truths about yourself. This is not an easy process. It's amazing how attached you can get to ideas and beliefs about who you are, even in the face of experience and awareness that tells a different story. We humans are extremely good at living with things that are diametrically opposite each other, and no one is better at it than Gemini. In fact, it's the downside of your gift for accepting all ideas as potentially valuable. However, reclaiming yourself requires a willingness to eradicate anything that interferes with a clearer self-portrait. And you will, years from now, identify this as a year when you truly got in touch with the length, depth, and breadth of who you are, what you are passionate about, and how you learned to be truly yourself.

Saturn

The challenge that Saturn presents to you in 2019 is an amplification of the issues he pushed onto your plate beginning in December of 2017. He is rarely high on your list of things you relish or look forward to at the best of times, but when he hangs out in his own sign of Capricorn, he is even less appealing. From your perspective, he is all work and no play. First of all, his method of getting your attention rubs you the wrong way. He doesn't entertain you or charm you. He just flat out puts what needs to be done right under your nose and asks you what you intend to do about it. What's more, it's done in such a dry, matter-of-fact way that your inclination is to ignore his call to action. Make no mistake, 2019 is a year when you definitely need not just to pay attention to the items he's put on your agenda but to act on them. And what are those items, you ask? Well, they run the gamut from making sure you take care of your debt load and your taxes on the mundane level to moving past any walls you have put up to avoid dealing with any lingering trauma, pain, or disappointment. Saturn isn't very comfortable with feelings and emotions, so he is reluctant to engage. However, when he touches any area of our lives, he is asking us to be accountable for making that part of our life work more satisfactorily. He is asking you to be more practical and sensible about all those deeply buried hurts that continue to affect you and keep you from building the kind of closeness, both with yourself and with others, that leads to creating a happier, healthier you.

Uranus

It's been quite the rollercoaster ride for the last seven years as Uranus has essentially played his own form of pinball in your life, leaving you wondering if there was anything you could hope for, dream of, or wish for. Plus he seemed to have people careening in and out of your life. Friendships you thought would last forever suddenly blew up; new people rushed in to take up the empty space and then departed as quickly as they arrived. Now, normally you don't mind a bit of bouncing around, but this was a little more intense than you are comfortable with. On March 6, this comes to an end when Uranus moves into Taurus. Initially, you feel he has completely disappeared and your response is to breathe a sigh of relief. That's okay. You deserve a respite, however brief. But you realize things are really changing when you find that your dreams are wild, unconventional, and somewhat overwhelming. Just remember—in case you've forgotten—that whatever Uranus touches gets a major shakeup. And your dream life is just the beginning, as Uranus will be putting you in touch with all manner of things you've been hiding from yourself, things that need to be released so that you are lighter and less burdened by events and experiences from your past that are casting long shadows in the present and keeping you from tapping into the inspiration that is waiting under all that detritus.

Neptune

So, have you figured out what you want to be when you grow up yet? No? The irony is that isn't always a question at the forefront of your mind, because it really doesn't interest you to try to figure everything out years in advance. On the other hand, you do like a path to wander down, and Neptune has been making it very difficult for you to even be clear about which end is up, never mind finding a forward direction or a purpose or even a sense of what's next. To add to your consternation, you wonder if you aren't slightly crazy because being around people is getting on your nerves. It's like you are plugged into them in ways you never have been and you can feel what they feel. All in all, the confusion and the overloaded circuits don't leave you in the best position to make long-term decisions or even short-term ones, for that matter. Be cautious about any pie-in-the-sky opportunities that come your way. Make sure you research everything down to the last detail before making any commitments. The most effective way to handle this energy is to take on something you have always wanted to experiment with. Just don't try to turn it into a career. It's too soon.

Pluto

Where Saturn fears to tread, Pluto jumps in full force and then some. Digging deep into one's emotional treasure trove to unearth all the dirt and anguish is the order of the day for him, because you can't transmute or transform yourself without engaging in some emotional excavation. This puts you in the middle between Saturn, who seeks an orderly, responsible way to deal with anything and everything, and Pluto, who doesn't care if things get messy. In fact, the messier the better, because that means you are getting somewhere. The key to mastering this intense showdown is to remember that Saturn can assist you in creating a process to deal with all the stuff that Pluto is unearthing, because sometimes messy is just messy, without a purpose or a plan. Accept that it will take some fierce dedication and determination on your part to find your way through the internal rumblings caused by the demands these two bring to bear. Never forget that they symbolize your own internal struggle between letting everything ride for as long as you can ignore or control it and a deep need to be rid of some very toxic stuff. You will emerge stronger, lighter, and much more in touch with what you are truly passionate about.

How Will This Year's Eclipses Affect You?

Eclipses signal intense periods that highlight major growth opportunities for us in the process of creating our lives. They are linked to the lunar phases—specifically the New and Full Moon—and involve the relationship between the Sun and the Moon and the Earth. A Solar Eclipse is a magnified New Moon, while a Lunar Eclipse is a magnified Full Moon. Eclipses unfold in cycles involving all twelve signs of the zodiac, and they occur in pairs, usually about two weeks apart.

In 2019 there are five eclipses, three solar (two in Capricorn and one in Cancer) and two lunar (one in Leo and one in Capricorn). The first Solar Eclipse arrives on January 5 in Capricorn, triggering the showdown between Saturn and Pluto over how to deal with all the long-buried secrets of your own psyche. Saturn just wants to control what he perceives as potentially overpowering, potentially dangerous, and potentially damaging, while Pluto invites you to see past the defenses and the coping strategies you have in place to find a deeper meaning and purpose to those experiences that you, in his mind, put in a safe place to be dug up when the time is right. And that time is now. This particular confluence of Solar and Lunar Eclipses, Saturn, and Pluto will not occur again in this lifetime, so take hold of the opportunity. It probably won't be pretty as you wrestle with the fear that delving too deep may shatter you and leave you broken.

Instead of feeding your fears, take the energy of the Lunar Eclipse in Leo on January 21 and build on your self-esteem by seeking new creative outlets, by celebrating yourself in some new and imaginative way. You will need a strong sense of self at your core to work with what is being stirred up, but work with it you can. Recognize that the best resource you have is your mental fluidity, because it allows you to move through things and see them quickly and accurately. That way you don't get lost in what surfaces and you are able to construct an approach to putting things in the proper perspective. That's imperative if you are to emerge a more integrated human being.

Your greatest asset is your brain, so use it wisely to create long-lasting life changes that the remaining eclipses of the year on July 2, July 16, and December 26 continue to provide the spark and the push to complete. One word of caution: Although the desire is to quantify the results of this yearlong process—and remember it really isn't a war, even if it feels like it—there really is no way to measure what you have accomplished, just a sense that you are a completely new person and a feeling that the world is a better place. The only thing that gives you a glimpse into what you actually did is how differently you respond to the same old situations, the same old input. In those aha moments, pat yourself on the back. You earned it.

Gemini | January

Overall Theme

The year begins with a quieter, more contemplative version of who you are. That's because you are trying to process a steady stream of input from deep within that causes you to take stock of your life in ways that are going to surprise you. Know this. It's necessary and it's just the beginning of a yearlong process to reinvent yourself.

Relationships

Don't be surprised if the people around you, including those you are closest to, wonder what's wrong with you. This irritates you so much that you find yourself snapping at people and being more than a little bit defensive because you aren't sure there isn't something wrong. Even you think you are too quiet. Relax and let the comments go in one ear and out the other.

Career, Success, and Money

You are feeling a distinct lack of satisfaction with what you perceive your future to be, leading to a series of disconnected thoughts about what you should do. Refrain from doing anything hasty. The timing couldn't be worse for making the kind of change that will really be meaningful to you. Continue to delve into the dissatisfaction to find out what's really underneath it.

Pitfalls and Potential Problems

Both the Solar Eclipse on January 5 and the Lunar Eclipse on January 21 hit you pretty hard, stirring up your subconscious. The best thing to do is to go with the flow, observing exactly how you feel and using it as a point of initiation for knowing yourself better—a much better approach than running from yourself and/or projecting stuff onto others.

Rewarding Days

13, 14, 21, 25

Challenging Days

5, 6, 28, 29

Gemini | February

Overall Theme

The bounce is back. Gone is your mind going in never-ending mental circles, covering the same territory again and again. No more living in slow motion—your mind is running at high speed. That is until February 10, when everything turns kind of soupy as Mercury enters Pisces, where it remains until April 17. One thing is certain: your imagination really knows no bounds.

Relationships

Again you feel out of sync with those around you. You are talking and you don't think anyone's listening because they are all so caught up in the demands of daily living that they aren't interested in a whole bunch of mental gymnastics. Now, if you offered to help them with life, you'd be better off.

Career, Success, and Money

Be cautious about taking any huge risks this month. It's okay to entertain yourself by thinking about what you could do with your career or your money, but be realistic. Too much of your life feels like an unknown quantity right now for you to be truly at peace with anything that requires a long-term commitment. Allow yourself to be mentally stimulated and entertained. You'll find it's enough.

Pitfalls and Potential Problems

Your life is in flux and, surprisingly, you don't like it. That's because last month's eclipses jarred loose a lot of hidden stuff and you are still trying to figure out what to do with it. Oh, your brain is dancing the dance, but it's not enough to bring you peace of mind. You find you need more than to be entertained, creating a crisis of confidence.

Rewarding Days

4, 5, 9, 10

Challenging Days

13, 14, 19, 20

Gemini | March

Overall Theme

The combination of Mercury going retrograde in Pisces on March 5 and Uranus moving into Taurus on March 6 knocks you off balance, stunning you into a level of confusion so unfamiliar that it overwhelms you. Accept that what is running around in your head isn't intended to make sense and you'll be fine.

Relationships

All the people in your life feel like a foreign country you've never had any desire to visit. Strange, isn't it? So strange that you don't know how to navigate this turn of events, leaving you with one simple solution: take a timeout. Just remember to let those you care about know how out of sorts you feel. That way no one hits a panic button, including you.

Career, Success, and Money

This is definitely not a month to do anything in these areas. You are so disconnected from your own life that you really have no idea which end is up. Any attempt to change this by making decisions or plans will only precipitate a crisis you don't need.

Pitfalls and Potential Problems

Life feels like a box of puzzle pieces that simply don't go together, leaving you grasping for anything that will give you a sense of security. Turn inward, because nothing in the outer world is going to allay this sudden fear that nothing is solid. And so begins a seven-year journey of dissolving the known to create a future that, in this moment, is entirely without form.

Rewarding Days

21, 22, 30, 31

Challenging Days

10, 11, 25, 26

Gemini | April

Overall Theme

You emerge renewed and ready to take on the world from last month's detour into all things intangible. Your engines are firing on all cylinders and everything glows with opportunity. The only challenge you face is figuring out where to focus all that enthusiasm and optimism. Just don't pick the first thing that catches your attention.

Relationships

You return from your self-imposed exile wondering where everyone is. The truth is they didn't go anywhere; you did. And as soon as you announce your arrival, you are surrounded by people and questions and concerns. Even though you are happy to see the hordes, you aren't sure you want to engage in a full-scale analysis of your life decisions. Just smile.

Career, Success, and Money

An idea, a project, or a proposal that's been waiting in the wings suddenly pushes itself to the forefront of your consciousness, and you are more than ready to move forward with it. First, make sure all the details are in order, and then refrain from taking action until April 17, when Mercury moves into Aries. Then go.

Pitfalls and Potential Problems

With your energy returning full force, be careful about acting without first taking stock of the current climate. This requires the recognition that you are likely to indulge in wishful thinking so you can finally get something done. After all, the first three months of the year felt like you were chasing your tail.

Rewarding Days

9, 10, 13, 14

Challenging Days

6, 7, 24, 25

Gemini | May

Overall Theme

You are still going full tilt, yet this month has more than its share of irritations and adjustments. Take this in stride because any perceived delays are actually opportunities to fine-tune the direction your life is going in, leading to a much-deserved reward by the end of the month.

Relationships

New people cross your path, including someone who will have a significant impact on your life for the foreseeable future. Don't hesitate to accept any invitations that have the potential to introduce you to both new experiences and new people. You won't be aware of it, but you are planting seeds for the future. Besides, you are ready for an infusion of anything new. Otherwise, boredom is on the horizon.

Career, Success, and Money

Optimism about the future rises and falls almost daily this month. Every time you turn around, the plans you put in motion falter when you least expect it. These are minor challenges and not the setbacks you perceive them to be. What little patience you have is tested. Count to ten and a solution emerges from your deep well of creativity.

Pitfalls and Potential Problems

You definitely don't like being required to revisit things that you believe you put the finishing touches on. However, once you get past this resistance, May promises to be a month when you emerge with a greater sense of satisfaction in how good you really are at mastering the challenges that come your way. Ease doesn't always equal fulfillment.

Rewarding Days

6, 7, 24, 25

Challenging Days

17, 18, 21, 22

Gemini | June

Overall Theme

As always, when your cognitive mind is overrun by the feelings that you keep so carefully camouflaged with words, conflict is inevitable. Why? Because you are never quite sure what you are supposed to do since you believe thoughts and feelings cannot comfortably exist in the same space. Time to change your outlook.

Relationships

Normally, you are not one to take offense at what people say to you. After all, you love verbal sparring. Just not this month. You feel that everything said in your general vicinity is designed to criticize you and/or hurt you. Take a hard look at what is triggering you, and some much-needed self-awareness will lighten things up considerably and give you the healthy space to let others know how you feel about what they've said.

Career, Success, and Money

Refrain from making impulsive, rash decisions about money, because the potential exists to create a drain on your resources, either financial or emotional. Money is so intertwined with your feelings of self-worth that being emotionally under siege can result in an internal battle around either hoarding or overspending.

Pitfalls and Potential Problems

If you aren't able to find a modicum of detachment, this could be a month when you create some long-term issues in various areas of your life by simply responding to what life dishes up with verbal tirades and a number of rounds of the blame game. Don't let the intensity of what you feel take control of what comes out of your mouth. Instead, take a step back before responding.

Rewarding Days

3, 4, 9, 10

Challenging Days

5, 6, 16, 17

Gemini | July

Overall Theme

Your confidence returns and just in time. The Solar and Lunar Eclipses on July 2 and 16, respectively, combined with your planetary avatar Mercury going retrograde on July 7 promise a potpourri of uncomfortable feelings and experiences that test your mettle. Use your considerable mental agility to put things in perspective.

Relationships

It's not so much that you want to be a hermit; you just don't feel like putting much effort into gadding about. Instead, you'd rather just hang out at home or, if you go out, it's to places that are warm and familiar. You need the security and comfort of the people who know you best, the tried and true, so you can deal with what is percolating within.

Career, Success, and Money

A lot of insecurity surfaces about the future and how prepared you are for it from a financial point of view. This leads to a full-on examination of whether your current career or work path is where your heart is. Be careful not to blow any qualms you have out of proportion. This is a time of recalibration, not hasty decisions to jump ship.

Pitfalls and Potential Problems

So far, 2019 has been a test of gigantic proportions. No part of your life seems to be functioning in a way that brings you consistent satisfaction. No time is this more true than in July. Ride out your discontent and refrain from extreme reactions, and a new sense of purpose will begin to take hold after Mercury goes direct on July 31.

Rewarding Days

4, 5, 27, 28

Challenging Days

15, 16, 20, 21

Gemini | August

Overall Theme

During the first ten days of the month, you feel like you are stuck in a never-ending loop of one step forward, two steps back. Yet your enthusiasm remains high and, for the first time in 2019, you know things are on the upswing. This leads to a renewed sense of purpose and the desire to get things done, no matter what it takes.

Relationships

What you seek in your relationships this month is simple: you want adventure. So don't be surprised if you find yourself organizing a getaway, a reunion, a camping trip—anything that involves a new location and as many of the people you love as possible. You just want to laugh and share and renew your connections.

Career, Success, and Money

You are definitely looking for new things to master, which helps you move through a lot of the nuts-and-bolts details that demand your attention this month. On a deeper level, you are a whirlwind of creativity, so make note of anything that pops into your head and then revisit these ideas every month until the end of the year. Not only does this give you a sense that you are in charge of your future, but it also reveals a possible new path.

Pitfalls and Potential Problems

The biggest threat to your renewed sense of joie de vivre is the sheer volume of itsy-bitsy details that somehow got overlooked last month and now need to be addressed. The truth is, the job isn't as big as you think. After all, you don't really like having to do anything over, so even one detail is one too many.

Rewarding Days

13, 14, 19, 20

Challenging Days

16, 17, 26, 27

Gemini | September

Overall Theme

Every area of your life is fraught with tension, and you aren't really sure why. The answer? You feel pushed to the brink by the demands on your time, both from the outside world and from within yourself. Normally you love to multitask, but this month you just want to take one thing at a time. That way you can take a breath and figure out what is going on instead of rushing headlong from one thing to another.

Relationships

The possibility is high that you will speak out of turn and then spend the rest of the month trying to smooth ruffled feathers and assuage hurt feelings. Part of the issue is that your circuits are overloaded trying to cope with a mountain of irritations, which leaves you with a short fuse and little capacity to edit yourself. Practice saying nothing if you are cranky.

Career, Success, and Money

No sooner do you get one pile of things accomplished than another appears. There's not much you can do about it except get things done. Such is the daily grind facing you on the job front. The antidote? Turn your attention to your home and take care of outstanding repair issues and/or renovation plans. It's definitely a good month to accelerate any plans to revamp your home, whether you want to redecorate or totally redefine your space.

Pitfalls and Potential Problems

The level of inner dissatisfaction you feel cannot be measured, nor should it be. Instead of focusing on all the things that annoy you, look past the list to what is at the root of your discontent. By doing so, you find the fuel to make change.

Rewarding Days

7, 8, 28, 29

Challenging Days

10, 11, 22, 23

Gemini | October

Overall Theme

You find yourself completely and utterly distracted by the constant mental noise in your head. Time to take a break from thinking everything to death and just get on with life. Otherwise you miss some great opportunities to apply, in very practical terms, the changes you feel compelled to make. Of course, this means moving past your default position of believing that your rational mind is the only source of awareness in your world.

Relationships

Socially, you are at the top of your game: lighthearted, happy to hang out, entertaining, and fun. On a deeper level, you find yourself seeking something that seems just out of reach. It shocks you to discover that what has always satisfied you in relationships is no longer enough. Time to begin the process of redefining what you really desire.

Career, Success, and Money

Follow your instincts when it comes to making decisions this month and you will find yourself with unexpected rewards, both in terms of strengthening your position and of creating long-lasting working relationships. Too much overthinking will only take you down a path that leads to a dead end, especially in the area of finances.

Pitfalls and Potential Problems

Please don't ignore any internal discomfort you feel. It's a sign that something isn't working for you, no matter what area of your life this unease is connected to. One of your biggest challenges in life is that you'd really rather keep everything light and on the upswing. Know this. Acknowledging the less attractive aspects of life keeps you from being blind-sided.

Rewarding Days

2, 3, 21, 22

Challenging Days

12, 13, 25, 26

Gemini | November

Overall Theme

Much of the month is spent recalibrating a number of stressful issues that keep surfacing in your life, in spite of your best efforts to resolve them. Go beyond feeling disheartened to recognize that you are in a long-term process of transformation that cannot be quantified. Dig in and you are rewarded with an infusion of relief.

Relationships

This is one area where you can expect to experience some real joy. You find that, rather than running away from you because you are deep in the swamp, those you love and cherish take time out to be there for you, to lighten your spirits, and to listen. The result is you open up in ways that surprise you, giving you an opportunity to acknowledge what you are really experiencing.

Career, Success, and Money

You struggle to do more than go through the motions. It seems that right now you don't feel particularly connected to your work, to where you might be going, or to seeing any value in pursuing long-term goals. Remember, it's okay to show up and do your job to the best of your ability without feeling over-the-moon excited or interested every day.

Pitfalls and Potential Problems

Be careful not to throw a month-long pity party. Oh, you are convinced that you are still the life of the party known as *life*, but that's not how you are acting. Far from it. You are feeling sorry for yourself underneath the usual mental gymnastics. Accept that you are totally disconcerted by the curve balls thrown at you in 2019. It's the first step to creating a new beginning.

Rewarding Days

3, 4, 20, 21

Challenging Days

11, 12, 28, 29

Gemini | December

Overall Theme

Life feels very weighty on and off for much of the month, as the majority of planets are in earth (Capricorn) or water (Scorpio, Pisces) signs. This makes you feel like someone clipped your wings. The key is to tend to practical issues. Don't let anything slide and you will enter 2020 with a greater sense of your own worth.

Relationships

Be very clear in your communication. No waffling, no changing your mind again and again, no making a promise just to please others and then backing out at the last minute. This is a month when you must follow through. Do what you say you are going to do and ask for what you truly desire. Otherwise, the fallout is unpleasant and you are disappointed in yourself.

Career, Success, and Money

Shared resources are in the spotlight, whether it's money, ideas, rewards, or time. Manage them well, making sure to talk everything out instead of going on your own merry way, and 2019 ends on a very positive note. You are full of hope for what you can accomplish in 2020 because you created space for both yourself and others.

Pitfalls and Potential Problems

Avoid feeling that everything is drudgery, another one of your default positions that gets you in trouble. Getting down in the trenches and working everything through with focus and commitment creates the space for more creative ideas and inspirations to flow. Understanding this is the best way to open the door to 2020.

Rewarding Days

3, 4, 17, 18

Challenging Days

6, 7, 15, 16

Gemini Action Table

These dates reflect the best—but not the only—times for success and ease in these activities, according to your Sun sign.

	JAN	FEB	MAR	APR	MAY	JUN	JUL	AUG	SEP	OCT	NOV	DEC
Move	21, 22			9, 10		8, 9		30, 31				
Start a class					1, 2				19, 20			
Seek coaching/ counseling	5, 6						3, 4			27, 28		
Ask for a raise				1, 2					3, 4			17, 18
Get professional advice			5, 6				10, 11				19, 20	
Get a loan		15, 16				4, 5				9, 10		
New romance			21, 22					4, 5				10, 11
Vacation		3, 4			23, 24						3, 4	

Cancer

The Crab
June 22 to July 22

Element: Water

Quality: Cardinal

Polarity: Yin/feminine

Planetary Ruler: The Moon

Meditation: I have faith in the promptings of my heart

Gemstone: Pearl

Power Stones: Moonstone, Chrysocolla

Key Phrase: I feel

Glyph: Crab's claws

Anatomy: Stomach, breasts

Colors: Silver, pearl white

Animals: Crustaceans, cows, chickens

Myths/Legends: Hercules and the Crab, Asherah, Hecate

House: Fourth

Opposite Sign: Capricorn

Flower: Larkspur

Keyword: Receptivity

The Cancer Personality

Strengths, Spiritual Purpose, and Challenges

You arrive on the planet brimful of sensitivity, adaptability, and the capacity to create a connection from something as simple as a good meal, a warm bed, or the best hug ever, because you put everything you are into everything you do. In your heart you feel everything but often aren't sure exactly how to take those feelings and put them into practice in the outer world, because your experience in that arena tells you that your gift of feeling—which is in fact your spiritual purpose—isn't valued the same way rational thinking is. This leaves you stuck in the belief that you are always at a disadvantage, that your gift is more like a curse. Therein lies your conundrum. How do you reconcile the truth that who you are and what you are doesn't always match what the world identifies as good and valuable? The answer? By constantly bending over backward to take care of everyone in hopes that it will get you the acceptance and sense of connection that you not only desire but need.

Surely fulfilling the emotional needs of others with your innate sensitivity will finally be recognized, celebrated, and honored, right? Not so much. Instead, it seems people just want more, with little or no gratitude, never mind any acknowledgment. This leads to moodiness and a lot of defensiveness, because you feel you are giving your all and nobody notices or cares. While that may be accurate—after all, your perception is your reality—remember this: Cancer is the first sign of the zodiac whose major focus is the need for a connection based not on what can be initiated or done or thought, but on simply being present and aware. That's a powerful invitation, but one that most people simply don't know how to respond to, so you shut yourself off, believing that you must protect yourself by hiding the very essence of who you are. You numb yourself, which leaves you devoid of a vital connection to yourself. This is the deepest cut of all, because you are placing more value on others than on yourself. Value yourself and respect yourself, and the world becomes a more positive place.

Relationships

Number one on your list of relationships is family. They always hold a special place in your heart, even when they don't live up to your needs or expectations. Your challenge is recognizing that who you are doesn't necessarily spring from them. It comes from deep within your own psyche, your own self. Of course, they had a hand in shaping you, but you actually provided the raw materials. This is important when it comes to forming relationships with the rest of the world, whether it's with your partner, your friends, your children, or your work colleagues. If you don't recognize yourself as an autonomous individual, you run the risk of not being able to relate to others without your family as a subconscious filter. This leads to many complications, including not knowing whether you are being authentic or are simply being what you perceive others want you to be, projecting subconscious family conflicts onto unsuspecting people, and not being able to work through issues with anyone because you feel you are somehow being disloyal. You have such a tremendous capacity to connect, to nurture, to support, and to love, provided you maintain a healthy relationship with yourself that is not clouded by the opinions and attitudes of others. One of your biggest challenges is to accept how sensitive you are and how easily offended you can be. Once you embrace those parts of yourself, you can remain true to yourself while putting what others say in the proper perspective.

Career and Work

It is in this area that the battle between what feels right to you and the inner demand for security often comes to a head. In order for you to be truly content in whatever career or job you choose, it has to be an emotional fit, one that makes you feel warm and fuzzy and comfortable. However, if the practicalities of life demand an infusion of money, the push for security easily overshadows the desire for something emotionally meaningful in your work life. Oh, you may plan to go back in search of that dream career or job, but the predictability of what you have often hijacks that intention. You end up convincing yourself that the time is not right, that you will do it next week, next month, or next year or that following your heart is a luxury you cannot afford. The key is to use your need for security as a foundation on which to build a plan to make your dreams come true while maintaining your security. Then, when everything is in place, you are able to make the move toward what resonates with you.

Money and Possessions

You really do get visceral pleasure as well as contentment and satisfaction from your physical surroundings, so you put a lot of planning and effort into turning where you live into the home of your dreams. It's not so much that you wish to accumulate a lot or own a lot. You want security and you want to be surrounded by what makes you happy. The challenge is that you can get carried away if you start substituting money and possessions for emotional satisfaction or the feeling that all is right in your world. Money and possessions can never be a substitute for what you require and value most in life: love and support, belonging and being seen, acceptance and nurturing. If you have those, then the money and the possessions are a nice bonus, making it easy not to hang on to them for dear life.

The Light Side of Life

Nothing is more fun for you than hanging out with those you love most in the world. Combine that with entertaining at home and you are in seventh heaven, sharing all that you have and all that you have created with those lucky enough to be invited into your world. Your home is more than where you lay your head at night; it is your sanctuary, your inspiration, your retreat, your source of energy, your mirror—your everything. So where else can you experience the things that bring you the most joy, the most serenity, and the most security? Your answer? Nowhere.

Cancer Keywords for 2019
Self-determination, self-nurturing, joy

The Year Ahead for Cancer

Get ready to be pushed outside your comfort zone again and again and again in 2019. Now, before you hit the panic button, take a moment to reflect on the feelings of dissatisfaction and confusion that last year brought to the surface, and then acknowledge them, out in the open for everyone, including yourself, to see. No hiding them or glossing over them or pretending they don't exist. Otherwise, you spend all of 2019 feeling like you are drowning under the weight of expectations and obligations, both your own and those of others. It's time to get clear about who is in charge of your life, which leads to a litany of things that need to be done before you can even give yourself permission to do that, much less hand yourself the reins. This process begins with you casting aside any thoughts, beliefs, or ideas that leave you struggling to feel that your life actually includes you. Now, there's no doubt that this feels like an enormous task, but it's a necessary one, because 2019 is a pivotal year in your development. Take one thing at a time. And while you are confronting these limitations in an orderly fashion, make time for what brings you contentment, emotional satisfaction, joy, a sense of fun, and connection. Shine yourself up every chance you get. In fact, make it a habit every day to find something that lights you up from the inside, whether it's making a gratitude list, buying yourself a treat, acknowledging something you've done, or recognizing a quality you like about yourself. Make sure you write down these rays of sunshine and look at them again once a week. Just one rule: Everything on the list has to be about you and who you are. Next, say no to anything that you quite frankly don't want to do, especially if there's a huge dollop of guilt attached to it. Refrain from offering reasons or justifications for your decisions. Just go with what feels right. This will take practice, but not only can it done, it needs to be done. Being able to say no is the first step in you being able to put yourself at the top of your list of priorities.

Saturn

Quite simply, Saturn can be and often is your archnemesis, because his approach to the world doesn't fit in with your sensibilities. This doesn't mean you don't recognize that life needs structure, purpose, and practicality. You just wonder why it has to be accompanied by the hard edges that you associate with Saturn. Is it not possible to take care of business at the same time that you demonstrate empathy, tenderness, and respect for the feeling, emotional side of life? This question remains foremost in your mind and heart for the second year in a row as Saturn hangs out in his own sign of Capricorn, demanding—in your mind, anyway—that you tow the line. Follow the rules, keep your feelings to yourself, and suck it up. It's true that Saturn doesn't have much time for the very things that make life important to you. It's not that he doesn't see value in them; he's too busy making sure you can survive to enjoy them. Granted, Saturn gets pretty stuck in that job, to the point that life is nothing but a series of duties and obligations. However, his deeper purpose is always to ask you to be accountable for your reality, both inside and outside. No matter what is going on, it truly is up to you to take charge and find a solution to the issues he presents. Since the end of 2017, those issues have a strong relationship flavor to them. Quite frequently, you find yourself at cross-purposes with just about everybody. Rather than lamenting what you think is an unfortunate turn of events, see these experiences as an opportunity to redefine where you want to make your mark, what your goals are and how you can achieve them. You can get so stuck in maintaining the familiar that you need a good challenge to get you to reexamine your life. And Saturn is more than ready to help you out.

Uranus

Well, there's one thing that offers you a huge sense of relief this year, and that's the shift Uranus makes from Aries into Taurus on March 6. No more topsy-turvy, chaotic, what-could-possibly-go-sideways-now moments. Before you get too comfortable, recognize this: all the things that Uranus touched still need attention. It's just that his job now is to mentor you in the areas you feel he more or less blew up during the previous seven years. His intention is not to abandon you and leave you to cope with the mess he created by pushing you outside your comfort zone. He challenges you to look beyond that to see what else is out there. Certainly his methods leave much to be desired, but much of that has to do with your inherent desire to hang on to everything, just in case. Instead of trying to put everything back together the way it was, you now have the opportunity to create a new foundation using the awareness that comes from recognizing that nothing is permanent. However, that doesn't mean you can't build a sense of security from knowing that not only can you weather big change, but you can actually grow and expand the boundaries of who you are and what you can accomplish from that well deep inside of you that you so carefully guard. It's time to draw on those resources if you are to make real use of Uranus in Taurus during the next seven years. Of course, the ride will be bumpy. There's no hanging out with Uranus without turbulence. Just remember, his job is to make sure you don't get so deeply entrenched in your comfort zone that you forget how to live.

Neptune

With Saturn, Uranus, and Pluto hammering away at your insides and your outsides, most intensely over the last two years, part of you would just like to disappear into the land of rose-colored glasses. And Neptune is definitely available to offer you that option. After all, he invented rose-colored glasses, illusion, and delusion. However, he can also be your guide to a deeper sense of clarity if you have the capacity to muddle through the fog that alerts you to the fact he is about to impact your life in a big yet indefinable way. Right now, he is busy vaporizing many of the things you hold dear, yet you can't get a handle on how or why. All you can do is stop trying to make sense of the big picture and take one minute, one hour, one day, one week, at a time. Accept that this is an inner journey and that much of the time you won't have a clue. Be in the moment and trust that creating space for a vision to emerge will lead to a new sense of purpose. This means immersing yourself in sensing, feeling, and knowing, acknowledging that your rational mind only inhibits the process and the experience of trusting the intangible. That way, a new vision of life's possibilities can emerge, you can appreciate the gifts you have in the feeling realm, and you can be more comfortable in your own skin instead of always trying to protect yourself by hiding from everyone, including yourself. One word of caution: Neptune can make anything seem possible. So ask yourself if what you are feeling is a fantasy (something totally improbable) or a dream (something founded in a real awareness of self).

Pluto

With Saturn cozying up to Pluto, it's going to be difficult to determine which one of them is annoying you, challenging you, or just generally getting in your way the most. So here's the litmus test: If you are fighting to take charge of your life, it's Saturn. If you feel like you are at the bottom of a swamp fighting desperately to breathe, it's Pluto. Granted, both descriptions are the extremes of what is possible, but they do give you a glimpse into the workings of these two heavyweight planets. When combined, they can create a deep and profound crisis that challenges you to take down any inner walls you have, to dig into your own psyche and clear away any emotional detritus cluttering up your path forward, to overcome fears and insecurities, and to be accountable for the role you have played in muddying up your own life. This might seem overwhelming, and at times it will be. There really is no way to get around that. Besides, trying to do that simply creates more problems than it solves. So give yourself completely to the process and a hidden treasure will emerge. (After all, we are talking about Pluto, who loves nothing better than to hide things that must be found at a later date.) The treasure? You discover just how strong and resilient you are. This allows you to let go of anything that no longer contributes to your life, creating the perfect starting point for the next phase of your life.

How Will This Year's Eclipses Affect You?

Eclipses signal intense periods that highlight major growth opportunities for us in the process of creating our lives. They are linked to the lunar phases—specifically the New and Full Moon—and involve the relationship between the Sun and the Moon and the Earth. A Solar Eclipse is a magnified New Moon, while a Lunar Eclipse is a magnified Full Moon. Eclipses unfold in cycles involving all twelve signs of the zodiac, and they occur in pairs, usually about two weeks apart.

In 2019 there are five eclipses, three solar (two in Capricorn and one in Cancer) and two lunar (one in Leo and one in Capricorn). The first Solar Eclipse arrives on January 5 in Capricorn, leaving you feeling emotionally like you've been hit over the head with a baseball bat—certainly not the beginning to 2019 you had in mind. Nevertheless, it signals a deep need to take care of yourself this year, rather than putting on hold your own feelings, desires, dreams, or plans. This comes with a challenge that has plagued you for much of your life: How much of your security rests in nurturing (or babysitting) those around you and how much of it actually resides in taking care of yourself? Too often, you feel these two things are mutually exclusive when, in fact, taking care of yourself actually amplifies the amount of love and energy you can give to others. The first step you need to take is to define what nurturing looks and feels like. To do that, it is imperative that you ask yourself if you can detach yourself from others. Or are you so entwined with them and their needs that you feel doing anything purely for yourself is selfish? Remember, detaching isn't the same as disconnecting. In order to be a healthy human being, to take a step back so you can be in your own space. Only then can you really know what works for you.

The Lunar Eclipse on January 21 challenges you to begin building your capacity to hang out with yourself, take care of you, and do what you want to do. Stepping into these unfamiliar waters promises two things: a deeper understanding of and appreciation for who you are and an abundance of life-affirming experiences for the rest of 2019. So stand tall and don't back down. No matter the stumbling block, know that you will prevail. Without this level of confidence and determination, the remaining eclipses of the year on July 2, July 16, and December

26 will continue to hit you hard instead of providing you with further opportunities to build a strong sense of your own identity (apart from what you can do for others) and to know just how deep the inner waters are that nurture you. Shocking, isn't it, to know that what you seek from others has always been inside, just waiting for you to recognize the truth and turn inward? This is the message of all the 2019 Solar and Lunar Eclipses, so take the risk and you will emerge from this year a more integrated and content human being.

Cancer | January

Overall Theme

No one is affected more by eclipses than you, because both the Solar and Lunar Eclipses involve the Moon, your avatar. The only thing that changes is the degree of impact, and this month brings you two extremely powerful eclipses designed to amplify issues connected to self-love versus your love of others. Take a stand and put yourself first. Resist the pull to give in to others.

Relationships

You feel under siege both within and without as you grapple with your innate inclination to take the road of least resistance when it comes to other people. It is natural for you to attend to the wants and needs of others. However, the relationship that is most important this month is your relationship with yourself. Remember, you are setting the tone for 2019. No more putting off the need to make yourself number one.

Career, Success, and Money

Be careful that you don't disappear into your work in an effort to avoid the emotional challenges rocketing around inside you, because in the end everything suffers. Accept that your attention is elsewhere and stick to maintaining the tried and true rather than initiating new projects or pathways. Your heart really isn't in the game.

Pitfalls and Potential Problems

January presents the first big test of 2019, and you aren't at all sure you are up to the challenge. Nothing feels the least bit secure, and your usual coping strategies don't bring any relief. The more you try them, the less effective they are. This further rocks your reality, and you aren't sure you know which end is up. Draw on the considerable emotional resources at your core to ride out the turbulence.

Rewarding Days

15, 16, 25, 26

Challenging Days

5, 6, 20, 21

Cancer | February

Overall Theme
There's a big push to get out into the world and make your mark, but after last month's challenges your inclination is to take a break, keep your head down, and refrain from drawing attention to yourself. This may seem like avoidance, but the truth is you are hard at work on a deep level and there isn't space for a lot of running around.

Relationships
You are certainly convinced that your only value to others is what you can do for them. Your greatest strengths—sensitivity and a profound capacity to care—often become your greatest weaknesses. The key is not to abandon who you are, but to recognize that it is entirely up to you who gets the benefit of your gifts. It's the only way you can begin to dismantle the pattern you helped create.

Career, Success, and Money
No matter what provokes you, triggers you, or just plain annoys you, don't act on impulse, whether it's connected to work, future plans, or money—especially at work, where the demands on your time are so far beyond the hours in a day that you are fairly certain you'll go crazy. Instead, make a list of all the things asked of you and forward it your boss.

Pitfalls and Potential Problems
You are highly resistant to being pushed in any direction, which leads you to dig in your heels, get defensive, and/or lose your temper. In turn, this leaves you feeling embarrassed and a little unsure about what exactly is going on. It's simple. You are shifting your priorities to yourself, and in order to do that, you find yourself taking things to the extreme.

Rewarding Days
11, 12, 24, 25

Challenging Days
1, 2, 21, 22

Cancer | March

Overall Theme

Take time to recognize that not everything is a life-or-death decision, even if it feels like it. The changes going on inside you feel like an internal earthquake, and in your quest for a release from the pressure, you need to be careful not to act out your inner five-year-old. Instead, find new creative or physical outlets.

Relationships

The truth is, you still like people, at least you think you do. You just aren't crazy about what they say, what they think, and how they act. The root of your discontent is a lack of authenticity. But the more you look at others, the more you become aware that your deepest desire is to become more yourself and less the picture of what others want.

Career, Success, and Money

A new path opens up unexpectedly, leading you to take stock of commitments and plans you thought you would never change or abandon. You find yourself reconsidering everything, from what type of work satisfies you to what your definition of success is to where money fits into your life. Just remember, you don't have to come to any conclusions this month.

Pitfalls and Potential Problems

This month brings a shocking insight that you are ready to turn your life upside down in order to create a new start. At the center of this awareness is the realization that what you thought was truly important, valuable, and sacred in your life doesn't seem to hold the same place in your heart anymore. Relax. This is not the end of anything, much less you. So don't put on the brakes or do anything hasty. Meditate and contemplate.

Rewarding Days

5, 6, 10, 11

Challenging Days

13, 14, 23, 24

Cancer | April

Overall Theme
Some of the tumult subsides, leaving you with the feeling that you can actually breathe three or four times consecutively without being consumed by a tidal wave of unresolved issues. It's just the respite you need to get yourself back on track in all aspects of your life. The result is that you get a lot accomplished and your self-confidence returns.

Relationships
Gone are those feelings of dissatisfaction that have been your constant companion for the first three months of 2019, and everyone notices. Just remember not to get upset when your loved ones, friends, and colleagues share their thoughts on how you've been acting. What's more, don't apologize or defend yourself. Some of the things you said or did were necessary. They needed to know your job isn't to be a doormat.

Career, Success, and Money
Now this is the month to get what you want at work, whether it's a raise, a promotion, or the green light for a new project close to your heart. It's also a good time to add to your skill set by going to courses or workshops that increase your value and your employability. As for money, don't buy all the bright, shiny things that seem to be calling your name.

Pitfalls and Potential Problems
Be careful not to forget the insights that opened up your eyes recently. It's okay to hang out in the world of Everything is Wonderful; just don't plan to make it your permanent residence. Otherwise, you will overlook some very real facts about friends and financial matters that could threaten your long-term prospects. Enjoy the blissful feeling while staying focused on what is happening.

Rewarding Days
1, 2, 6, 7

Challenging Days
9, 10, 24, 25

Cancer | May

Overall Theme

You can't decide whether the most important thing to do is rush around as if there were no tomorrow or kick off your shoes, have fun, get creative, and socialize. It's not really a case of either/or. Too much rushing around leaves you exhausted and dissatisfied. Too much taking it easy creates a guilt complex. Find a happy blend of the two.

Relationships

Accept all social invitations, because it's time to meet new people. This means setting aside your natural reluctance to go into unfamiliar territory. But it's definitely worth it. First, you'll have fun, something that's been in short supply lately. Second, you'll cross paths with the kinds of people with whom you truly connect. Third, you'll meet someone who promises to have a long-term impact on your life.

Career, Success, and Money

The message is to hold steady in all three areas. No rocking the boat, no pushing the envelope, no taking big risks. That's because you are really feeling like you have one foot on the brake and one on the gas pedal, which creates the kind of internal insecurity that could undermine any deviation from the usual.

Pitfalls and Potential Problems

The biggest lows this month come from you spending too much time questioning yourself. The key is to go with what feels right to you. It may not be a good time to do a major overhaul on the structured parts of your world, but it is a good time to expand the length and breadth of you.

Rewarding Days

4, 5, 16, 17

Challenging Days

8, 9, 20, 21

Cancer | June

Overall Theme

Be careful to count to ten before you open your mouth, as the impulse to speak before thinking hits the stratosphere, leaving you a little dumbstruck that you could be so foolhardy. How could you say those things? Easily, when the internal pressure of feeling that no matter what you do it isn't enough boils over. Be kind to yourself and know that what you bring to the table is worthwhile, not just necessary.

Relationships

You definitely want to speak your truth this month. Your challenge is doing so without needing or worrying about the kind of response you will get. Part of this process is sharing, with no expectations, your stress, your insecurities, your fear of loss, and your feeling that you are invisible. This is powerful and liberating, as well as an important step in honoring yourself and nurturing yourself in a newer, healthier way.

Career, Success, and Money

Expect to work hard, put out a lot of fires, and feel like there is no end to the feeling of drudgery that threatens to overwhelm you every second or third day. And the reason why is simple: everything on your plate isn't yours. So return the work that isn't your responsibility to the person it belongs to. That way you can breathe again.

Pitfalls and Potential Problems

The ups and downs of this month signal an important step in your development as you stretch yourself beyond your comfort zone, beyond the subconscious belief that you are only as important as the last thing you did for someone, beyond the well-developed ways you created to hobble yourself to fit other people's expectations. It's a big job. Take care not to judge yourself too harshly.

Rewarding Days

9, 10, 27, 28

Challenging Days

16, 17, 25, 26

Cancer | July

Overall Theme

One day you feel like a million dollars and the next you want to crawl under a rock. This symbolizes your ongoing life's struggle, which is in high relief in 2019: trying to integrate how to take care of yourself at the same time you exemplify your deep dedication to the welfare of others. Make this a time to celebrate yourself every day by doing what brings a smile to your face.

Relationships

Every time you turn around, you find yourself wondering why you worry more about others than yourself, why you often don't consider your desires or needs important. This is a watershed month for taking deliberate steps to put yourself at the top of your list of priorities. Start with small things, like making your favorite meal or letting someone else take care of the chores. Time to let go of the need to be indispensable.

Career, Success, and Money

As you take charge of yourself and your life, you also examine the roles you play in the work world. Are you primarily a helper, a cheerleader, a support to others, while playing down your own skills and abilities? Do you give yourself permission to dream beyond your comfort zone? Those are big questions that need answers.

Pitfalls and Potential Problems

Pushing yourself outside the spaces and places that make you feel safe comes with a mountain of resistance, especially if you find yourself absolutely overwhelmed by the call to shift old patterns and create new beginnings. Your tendency is always to opt for the known, yet that has become more than unsatisfying and uncomfortable; it is now unbearable. So take the risk and step over the line.

Rewarding Days

6, 7, 25, 26

Challenging Days

2, 3, 15, 16

Cancer | August

Overall Theme

After a month of soul-searching, you are now ready to conquer your inner fears, stand up for yourself, and take charge of the parts of your life that need an overhaul. You feel ready for any challenge that comes your way because your optimism is founded in reality and in a confidence you didn't know you were capable of. Courage, thy name is Cancer.

Relationships

So far it's been a difficult and challenging journey to selfhood, and you know there are a few more hurdles to overcome before you can feel you are living life from your own core, not from the center of other people's demands. Take a moment or two to acknowledge what you've accomplished before you turn to the next task. Not only do you deserve it, but it's important to refresh yourself.

Career, Success, and Money

Financial resources take the spotlight and you find yourself caught between the desire to hold on for dear life to what you have and the need to spend at least a little of your abundance on yourself. Accept that this is an important way to demonstrate—to yourself—that you are valuable. So buy what's at the top of your wish list.

Pitfalls and Potential Problems

You are pretty pleased with the changes you are making. Life feels expansive and hopeful and full of all the possibilities that you can imagine. Not that you expect all that you daydream about will happen. It's just life-affirming to entertain them all. However, not everyone in your world sees it the way you do. Just remember that their resistance is their problem, not yours.

Rewarding Days

4, 5, 30, 31

Challenging Days

11, 12, 23, 24

Cancer | September

Overall Theme

The faceoff between what is real and what is fantasy, between perfection and imperfection, and between facts and knowing creates confusion and challenges your newfound commitment to trust life as it unfolds, without an attempt on your part to control the outcome. This kick-starts a compulsion to hyperanalyze everything. That's fine. Once you are done, trust your instincts. This yields better results.

Relationships

What you seek is a good conversation, one that illuminates, challenges, lightens things up, expands your horizons. Translation? You are easily bored with people this month. Normally you are happy to hang with others if that connection is there. After all, your primary need is comfort. Well, you discover that your definition of comfort isn't predictability.

Career, Success, and Money

Your need for more stimulation extends to your career, your work, and your purpose. You want more, but you aren't sure what that is or what it looks like. Talk to those at work who know you best. Ask for their input and invite them to give you a vision of what your next steps might be. Let them know you truly want to challenge yourself and expand your capabilities.

Pitfalls and Potential Problems

Your willingness to question everything and entertain every possibility while demanding an immediate resolution to the problems this creates is likely to leave you feeling like you are spinning your wheels. Instead, take time to sit with how you feel about what comes your way, rather than overthinking everything. This will make it easier to find the treasure you are seeking.

Rewarding Days

3, 4, 28, 29

Challenging Days

12, 13, 22, 23

Cancer | October

Overall Theme
This is the time of year when you find yourself wanting to hunker down and take a break from the world at large. Home is your favorite place to be, and you turn your attention to changing your physical surroundings to match the shifts going on inside you. It's a perfect time to purge anything that doesn't reflect how you feel right now.

Relationships
You gradually begin to understand that life truly is a circle, and that in order for the circle to be complete, there has to be reciprocity. No more giving more than you receive. That means the people in your life must demonstrate the same level of commitment on a heart level that you do. You may find that it's time to close the door on some of the relationships in your life.

Career, Success, and Money
Just when you are ready for some peace and quiet everywhere in your life, an unexpected challenge in your professional life leaves you wondering who you can trust. The first thing you need to know is that you will get the support you need to weather this tempest in a teapot created by someone else.

Pitfalls and Potential Problems
Because life has been so taxing for much of 2019, your resilience is a bit low this month. Hence your need to be at home to recharge your batteries. Recognize that this is a wonderful step toward taking care of yourself and that you know how to do that when you give yourself the space and the permission to listen to your inner voice.

Rewarding Days
10, 11, 28, 29

Challenging Days
4, 5, 12, 13

Cancer | November

Overall Theme
You begin this month feeling rested and rejuvenated, only to find your stress level rises quickly as you take stock of the various parts of your life and find that things still aren't quite coalescing the way you desire. Refrain from going into overdrive to fix what you perceive to be a multitude of issues. Take a step back and see that some of what is going on is just life, not a crisis, and trust yourself to do what is needed when the time is right.

Relationships
Recognize that you need space right now. That way you can ask for it, create it, and enjoy it without having to be cranky, feel guilty, or run away from everyone in your life. It's not that you've stopped loving or caring about others. It's that the simplest request feels like a prison door slamming shut on you at a time when the only person you are interested in is yourself.

Career, Success, and Money
This area is the least of your concerns, not because everything is smooth sailing, but because you are emotionally occupied with the essentials of who you are. This means a lot of your outer world feels a little like window dressing right now. Accept that's how you feel, take care of business, and just be.

Pitfalls and Potential Problems
It takes a lot of courage to turn inward and unearth all those emotional truths and realities that you tend to hide from yourself. Just be careful not to minimize or react in the extreme to what you find. This will lead to an internal polarization that divides you and then shuts you down. Instead, remain present and handle yourself with TLC. That way you can separate the wheat from the chaff.

Rewarding Days
6, 7, 20, 21

Challenging Days
2, 3, 13, 14

Cancer | December

Overall Theme

You are running this month, literally and figuratively, and you aren't sure why. The only thing you know for sure is there's a compulsion to keep moving and it's not fear that is driving you. Recognize that it's a search for passion. What you need right now is to find something new, something that ignites you from the inside out.

Relationships

You suddenly feel free to ask for what you truly desire from the people in your life, and with that comes a huge sense of liberation. The mere act of telling others what works for you creates something you weren't expecting: a space in the world where you include yourself. You discover, much to your surprise, that that's more important than whether everyone listens to you. You are listening to yourself.

Career, Success, and Money

Take time to keep this whole part of your life in the proper perspective because there's just no predictability you can count on. It's not that there is any real chaos; it's more that things feel consistently inconsistent. Yes, it's that kind of month: paradoxical, with no way to make sense of it in the moment. Just know that everything will sort itself out.

Pitfalls and Potential Problems

As you take a stand and declare yourself to be just as important in your own life as you have made everyone else, be prepared for disapproval, discontent, and, in some cases, backlash from those who depend on you remaining the same reliable, dependable person you have always been. Be clear that your job isn't to babysit others. That might work for them, but you now know it doesn't work for you.

Rewarding Days

3, 4, 17, 18

Challenging Days

6, 7, 26, 27

Cancer Action Table

These dates reflect the best—but not the only—times for success and ease in these activities, according to your Sun sign.

	JAN	FEB	MAR	APR	MAY	JUN	JUL	AUG	SEP	OCT	NOV	DEC
Move					1, 2		4, 5		28, 29			
Start a class		6, 7						30, 31			5, 6	
Seek coaching/ counseling			9, 10			15, 16						10, 11
Ask for a raise	20, 21					4, 5			7, 8			
Get professional advice	5, 6						15, 16				22, 23	
Get a loan								5, 6				1, 2
New romance			27, 28		17, 18					28, 29		
Vacation		23, 24		1, 2						9, 10		

Leo

The Lion
July 23 to August 22

♌

Element: Fire	Glyph: Lion's tail
Quality: Fixed	Anatomy: Heart, upper back
Polarity: Yang/masculine	Colors: Gold, scarlet
Planetary Ruler: The Sun	Animals: Lions, large cats
Meditation: I trust in the strength of my soul	Myths/Legends: Apollo, Isis, Helios
Gemstone: Ruby	House: Fifth
Power Stones: Topaz, sardonyx	Opposite Sign: Aquarius
	Flowers: Marigold, sunflower
Key Phrase: I will	Keyword: Magnetic

The Leo Personality

Strengths, Spiritual Purpose, and Challenges

Perhaps your greatest strength is just how much you like yourself. This is the key to you maintaining your equilibrium as well as greeting life's challenges and difficulties with determination, dedication, and aplomb. Nothing much rattles you, unless it's a personal attack on your basic character. That is something you just can't tolerate, because you believe with absolute certainty that you always operate from a place of honesty and integrity. Any suggestion to the contrary is a profound insult, which, of course, deserves the loudest roar and the biggest swat of your paw that you can muster. Meanwhile, you nurse a very bruised ego, privately wondering how anyone could misunderstand you or your motives. For all your charm, bravado, and inner confidence, you are easily wounded by the inconsistencies that characterize human behavior. Knocked off balance, you draw on your natural inner authority as a way to protect yourself from what you perceive to be injustice, and you adopt an outer shell that you hope makes you impenetrable. This, in turn, leads people to assume that you place yourself above and apart from others. More than that, it cuts you off from your spiritual purpose in being here. It's hard to create when you are out of touch with your true spirit, hiding away all that love that springs effortlessly from the core of who you are.

For you, love is the purest source of energy and it must be expressed in all areas of your life. Any distortion of that commitment diminishes you in ways that rob you of any sense of purpose, leaving you deflated and disconnected from yourself. You also operate with an unflinching demand that you always do your best. After all, isn't that one of the basic tenets in your operator's manual? No slacking off, no halfway measures, no abandoning the mission before it's complete. Not only does it seem illogical to you to do anything less, but it's imperative that you be able to look in the mirror and like what you see. The truth is, you always set the bar high for yourself. There's no fun—and you know how much you like fun—in not pushing yourself to see just how much you can accomplish.

Relationships

Love is the true center of how you connect to others. That doesn't mean you love everybody; it means that you draw from that infinite capacity you possess to act with kindness and generosity toward others. Meeting people is something you excel at, always open and curious and ready for new experiences. However, you aren't always prepared for what comes next ,because at your core you are a bit naive. Manipulation, dishonesty, game playing, pretense, and boasting (to name just a few aspects of human behavior) seem like such a waste of time to you, and often not worth any effort on your part, other than a shake of your head. However, when you give your heart, you hold nothing back and your commitment is total. No equivocating, no negotiating terms, no betrayal. So if you encounter any of this behavior in the people you love, it breaks your heart. And that's no small thing in the Lion's world. It can take a long time for the pain to subside and an even longer time for you to open your heart again.

For you, a promise is something truly sacred and not to be trifled with, so it's a challenge for you to understand that everyone's definition of love isn't the same as yours. Your other difficulty in dealing with people is understanding that not everyone is blessed with the confidence that seems to just ooze out of your pores. It's always a huge surprise when you discover that not everyone likes themselves, much less loves themselves. However, once you acknowledge the insecurities of others, you can be their biggest cheerleader and support system because you have a tremendous capacity to see other people's true value and true talents.

Career and Work

The truest definition of success in your life is to do something you love. This is at the heart of what you desire in choosing a career. Of course, you understand the necessities and practicalities of life. You just believe that all of that can be accomplished by doing something that brings you satisfaction on all levels, practical, intellectual, emotional, and spiritual. Not only do you expect this, but you will give your all to find the right niche for yourself. If circumstances dictate that your job doesn't satisfy this intrinsic need, you turn your attention to your playtime to fulfill your dreams. You simply cannot imagine life without the joy of exploring the things you love. This is the most fertile ground for you to stretch yourself, find the depths of your talents, and remain connected to the best parts of yourself.

Money and Possessions

Money is a means to an end, nothing more, nothing less. That doesn't mean you don't like money. You do. But only as a way to create comfort, joy, and happiness in your life. Its value is in providing you with the capacity to get whatever makes your heart sing. The same goes for possessions. You don't see any purpose in accumulating things that hold no meaning. The result? Rather than getting stuff to have stuff, what you include in your life adds color and depth and actually says something about who you are. It doesn't have to be the most expensive, but it has to be of good quality. You are more likely to save up to buy the one thing you desire than to settle for something cheaper. As much as you like gratification, you are capable of waiting for what you really desire.

The Light Side of Life

It often feels to you like no one knows how to play better than you. In fact, you are certain you invented it. Well, that's debatable, but you definitely know how to find fun and laughter in any situation. It is a gift that carries you through a lot of life's difficulties because it helps you see past the sadness, the challenges, and the ugliness to the source of what really matters: the human spirit. Nothing is as important to you as the wellspring of faith you have in yourself and others. And being playful, engaging in goofy things, and being childlike is your way of continually nourishing that source.

Leo Keywords for 2019
Purging, adapting, structuring

The Year Ahead for Leo

The message for 2019 is a consistent one: Be fully engaged in the process of recognizing that not only do you need to overhaul a significant portion of your life because it really isn't working for you, but you are at heart worn out and exhausted by the complications that you inadvertently created for yourself. Life—and by that I mean forces outside of our control—always presents us with experiences, opportunities, events, and encounters we never envisioned, at least not on a conscious level. This is true for everyone, even you. What always shocks you is that your commitment to always showing up and doing your very best in any situation doesn't guarantee that the outcome actually paves the way for a life of happiness, bliss, and joy. It's not that you are opposed to overcoming difficulties, challenges, and even crisis; it's more that you believe that how you handle them ought to create ease in your life, not the contrary. Time to use your strong inner strength to jump into the deep end of your dissatisfaction, confront it head on, and transform your frustrations, your complaints, your disillusion, and anything that continually interferes with the feeling that who you are, not just what you do, means something. And the best way to start that process is to dust off your faith in yourself, your awareness of who you really are at your core, and begin an inner dialogue with the disaffected parts of yourself.

Face it: you are disenchanted with the status quo. Forget about being the noble Leo. Resist the temptation to continue to sacrifice yourself on the altar of I Am Always Fine, or the altar of I Can Handle Anything. This is a year when you are pushed to recognize that you don't have to prove yourself again and again. In fact, the question is not, can you handle something, but should you? Not everything that happens is your responsibility. Nor is it supposed to be. So take stock of all the situations in your life that robbed you of your sense of well-being, your innate love of life and people. Tap into the feelings those experiences created. Acknowledge the residue of resentment and anger that still exists. Then find a way to release it all. Meditation, massage, writing a letter and burning it, and therapy are things to consider. Find a way to do it that resonates with you. Doing this will liberate you and leave you with the energy and the space to begin a new phase of your life.

Saturn

If you thought Saturn symbolized the thorns continually poking at your life in 2018, be prepared for things to get more intense in 2019 as Saturn joins forces with Pluto and Neptune to challenge you in ways that test your resilience, your fortitude, your faith, and even your confidence in yourself. Make no mistake, Saturn is the coalescing agent for either an initiation into a new way of living your life or a stark reminder of what you fail to take care of because you believe that you are indestructible. The choice is yours. There is no right or wrong, just what is, and this year Saturn insistently asks you to be accountable for what you have done in your life so you can completely understand the impact your choices have had on you—not for the purpose of finding fault, but so you can use this awareness as a jumping-off point for a renewed commitment to your own well-being, physically, emotionally, mentally, and spiritually. You definitely have the necessary courage to do this. The question is, are you willing? Because you believe that your course of action is always the right one and any scrutiny or assessment of what you have done is tantamount to saying you did something wrong. And that's not something that appeals to you in the slightest.

Let's be clear. That's not what Saturn is pushing you to do. He is inviting you to move past any inclination to judge yourself as lacking and instead begin a process of taking what you have accomplished and where you are at in life to build a new foundation. This does require some serious adjustments, taking time to look at what works in your life and what doesn't. And as much as Saturn may not be a big fan of making adjustments any more than Sun in Leo is, the energetic relationship between you and Saturn demands this. Be aware that trying to stick to the status quo may have some serious effects on your overall health, whether physical or emotional. So take stock of your life objectively, overlook, or avoid nothing, and release anything that is not useful or helpful. This promises to lighten your load and renew your vitality.

Uranus

As Uranus ends his sojourn in Aries, he insists that you pull together any insights gained during the last seven years—insights that changed how you perceive life, how you look at where you fit in the universe, how you find meaning in your life, how you connect to your higher self...and the list goes on. In short, Uranus set you off on a trek to find out what truly makes life worth living, and it's been quite the journey. Now, as Uranus enters Taurus on March 6, it's time to apply the perceptions that have shifted your inner life in a practical, external way. It's one thing to say you believe something, but it's another to embody it in your everyday life. Of course, as a Leo, as a fire sign, actions are more important than words, so it is natural for you to truly exemplify your values. However, in putting into practice your newfound awareness and wisdom, you may be confronted with the depth of change this actually requires. It may come as a shock to you to find that there is a lack of congruity between your inner and outer worlds, leading to a complete change in life direction as you come face to face with any dissonance between the realities of your life as it currently stands and the growing inner need to follow your heart by walking away from what you have built to create something new, something more reflective of your deeper understanding of yourself and your place in the world. One thing to remember: this is year one of a seven-year process. Take time to truly survey the landscape before initiating the big changes you desire.

Neptune

You do really appreciate Neptune's invitation to play with all possibilities. What you aren't fond of is the feeling that, as much fun as it is, nothing really ever comes together in what you consider a concrete way. After all, as a Leo, you like things to have a tangible, actionable aspect to them. Otherwise, it remains nothing more than a fancy, a whimsy, an illusion, and that just won't do. So when Neptune invited you to join him in delving into the world of all that's hidden from the naked eye in 2012, you balked. Why? Because it felt like groping around in the dark without a clue, not something you find terribly appealing. For you to engage in anything, you definitely need things to have a distinct shape, even if the whole picture hasn't been filled in. Well, Neptune persisted, and in 2018 he challenged you to move past your reluctance to come and play with him. In 2019 he turns the heat up even more as Saturn amplifies your fear of the unknown at the same time he combines with Neptune to let you know that you must trust that you can reap something valuable from plunging into the less definable but nevertheless deeply felt areas of both your life and your psyche. So let down your guard and you will be amazed at what you gather from this process.

Pluto

When Saturn entered the sign of Capricorn at the very end of 2017, he moved into what had been Pluto's exclusive territory since 2008. During those nine years, Pluto pushed you to transform any rigid or immovable walls that created feelings of being trapped, stuck, and/or limited. Pluto's job is always to ask us to dig deep to find the detritus we are hanging on to so we can create space for growth and real passion. Saturn isn't always comfortable with space—he often interprets it as emptiness that needs to be filled. So this basic difference in approach has caused a serious internal struggle for you as you try to free yourself from what no longer serves you—which requires a willingness to be vulnerable—while simultaneously trying to protect yourself. The key is to tap into the healthiest way of expressing these two very disparate energies. Move through the fear that Saturn naturally stirs up. Realize you can use his tremendous call to create practical outcomes and build a new foundation in your life, based on the clearer, healthier version of yourself that you initiated following Pluto's demand to transform the ineffective, unsatisfying ways you were living life.

How Will This Year's Eclipses Affect You?

Eclipses signal intense periods that highlight major growth opportunities for us in the process of creating our lives. They are linked to the lunar phases—specifically the New and Full Moon—and involve the relationship between the Sun and the Moon and the Earth. A Solar Eclipse is a magnified New Moon, while a Lunar Eclipse is a magnified Full Moon. Eclipses unfold in cycles involving all twelve signs of the zodiac, and they occur in pairs, usually about two weeks apart.

In 2019 there are five eclipses, three solar (two in Capricorn and one in Cancer) and two lunar (one in Leo and one in Capricorn). The first Solar Eclipse arrives on January 5 in Capricorn, stirring up an overwhelming feeling of powerlessness and insecurity that rocks the very foundation of your life. Take a deep breath, look beyond your initial reaction, and accept that you are being asked to strip away some unnecessary ego trappings that you have developed as a way to protect yourself. The real value of who you are cannot be found in the parts of yourself that no longer serve any useful purpose, other than to keep you from looking realistically and truthfully at where you are instead of where you thought you would be. Life really is what happens to us, as opposed to what we thought would happen to us. In resisting this, you empty out the best parts of yourself in a vain attempt to avoid the fact that, like everyone else, your life is beset with problems and adjustments. And worst of all, you miss the chance to use your experiences to know yourself better and expand beyond the already well-developed sides of who you are.

It's time to remove your pride from the equation of how you live your life—at least in 2019, because it only inhibits the growth opportunities contained in this year's eclipse cycle. It's definitely a necessary step as you approach the Lunar Eclipse on January 21, which takes place in your sign of Leo. Otherwise, you engage in a lot of self-congratulatory behavior rather than reconnecting with the true source of your confidence: your intrinsic sense of honor, your capacity to love unreservedly, and your commitment to being the best person you can be. Once you've tuned in to the core of who you are, the remainder of the year's eclipses on July 2, July 16, and December 26, open some surprising doors to seeking more meaningful ways to be of service, to finding new ways to express your deep need to create something long-lasting as a reflection of your authentic self, and to connecting to a renewed feeling of peace about who you are, where you are going, and what really makes your world go round.

Leo | January

Overall Theme

The year begins on something of a sour note as you fall into a pit of uncertainty and lack of focus. Time to recalibrate your inner core by making sure that your sense of duty and responsibility isn't taking up all the space in your life. First step? Find something that ignites your natural sense of fun. That lifts the cloud you feel hanging over your head.

Relationships

Your world feels dark and dingy, making you a little cranky with everyone from those closest to you to the person who delivers the pizza. You need some quality time with yourself to shake off the blues. If you do that, the Lunar Eclipse on January 21 triggers a return to your usual charming, kind, and affable self. Finally feeling like yourself again, you are ready to party, figuratively if not literally.

Career, Success, and Money

Satisfaction isn't easy to find; in fact, it seems to have taken a vacation from your life. This isn't something you easily tolerate, but you really have no choice. The things you are committed to must be done. Take the opportunity to rethink how easily you agree to do things that you simply don't care about. For you, this is always a recipe for discontent.

Pitfalls and Potential Problems

Your inner fortitude seems to be in short supply as a series of problems, substantial and petty, constantly drain you. The solution is to recognize that you don't have an inexhaustible supply of energy, generosity of spirit, and nobility. Even the Queen must be nourished. Make time every day to play. This restores that feeling of contentment that is so necessary to your well-being.

Rewarding Days

2, 3, 30, 31

Challenging Days

4, 5, 6, 19, 20

Leo | February

Overall Theme

You certainly feel better equipped to successfully manage the hurdles that present themselves now that you have regained your natural confidence. This, in turn, leads to a month where nothing gets you down or gets in your way. At least, not for long. You are definitely at your best.

Relationships

The way people behave is often a mystery to you, testing your core value that everyone deserves to be loved. Your problem? Inconsistency and failure to conform to your picture of how to be human doesn't determine whether a person is lovable. Be prepared to be tested. Time to discern the difference between love and approval.

Career, Success, and Money

Take time to review your commitments in these areas in preparation for major changes on the horizon when Uranus moves into Taurus on March 6. You are definitely feeling more optimistic about future endeavors, because you do feel a shift bubbling just below the surface. However, make sure you take care of any unresolved issues that could cause future complications.

Pitfalls and Potential Problems

This is not a time to indulge yourself by pretending that your life is all settled and fine, thank you very much. Expect some disturbance at a deeper level that demands much of your attention next month. There's nothing much you can do except acknowledge the discomfort you feel. No amount of thinking, analyzing, or probing improves the situation. Instead, enjoy a brief respite while strengthening your body, your spirit, your mind, and your feeling nature.

Rewarding Days

3, 4, 9, 10

Challenging Days

11, 12, 24, 25

Leo | March

Overall Theme

There are days when you feel you just want to crawl out of your skin, certainly not a typical state of affairs for you. The more you try to stabilize things by using your usual coping strategies, the more you feel out of control. Welcome to the new reality of Uranus in Taurus, an initiation into questioning your purpose, your status, and what you truly value.

Relationships

It really is okay to turn to your nearest and dearest for reassurance and support. But before you can get past your reluctance to do so, you need to relinquish the belief that you never need help. Yes, your capacity to master most of life's situations is beyond compare (well, most of the time), but right now you feel so untethered that you cannot let your pride interfere with getting the support you so readily give to others.

Career, Success, and Money

Suddenly, nothing about your career makes any sense to you, no matter how many times or ways you rearrange the truth. This doesn't mean you need to take drastic action to resolve the situation. The time for that couldn't be worse. It's best to take a step back and observe, knowing this is the start of a seven-year process of overhauling a major facet of your life.

Pitfalls and Potential Problems

Resist the temptation to stomp your feet, plug your ears, and sing loudly. Being petulant and childish (yes, I said childish) doesn't change the reality of what is on the horizon. Now, you don't have to enthusiastically embrace change by turning your life upside down, either. The only thing required of you now is to accept that change is inevitable. Once you do that, you create space for growth.

Rewarding Days

2, 3, 21, 22

Challenging Days

10, 11, 17, 18

Leo | April

Overall Theme

The push to get moving in a forward direction comes into direct conflict with an inner compulsion to retreat and take a deep breath. The difficulty is that your circuits are still all twisted up and you don't feel you have a clear sense of direction. Remember, action doesn't always have to move out into the world; it can move inward. Do that and the results surprise you in delightful ways.

Relationships

The only kind of contact you seek this month is one without subterfuge, superficiality, and all the trappings of niceness. You want something with depth, profundity, and complexity, because your soul is reaching out to go beyond the socially acceptable to the kind of intimacy that has no walls, only truth and vulnerability. Be ready to take the first step. You can't ask of others what you aren't willing to do yourself.

Career, Success, and Money

You are content to let things continue on the path you have already set. Without any idea what you want, you are wise enough to know that what truly feeds you right now is to stand pat. That way you can focus your energy on sorting through all the confusion bouncing around in your brain.

Pitfalls and Potential Problems

Let's face it: you need a vacation. So take one. It's ironic to think that a holiday amounts to a problem, but in this case you are reluctant to leave the scene of your everyday life for fear that something untoward, disastrous, or irritating could blow something up when you aren't around to take care of it. Relax. The biggest challenge to your equilibrium is inside of you.

Rewarding Days

5, 6, 13, 14

Challenging Days

1, 2, 25, 26

Leo | May

Overall Theme

The beginning of the month finds you feeling fresh, energized, and less burdened by the combination of uncertainty and insecurity that has been your constant companion for quite a while. You are ready to look the future squarely in the face. You realize that not only do you need a new beginning, but you truly desire it. Game on.

Relationships

Be cautious when making promises to anyone and everyone. You have a tendency to agree to things without truly thinking about the level of commitment being asked of you. So before saying yes, ask some very practical questions so you know exactly what you are consenting to do. Otherwise, this leads to resentment on your part, not to mention anger and/or hurt feelings on the other side. After all, you hate to break a promise.

Career, Success, and Money

New opportunities cross your path through old connections. Of course, you are interested. However, if the doors that open lead you down the same old path, you need to recognize that new window dressings can't camouflage the very things you have already decided you need to leave behind.

Pitfalls and Potential Problems

Yes, you are filled with enthusiasm and anticipation now that you want to take that leap of faith to create not just a new future, but a new you. But it can't and won't take place overnight. This kind of profound recalibration takes intent, vision, preparation, and execution. You are still at intention. So play with that intention, mentally, emotionally, and spiritually. That creates the fertile space for the necessary vision.

Rewarding Days

1, 2, 10, 11

Challenging Days

9, 21, 22

Leo | June

Overall Theme

The stuff running around in your head offers a whole series of possibilities you hadn't considered when it comes to fashioning a new future. This is your imagination at work. You really are opening up to that new vision you seek, so enjoy the process. Let things flit in and out of your consciousness. Contained in these ephemeral wonderings is the potential for a new beginning that isn't quite ready to reveal itself yet.

Relationships

The number-one thing on your agenda is fun, so you find yourself looking around to see who wants to join you in doing just that. Recognize that you may not have a clue how you want to have fun, because it's not an activity you are looking for. What your heart desires is people who are fun themselves, who invite you to shine a light on your fun side, and who see the lighter side of you.

Career, Success, and Money

The potential for conflict is a strong possibility as you contend with people who appear not to be listening to you. This is serious because there are some important decisions that need to be made and you just want to get on with it. The solution is to use written communication to get your point across. Be careful not to overspend because you are frustrated.

Pitfalls and Potential Problems

It's not just your inner self that wants to play. The rest of you is also definitely interested in some serious fun. Sounds paradoxical, right? In your mind, it isn't. You rarely engage in anything without purpose and determination. However, sometimes this attitude can create complications. The key is to have fun—spontaneous fun, not planned fun.

Rewarding Days

9, 10, 22, 23

Challenging Days

7, 8, 18, 19

Leo | July

Overall Theme

You feel like someone turned out the lights and you are sitting all alone in a dark room with no idea what is happening. Don't worry. There's a purpose to this. For too long, your focus has been entirely on taking care of any and all duties, obligations, and responsibilities. Time's up. In order for your new day to dawn, you need to turn inward and take care of yourself.

Relationships

The year 2019 has been a rollercoaster for you in this area. One minute you are your usual social self and the next you aren't sure you ever want to talk to anyone again. Your challenge this month is to maintain some equilibrium by responding to your needs and desires in the moment. It's just one of the ways of determining how to honor yourself.

Career, Success, and Money

Serious obstacles crop up in achieving goals set months ago. The cause? Those around you haven't done what they were supposed to do. Refrain from taking all the responsibility for this state of affairs by being clear with yourself and others that you have done your job. Now it's time for them to do theirs.

Pitfalls and Potential Problems

You have excellent hunches, gut instincts, intuition, and awareness. What you call it isn't as important as truly trusting it and using it to your advantage, not in a way that is dishonorable or hurtful but in a way that supports who you are, first and foremost. The Solar Eclipse on July 2 and the Lunar Eclipse on July 16 test you to see if you know how to do that.

Rewarding Days

12, 13, 25, 26, 31

Challenging Days

2, 3, 15, 16

Leo | August

Overall Theme

This is your time of the year to shine, and this year is no different. In fact, you feel like the most luminous star in the universe. Never have you been this content or at peace with yourself or your world. So much so, you are convinced that life is about to gift you with everything you desire.

Relationships

You aren't the only one who notices the deep change in you. Everyone around you lets you know how glad they are that you are happy again. On the surface, this may annoy you because you are totally aware that it's so much more than happiness. The difficulty is you can't really explain it because it is indescribable. Relax and find joy in their good wishes.

Career, Success, and Money

Suddenly all the issues of the last couple months vaporize in what seems like a puff of smoke. Everything comes together as if by magic, and you get a lot of the credit for making that happen. This stuns you until you realize that letting other people be responsible for their part actually reaps dividends.

Pitfalls and Potential Problems

Don't overdo it, and by it I mean everything. Your energy is high, your confidence stratospheric, and your awareness stellar. This doesn't mean that you need to push yourself beyond your limits or capacity because you are determined to make sure you succeed in moving your life forward *right now*. You have lots of time.

Rewarding Days

9, 10, 30, 31

Challenging Days

11, 12, 23, 24

Leo | September

Overall Theme

Practical matters take center stage, and your life is consumed by a never-ending barrage of details, with little room for anything else until the middle of the month. This focus on getting all your ducks in a row will be tedious at times, but there's an unexpected reward accompanying your hard work, something that brings the kind of satisfaction that makes life worthwhile.

Relationships

Even this area of your life is full of tasks, jobs, and duties. It seems everyone you know has a problem only you can solve. While that definitely strokes your ego, it's only transitory, leaving you irritated, cranky, and out of sorts, especially when you realize that you aren't the only one who can take care of the problem. Set aside your sense of duty and decline gracefully.

Career, Success, and Money

This is definitely a month for examining your financial reality and making some necessary plans. Now, that could mean you choose to reward yourself for all your hard work, or you maybe need to consult a financial planner or begin to make plans for your retirement. No matter the need, this is a month when excellent progress can be made.

Pitfalls and Potential Problems

There was a time when you took great pride in being able to master everything thrown at you, big or small, but you are beginning to realize that you are tired of juggling it all, that what you need is joy in your world, not just satisfaction. Hang in there. Take stock of what you truly love. That's the next step in creating a new you.

Rewarding Days

3, 4, 24, 25

Challenging Days

10, 11, 22, 23

Leo | October

Overall Theme

Your patience is tested as any action you take hits obstacle after obstacle. It leaves you shaking your head because you know that there's no logical reason for all these roadblocks. Well, you are right. However, that doesn't change the reality. Maybe it's a sign that you need to get away until things resolve themselves.

Relationships

You feel warm and fuzzy. Sort of. That best describes your overall approach to relationships this month. The idea of connection is attractive, but the reality of being with others leaves you lukewarm—and confused. You are not one to live in gray areas, especially when it comes to love and attachment. Well, you'll be happy to know this is temporary, so don't read too much into it. Just honor how you feel and act accordingly—with your usual grace and diplomacy.

Career, Success, and Money

With all the challenges facing you every time you try to get something done, part of you just wants to throw up your hands and walk away. Recognize that your tolerance is at a low ebb, and refrain from sharing your frustration too loudly. Petulance never looks good on you.

Pitfalls and Potential Problems

There is a distinct possibility that you could lose your temper more than once during October. The year 2019 has not been your best friend at all, and you are suddenly aware of all the resentment you've somehow accumulated while dealing with the turmoil that you feel is the hallmark of this year. Your discontent is understandable. Just make sure you don't dump it on the rest of the world.

Rewarding Days

7, 8, 23, 24

Challenging Days

12, 13, 17, 18

Leo | November

Overall Theme

The month begins with you deep in thought about what your life is truly based on. Suddenly the external world, with all its demands, its plans, its duties, and obligations, seems less important to you than your roots, your home, and your family. The reason? You are in search of what nourishes you, because you feel all wrung-out, with no resources to back you up.

Relationships

Every relationship you have or have had is under the microscope as you analyze just who you are in your relationships and whether you know how to ask for what you desire—which is love, of course. But not everyone's definition of love is the same. This creates a double conundrum for you. First, your pride makes it hard for you to ask for anything. Second, even if you do ask, can you be sure it's clear what you are asking for? Ask anyway. At the very least, you'll learn something about yourself.

Career, Success, and Money

It's a good time to put one foot in front of the other and not worry too much about what's next. You simply don't have the resources to think beyond today. That's okay because so much piled up after the various and sundry delays that occurred last month.

Pitfalls and Potential Problems

The fatigue you feel when it comes to dealing with anything of a practical nature is real. Just make sure you tend to the matters that really need your attention, especially any household repairs. This is a good month to move forward with any renovations you've been thinking about. It will do a lot to revive you.

Rewarding Days

18, 19, 28, 29

Challenging Days

11, 12, 16, 17

Leo | December

Overall Theme

You find yourself looking to the future with a steely-eyed strength and determination, buoyed by the fact that you have survived much of what 2019 triggered in you. This has restored your belief in your capacity to thrive in the face of adversity, whether it's an external problem or an internal challenge. You know you will prevail no matter what.

Relationships

Having decided that you need not be a role model of love and generosity *all* the time, you find that you are feeling far more interested in actually being yourself with the people in your world. And much to your surprise, you find they don't expect as much of you as you expect of yourself. What's in your heart is far more important than playing the role you put yourself in.

Career, Success, and Money

The thought of changing the entire foundation of this part of your life is a welcome one now. Gone is the resistance you experienced earlier in the year at the mere suggestion that a complete overhaul might be in the cards. You realize that the success you created is about you, not the career or job you chose.

Pitfalls and Potential Problems

The final Solar Eclipse of 2019 on December 26 again tests your resolve to ground your life in hope and optimism, but not for long. Oh, the feelings of insecurity and uncertainty rear their heads again, but this time you recognize them for what they really are: symbols of accepting what no longer works for you, believing you have no choice but to remain stuck.

Rewarding Days

3, 4, 17, 18

Challenging Days

10, 11, 26, 27

Leo Action Table

These dates reflect the best—but not the only—times for success and ease in these activities, according to your Sun sign.

	JAN	FEB	MAR	APR	MAY	JUN	JUL	AUG	SEP	OCT	NOV	DEC
Move					10, 11			13, 14		28, 29		
Start a class			21, 22			2, 3			28, 29			
Seek coaching/ counseling	5, 6		10, 11			17, 18						
Ask for a raise		19, 20					25, 26					11, 12
Get professional advice		11, 12						5, 6			1, 2	
Get a loan				1, 2					3, 4		19, 20	
New romance				25, 26			4, 5			2, 3		
Vacation	25, 26				1, 2							23, 24

Virgo

The Virgin
August 23 to September 22

♍

Element: Earth

Glyph: Greek symbol for containment

Quality: Mutable

Anatomy: Abdomen, gallbladder, intestines

Polarity: Yin/feminine

Colors: Taupe, gray, navy blue

Planetary Ruler: Mercury

Animals: Domesticated animals

Meditation: I can allow time for myself

Myths/Legends: Demeter, Astraea, Hygeia

Gemstone: Sapphire

House: Sixth

Power Stones: Peridot, amazonite, rhodochrosite

Opposite Sign: Pisces

Flower: Pansy

Key Phrase: I analyze

Keyword: Discriminating

plished because you are in a constant state of adjustment. Or is
xiety? Or is that fear? Or frustration? Or recalibration? Or all of
ve? So, as this abates, you finally have a clear sense of where you
ng, even if it comes and goes. It's better than the general feeling
previous two to three years, when it seemed nothing ever truly
nto focus long enough for you to make sense of it. It was like
iven only 250 pieces of a 500-piece jigsaw puzzle. The more you
d, the more it felt like things went sideways or didn't materialize
Of course, you thought it meant your plans were somehow wrong.
wasn't that, as much as you were plotting a course of action with-
remaining 250 pieces.

s year feels quite different because you have the chance to at least
framework to guide you through the remainder of the shift sym-
by Neptune and Pluto. These are long-term shifts that take years
into practice. The year 2019 is a bit of a respite from all this, giv-
a chance to catch your breath and begin to put the pieces of the
together, provided you know that you can no longer hang on to
moded, outworn, and antiquated aspects of your life. Just know
create some truly worthwhile, powerful, and beautiful things to
se spaces.

n

2018 finally saw you feeling focused and accomplished for a
, although life still felt on the verge of upheaval at its worst and
niggling annoyances at its best. It's all down to Saturn, who has
magnificent job of convincing you that all is right in your world.
because he has a tremendous capacity to keep things on the
t and narrow, so much so that you can and probably have been
ng issues that exist outside the lines he is so good at drawing. For
's all about the job at hand. How could anything else be impor-
The difficulty is he tends to apply this approach in an extremely
d way, ignoring those things that do not have an immediate,
cal solution. He really doesn't know what to do with feelings,
vity, imagination, matters of the heart, or the need for change, so
ids them or suppresses them. As an earth sign, you understand
itude. However, you cannot do this in 2019. Otherwise, you will
ourself in the midst of a logjam of confusion, frustration, and
ment. Take care to use Saturn's energy in clear, positive ways—to

The Virgo Personality

Strengths, Spiritual Purpose, and Challenges

For you, life boils down to one thing: How do things work? You have to
know that, or else life is meaningless, without a sense of order or consis-
tency—both of which are deeply necessary to how you function in the
world. You simply cannot move forward without knowing the various
steps required to achieve your goal. This is mirrored both in your spiritual purpose and in your motto. The former is to process; the second is
to be prepared. You will go to the ends of the earth to honor both, so
much so that you often get tied up in knots of insecurity because you
have difficulty understanding that the best-laid plans often go awry—not
because you failed to do anything but because life just isn't as predictable
as you prefer.

Being prepared means developing your natural skills so you can draw
on them in any situation, not anticipating all eventualities so things go
off without a hitch. The irony is, even though you don't like to make
adjustments, you are good at handling crises. While everyone else is
panicking, you are cool, calm, and collected, surveying the situation
quickly and effectively and moving forward confidently to take care of
business. This is the definition of you being perfect: handling whatever
comes your way without hesitation, without self-consciousness. It's only
when things have settled down that you fall to pieces, often beginning
the inner drama of asking yourself how the whole thing happened in
the first place and completely overlooking just what you did under trying circumstances. This is not only counterproductive but is also harm-
ful to your self-esteem.

Your penchant for self-criticism ignores the reality that growing as
a human being doesn't come from being perfect but from taking on
life's challenges, mastering them, and using the wisdom that is gained
to create a life lived more effectively. So accept life's vicissitudes. You'll
like yourself more and it'll be easier to release yourself from the analysis
paralysis to which you are prone. Getting so caught up in the whys and
wherefores makes it difficult for you to make decisions or move forward,
which in turn undermines your self-confidence. It's a vicious circle.
Instead, take your experiences and find the wisdom in them.

Relationships

You are profoundly sensitive to anything you perceive to be criticism, which can often make relationships a minefield for you. Because you are so invested in being perfect, you have difficulty understanding the difference between a comment and a critical remark. So in order for relationships to be a positive experience, you do need to learn how to discern the difference. That means moving outside your own reality and paying attention to the cues you are getting, being able to express how you feel about what has been said to you, and working at being kinder to yourself. All these are necessary so you can move beyond your automatic assumption that if something is off kilter, you must be to blame. This makes it so easy for others to use you and even abuse you, which, in turn, makes it hard for you to trust that you are worthy of love, respect, and even basic courtesy. The solution is to remember your innate commitment to being the best person *you* can be, not to being the best person other people want you to be. The only standards in life that truly matter are your own. So be clear what they are, trust yourself, and weigh everything that people say to you about you very carefully. It really is easier to connect to others when you are authentically connected to yourself.

Career and Work

Working hard comes naturally to you, so provided you are doing something that is purposeful and practical, you have no difficulty succeeding. Your biggest challenge in this area is determining what success for you truly is. It begins with your need to be of service, which is completely different from being a servant. Too often you get these confused, and it can make you resentful if you feel you are consigned to a menial position with no respect or appreciation for the effort that you put in. You will always feel like a failure if what you do is taken for granted or not valued at all. The antidote to this begins inside you. Set aside the thoughts and attitudes of others and recognize that you doing something automatically makes it valuable.

Money and Possessions

You really have no difficulty using money to take care of the necessities of life. That's a given. Your challenge is recognizing that you can use it to value yourself by spending it on things that are not practically necessary but are emotionally satisfying. In fact, you make sure everyone else's

needs are met before thinking it might be a good idea to t something you so richly deserve. Taking care of life means yourself, something you are certain wasn't included in yo manual. This is something you need to practice, just as yo tice learning a new skill. As for possessions, you do love be and you are quite discerning about the finer things in life, old thing is satisfactory. No sloppiness, no unrefined ed and no cheap-looking things for you. Things must always

The Light Side of Life

The things that bring you pleasure range from anything lating to any kind of improvement. In fact, Virgo is the sig improvement, because on a deeper level you are aware th in a state of becoming. This often gets turned into a searc that fuels your drive to improve everything, from your ho to your lot in life. It may be hard for others to understar to do this and it makes you happy—which it does as lo become a compulsive need. Instead, do the other thing new things, have great conversations (you make a grea master a game, or help someone through a crisis. Re body's definition of fun is their own.

Virgo Keywords for 2019
Discernment, objectivity, self-compassion

The Year Ahead for Vir

Things feel less like you are hanging by a thread in 201 takes the reins and gives you the opportunity to feel He hinted at it last year, but he had to contend wi and Neptune constantly challenging your sense of wl not fond of constantly shifting landscapes, in spite o capacity to adapt, and that trio has been creating your mind—all over your life, taking you places whe everything that holds value for you. Well, with Ui Taurus on March 6 and Saturn taking charge of P there really is an opportunity to use all the experien Uranus, Neptune, and Pluto to start the process of worthwhile in your life, instead of feeling that no

find focus for your ongoing journey to unearth your creative self, to include more of the things that bring you joy in life, and to be more loving toward yourself. Use Saturn to build the appropriate framework for these activities. It's definitely his job to provide structure, but he's not always the best planet to rely on for content. That will come from the less exact parts of you. But this way you satisfy your desire for something you can depend on while creating space to move your life forward.

Uranus

You are never quite sure who is the bigger problem in your life, Uranus or Neptune. Truly it depends on which one is knocking on your door the loudest on any given day. At least since 2012, as Uranus pummeled you from Aries and Neptune mystified you from Pisces. Well, Uranus is about to make his way into Taurus and you couldn't be more relieved. Finally, he will stop adjusting your reality, or is that turning everything upside down? Instead, he will offer his support for change from a friendly earth sign and things will settle down. But only if you actually take the awareness he offered you in Aries and use it to actually grow, to recalibrate the things that don't work for you instead of analyzing them to death. And if you think you can return to the same old, same old, you'll find things still going bump in the night. So be forewarned: Uranus in Taurus can bring all kinds of rewards only if you are willing to take a look at the things you insist on hanging on to for dear life and ask yourself if they hold value for you. It can be difficult for an earth sign such as yourself to realize that change is inevitable, because you want things to stay put. After all, you need to be able to rely on something. One of Uranus's strongest messages always is to rely on yourself—not to the exclusion of others, but to know that being who you are is the rarest possible gift you can give yourself.

Neptune

For you, Neptune energy doesn't make much sense. You just don't like the wispy, the foggy, the insubstantial. How can you make anything out of what you consider to be nothing at all? So, Neptune's insistence, since 2012, on playing hide and seek with your basic sense of self, your core, has created a level of anxiety that has often disconnected you from any applicable sense of reality. Normally you can count on your capacity to sort through all incoming data to paint a picture of what's happening, but when it feels like you are wearing a pair of glasses that cause the world to disappear, you are completely at a loss as to what to do. The key here is to understand that Neptune's purpose is to get you to turn inward to your imagination, to the source of your own creativity, so you can envision a new beginning in your life. This Neptune-in-Pisces journey is like a vision quest. You must be prepared to empty yourself of any negative ego qualities you have accumulated so you can see clearly what your truth is. Of course, along the way you confront any illusions or fantasies about yourself, created by you or others. And that is quite a daunting prospect. Just know that as Neptune hits the halfway mark of his trip through Pisces, you are on the verge of really understanding the potential offered to you by this process. Even the most difficult experiences offer a blessing.

Pluto

Quite frankly, you aren't prone to viewing yourself as a creative person. Of course, this ignores the reality that living is a daily act of creativity, because, like most people, your definition of creativity is limited to anything artistic. But humans by nature must create, whether it's plan something, play something, build something, paint something, write something, theorize something, enact something, cook something, etc. So, since 2008, Pluto has challenged you to get in touch with your creativity and apply all your passion to whatever projects call to you. The key is to do what your heart desires, what your intuition illuminates, not to use your logical brain to chart the course for you. Pluto signals that this requires you dig deep, past your usual modus operandi, to uncover that wellspring of feeling that can fuel how you express yourself and transform your fear of not being good enough. It's time to release the notion that it's your perfectionism that gets things done when it's actually your commitment to always doing your best. When you recognize that, you will see clearly that perfectionism is a trap, and your gift of always doing your best is the very thing that frees you to create things from your heart instead of from your fear of inadequacy. This is a risk, no doubt. However, Pluto doesn't take no for an answer. So acknowledge the challenge and know you can meet it.

How Will This Year's Eclipses Affect You?

Eclipses signal intense periods that highlight major growth opportunities for us in the process of creating our lives. They are linked to the lunar phases—specifically the New and Full Moon—and involve the relationship between the Sun and the Moon and the Earth. A Solar Eclipse is a magnified New Moon, while a Lunar Eclipse is a magnified Full Moon. Eclipses unfold in cycles involving all twelve signs of the zodiac, and they occur in pairs, usually about two weeks apart.

In 2019 there are five eclipses, three solar (two in Capricorn and one in Cancer) and two lunar (one in Leo and one in Capricorn). The first Solar Eclipse arrives on January 5 in Capricorn, inviting you to confront any limitations you have at deeper levels that interfere with you loving yourself, appreciating yourself, and embracing yourself with total grace. Not an easy thing to do, as the parts of you that are comfortable with old patterns and old attitudes will question whether this is even necessary, triggering a push to shut down and accept reality as it is. The key here is to recognize that we all accumulate perceptions, beliefs, and thoughts about ourselves that need overhauling, and that maintaining a static view of ourselves is detrimental to our well-being. No one needs to understand this more than you do.

You are not the sum of your past choices, behaviors, and experiences. What you did says more about you than what happened to you. So this eclipse combined with the Lunar Eclipse on January 21 gives you a chance to enroll and participate in the School of Self-Appreciation. Strip away any automatic, self-critical responses that surface when you look at yourself. Self-examination is a useful tool only when you use it to make your life work for you. Otherwise, it becomes an exercise in self-torture and self-condemnation.

There isn't a single person on the planet who can be harder on you than you are on yourself. All the eclipses of 2019, including the Solar Eclipse on July 2, the Lunar Eclipse on July 16, and the Solar Eclipse on December 26, offer you the opportunity to deal with this and to put a halt to your compulsive need to put yourself in an emotional choke-hold, the one that says you are always one breath away from making a big mistake. Now's your chance to define what healthy self-nurturing looks like by stepping outside your insecurities and asking for insight and support from the people in your life, especially your friends. You'll be shocked by how much they are there to help you.

Virgo | January

Overall Theme

The year begins with a mixed bag of emotions. On the one hand, you feel hopeful and optimistic, ready to tackle the new year with gusto. On the other, you are cranky and out of sorts because you are convinced that something or someone is waiting just out of sight to rain on your parade. The best thing you can do is trust yourself to do your best, no matter what happens. It's your greatest strength.

Relationships

If anyone comes knocking on your door looking for any kind of a hand-out, whether it's support, the answer to a problem, or even money, you find yourself not particularly receptive. The reason? There is a push from inside you to be free from the responsibility for fixing everyone else's life and ignoring your own well-being. Bravo! This is the beginning of a yearlong process of nurturing yourself first. Just remember to be polite.

Career, Success, and Money

Your intent is simple: to rid yourself of duties and obligations that not only drag you down but weren't yours in the first place. You understand that this is an important step in valuing yourself and what you do. Doing this opens the door to the kind of success you dream of. It's hard to accomplish what you are truly capable of when you are busy cleaning up other people's messes.

Pitfalls and Potential Problems

Expect, at the very least, to second-guess yourself continually this month. It's your natural state, even when life isn't asking you to shift gears and change the very ground you stand on. The challenge is to avoid getting caught up in a spiral of overthinking by constantly revisiting every potential outcome three or four or five times. That will only wear you out.

Rewarding Days

14, 15, 29, 30

Challenging Days

4, 5, 12, 13

Virgo | February

Overall Theme

You feel a deep shift that you can't quite explain. Just let it percolate, because that's the most effective thing you can do. Any effort to quantify or even qualify what's happening only leads to frustration and anxiety. This amplifies your worry quotient all out of proportion. As hard as it is to accept, all you need to know is that nothing is broken or needs to be fixed.

Relationships

Don't be surprised if the communication between you and everyone else has entered some sort of twilight zone. No one, including you, seems to be speaking clearly or listening or understanding. This, combined with unspoken demands and expectations, results in bad tempers and questionable behavior all around. To circumvent this as much as possible, try writing down what you want to say.

Career, Success, and Money

Stick to the boundaries you set last month. Otherwise, you find yourself yet again taking care of other people's responsibilities at a time when new opportunities for advancement present themselves. A new project comes along offering you the chance to flex your creativity, and you definitely don't want to be bogged down and unable to rise to the challenge—and reward—it promises.

Pitfalls and Potential Problems

It drives you crazy when you can't get a handle on what things are all about, so this month is a definite challenge on two fronts. First, new things are sprouting up in your consciousness, but they have no definition. Second, there's a push to wrap up some old subconscious beliefs and attitudes that have been blocking your path. On the surface, they don't appear to have much in common, but their intent is the same: moving you forward.

Rewarding Days

10, 11, 19, 20

Challenging Days

1, 2, 17, 18

Virgo | March

Overall Theme

You know change is in the wind. You can feel it. Of course, this means you are stubbornly trying to keep yourself at a standstill. Your preference is always the devil you know—at least you know what you can expect. However, resistance is futile. Uranus changes signs on March 6, bringing a whole new set of opportunities for growth. Take the risk. It won't hurt as much as you think.

Relationships

Well, you probably emerged from last month thinking relationships are nothing but a quagmire. That may be true, at least some of the time. However, it's best to set that opinion aside in favor of detachment. You'll need it to work through the misunderstandings created by the fuzzy, incomplete, and inaccurate communication that typified your connections with others in February.

Career, Success, and Money

Again, it seems that your forward momentum is stalled. Step back from that hasty assumption and realize there are some things that need to be recalibrated before you will be able to institute the larger changes you want. It's major cleanup time, not just when it comes to your career and future success but in financial matters, too.

Pitfalls and Potential Problems

You don't mind taking time to reexamine all aspects of your life. It comes naturally. What creates turmoil for you is not being able to gather any useful information from that process. Well, when Mercury, your planetary avatar, is in retreat in Pisces, it's time to follow your hunches, not your rational meanderings. You'll be astounded at how much is revealed to you and how much you truly know.

Rewarding Days

9, 10, 27, 28

Challenging Days

5, 6, 17, 18

Virgo | April

Overall Theme

Your usual patience and adaptability are in short supply for much of April. Quite simply, you are ready to move forward and the rest of the world is on a coffee break. Instead of clenching your teeth, see this not as a delay but as a pause. The timing is not quite right to take the steps you envision.

Relationships

Now that a state of equilibrium is restored in the most important relationships in your life, you are content and happy. So get out and enjoy yourself. Gone are those testy moments when you were convinced that the only function others served in your life was to let you know how inadequate you were. It really is nice to know you are loved and accepted.

Career, Success, and Money

Time to take care of financial matters, including asking for a raise or seeking a promotion. Money is a reflection of how much we value ourselves, and you need to step up to the plate and be clear that it's not inconvenient to ask for what you deserve. Also be wary of any requests to invest your money in other people. Your emotional and intellectual support is sufficient.

Pitfalls and Potential Problems

It feels like Uranus lit a fire under you. Once reluctant to make any change without considering the ramifications for what seemed like a millennium, you are now more than ready to rush headlong into the future. Relax. Realize that even though you don't want to wait any longer, you need more time to rejuvenate your body, soul, and spirit. After all, you exhausted yourself fighting the need for change.

Rewarding Days

6, 7, 21, 22

Challenging Days

10, 11, 17, 18

Virgo | May

Overall Theme

You find steady ground for the first time this year. Once again, life feels dependable and reliable and you flourish. Gone is the apprehension, lurking just under the surface. In its place is a wellspring of newfound confidence, built on mastering all the ups and downs you've experienced over the last seven years.

Relationships

Things settle into a comfortable routine, something that truly nourishes your whole self. This restores your trust in others, which has been in short supply lately. You always struggle when you don't understand what makes other people tick. Your challenge is knowing that caring about others doesn't mean you always understand them.

Career, Success, and Money

The keyword in May is *satisfaction*. No big messes, no big challenges, and no major irritations crop up, leaving you with a whole month to truly get things done. You are in your glory, not only because work is going smoothly but because you have an increased sense of your own worth.

Pitfalls and Potential Problems

There really isn't a lot that's going to upset your apple cart this month. Even the usual stuff that irritates you doesn't even make a blip on your radar. This, in itself, may make you wonder if you're okay. Only you could find a reason to be worried about being happy. Just enjoy the experience. You deserve it.

Rewarding Days

12, 13, 26, 27

Challenging Days

8, 9, 19, 20

Virgo | June

Overall Theme
New pathways for creating the kind of future you desire open up, but not without some deep soul-searching on your part. You can't ignore any deep insecurities you keep hidden to hijack your forward movement. Whether you realize it or not, you've been preparing for this for a long time. And you are prepared. Just trust yourself.

Relationships
Think before you speak. It keeps you from saying things you'll regret. It's true that there's a lot going on emotionally for you right now, making you deeply aware of any anomalies in the way others respond to you, either through words or actions. However, you are in the midst of a powerful shift in the way you think about yourself, so don't derail this process by putting any emphasis on how others treat you. It's not important right now.

Career, Success, and Money
You want everything in this part of your life to be clear, organized, and on point. So do it. Forget about what everyone else is doing. Take care of your responsibilities and you'll find yourself on the receiving end of some unexpected praise as well as a big opportunity for advancement. Oh, and keep an eagle eye on any spending connected to your home. You might overdo it.

Pitfalls and Potential Problems
There's no really polite way to say this: You find yourself in a highly reactive state this month, and almost anything is likely to trigger hurt feelings, insecurity, and inadequacy. Trust that this is old stuff you've kept buried for a long time. Allow it to surface, but don't act on it. Instead, find some healthy ways to nourish yourself. This reveals how much you believe yourself to be imperfect. Time for a makeover.

Rewarding Days
8, 9, 22, 23

Challenging Days
4, 5, 17, 18

Virgo | July

Overall Theme

The battle between old patterns and new hopes makes you wonder if you know which end is up. The pull of the familiar is so deeply ingrained that it's a big challenge to realize the time has come for you to set aside any definition of what you are responsible for and create a new life template where your number-one priority is you.

Relationships

You find yourself taking a long, hard look at just what you need in relationships. The result is you are surprised to discover just how many relationships you have in which you are giving a lot and not receiving much in return. Refrain from getting caught up in trying to balance the scales. Respect your choices at the same time that you decide how you are going to alter this imbalance.

Career, Success, and Money

The more things change, the more they stay the same. This describes just how you feel about your job and your workplace. Mostly it's the people you work with. Once again you are reminded that the only person you can take charge of is yourself. Otherwise, trying to fix someone else's problem gets you in trouble.

Pitfalls and Potential Problems

It takes a lot of heavy lifting to shift patterns that you've lived with your whole life, so you are overwhelmed. Just don't turn this response into another way to find fault with yourself. You may believe that if you really knew what you were doing, you wouldn't feel this way. Well, overwhelmed is not the same thing as inadequate. Accept that life has a habit of stretching us all beyond our limits, and that includes you.

Rewarding Days

6, 7, 25, 26

Challenging Days

2, 3, 15, 16

Virgo | August

Overall Theme

You feel a lot of fire in your soul. However, it doesn't translate into much outward action, as you aren't quite sure where to put all that energy, partly because one minute it's larger than life and the next it vaporizes. Recognize that you are awakening your intuition, your imagination, and your dreams so a vision can emerge. This removes the need for you to *do* something.

Relationships

Your softer, fuzzier side takes center stage. This makes connecting to people a more attractive proposition than it has been recently. The key is to remember to apply this to yourself as well. You need compassion and a cuddle as much as anyone. Remember, being kind to yourself—which doesn't come easily to you—shows everyone just how you desire to be treated. Plus, you set a new standard in your relationship with yourself.

Career, Success, and Money

It's hard for you to seek attention, or even accept it when it shows up. Why? First, because you aren't sure you deserve acknowledgment. In your mind, that symbolizes perfection, and you know perfectly well you haven't achieved that, or ever will. Second, because then you run the risk of feeling less than, no matter what accolades you get. Well, this month everyone notices you. Embrace the attention.

Pitfalls and Potential Problems

As your connection to life shifts at ever-deeper levels, welcome the experience. That's all that is required. Hard to believe, right? What exactly does that process look like? And where's the set of directions? Yes, it's difficult to function without answers to those questions. But you must. You are creating a new path by being open and vulnerable rather than organized and structured.

Rewarding Days

9, 10, 30, 31

Challenging Days

1, 2, 11, 12

Virgo | September

Overall Theme

All systems are a go. The time to take action finally arrives and you are ready, willing, and able. The interesting thing is you are much more interested in taking a risk than managing the outcome. You're drawing on your burgeoning awareness that being able to adapt to whatever life serves up is definitely your gift.

Relationships

You are more at ease with yourself and, consequently, with others. Too often you spend time on high alert, trying to figure out how to protect yourself from any possible slings and arrows that you are sure are just around the corner. Or you are compulsively focused on making sure that whatever you do in relationships is correct. Becoming more comfortable in your own skin takes the pressure off and gives you the chance to truly be yourself.

Career, Success, and Money

Your increasing self-assurance reaps huge benefits this month. First, you create a solution to a long-term work problem that demonstrates your profound ability to understand complexities. Then you get a sudden insight that not only inspires you but causes you to see yourself in a whole new light. You don't always have to be the support person. You can be the initiator.

Pitfalls and Potential Problems

There's no doubt that you are on the verge of creating your own brave new world. After all, you are taking the first steps toward it. Be aware that the old, worn-out, not-very-effective parts of you, parts that have definitely outlived their purpose, are deeply ingrained and you will experience them again. That's not bad or good. It just is. So don't judge yourself. Not even a tiny bit.

Rewarding Days

3, 4, 7, 8

Challenging Days

10, 11, 15, 16

Virgo | October

Overall Theme

Don't be surprised if you find yourself taking a step back from all the things you initiated in September. Life is an ebb and flow, and although you pushed forward without overthinking anything or getting in your own way, you naturally need to take time to examine what you created. You are not retreating, just sorting and sifting. That's how you do life.

Relationships

You are deep inside yourself, so people may wonder where you went, both physically and emotionally. It's not that you are ignoring anyone. You are busy observing all the changes you created in your life and creating a new framework for who you are becoming. So let your partner, family, friends, and peers know you really are available. They just have to ask.

Career, Success, and Money

This area of life is the least of your concerns, not because you are neglecting anything but because there is truly nothing you are worried about. Everything is humming along and you are content to support what you've set in motion, instead of micromanaging it—another step forward in reinventing the way you do life.

Pitfalls and Potential Problems

What this month brings is a chance to relinquish the notion that easy is bad. And you can't help going there, because things went so smoothly last month. Life doesn't always need to be hard. It really can be easy—and that isn't a sin or a problem. Accept that this is part of the process of creating a life more lived than planned. It's okay to be present and let life unfold.

Rewarding Days

9, 10, 24, 25

Challenging Days

12, 13, 19, 20

Virgo | November

Overall Theme

Your focus shifts to refining and smoothing out any rough edges that accompany the major changes you've embarked on in 2019. Much to your surprise, there's not much to do, partly because your attention to detail is legendary and partly because following your heart didn't turn out to be as undisciplined as you feared. Time to celebrate. Growing yourself is worthwhile.

Relationships

You definitely feel new and improved. Buoyed by your own optimism, you check in with those most important in your life for their input. The key here is not to play games or camouflage your intent because you are afraid you won't get positive reviews. Be clear and direct. Be prepared for what you may hear. This isn't as much about what people think as it is about you knowing who you are, no matter what.

Career, Success, and Money

This is a time for clear, written communication because the potential for misunderstanding what is needed on a very important project runs high, leading to an unnecessary and expensive redo. Even though the problem isn't on your end, take the initiative in establishing the procedure that avoids the issue entirely.

Pitfalls and Potential Problems

As you review your 2019 journey, be careful not to nitpick yourself to death. Examining your life's experience to find what is more effective and useful is healthy and nurturing, as long as it doesn't lead to slicing and dicing every little thing you could, should, or might have done differently. That nullifies the whole purpose of the process, which is to gain valuable awareness.

Rewarding Days

3, 4, 20, 21

Challenging Days

11, 12, 26, 27

Virgo | December

Overall Theme

The biggest gift of 2019 is opening up to the reality that purpose and passion can occupy the same space. You now understand that passion is a source of energy, not a threat to your stability. Of course, this required that you let go of your reluctance to be vulnerable and open. But now that you've crossed that threshold, you are reenergized, inspired, and truly enthused.

Relationships

Your new boundaries in relationships really take hold as you work to let go of old patterns in dealing with others. No more feeling that it's okay for others to guilt you into doing things you don't want to do. Now that you feel you have a choice, your irritation and resentment begin to disappear. And as you change the dynamic, you notice that some people shift with you while others don't. That's their issue.

Career, Success, and Money

All in all, you feel very positive about what 2019 symbolizes in this area of life. There were far more good things than negative, leaving you feeling satisfied and eager to get to the next chapter of your life's purpose. Not only that, but you know you are better equipped to make the most of any new opportunities.

Pitfalls and Potential Problems

The eclipse on December 26 again calls into question whether structure is more important than content. Avoid the trap inherent in that question. True, you can have structure without content, but if this year has shown you anything, it's that you need both. Otherwise, there's an emptiness that drains you deep in your core. For you, structure is not the end result. It's just the container for what's really valuable.

Rewarding Days

3, 4, 17, 18

Challenging Days

6, 7, 26, 27

Virgo Action Table

These dates reflect the best—but not the only—times for success and ease in these activities, according to your Sun sign.

	JAN	FEB	MAR	APR	MAY	JUN	JUL	AUG	SEP	OCT	NOV	DEC
Move	2, 3					15, 16		30, 31				
Start a class		15, 16			17, 18					27, 28		
Seek coaching/counseling				4, 5			1, 2					3, 4
Ask for a raise			21, 22					6, 7			24, 25	
Get professional advice		19, 20				2, 3			13, 14			
Get a loan					1, 2					2, 3		19, 20
New romance	10, 11			15, 16					7, 8			
Vacation			10, 11				20, 21				11, 12	

Libra

The Scales
September 23 to October 22

Element: Air

Quality: Cardinal

Polarity: Yang/masculine

Planetary Ruler: Venus

Meditation: I balance
conflicting desires

Gemstone: Opal

Power Stones: Tourmaline,
kunzite, blue lace agate

Key Phrase: I balance

Glyph: Scales of justice,
setting sun

Anatomy: Kidneys, lower back,
appendix

Colors: Blue, pink

Animals: Brightly plumed birds

Myths/Legends: Venus,
Cinderella, Hera

House: Seventh

Opposite Sign: Aries

Flower: Rose

Keyword: Harmony

The Libra Personality

Strengths, Spiritual Purpose, and Challenges

Your capacity to accept one and all comes from a deeply authentic desire to know people, to create true bonds. This speaks to your spiritual purpose, which is to be a bridge, a connector, a conduit. You aren't always sure exactly how that's supposed to work, but you are open to finding that out as you welcome others with open arms and an open heart. You cannot help but be inclusive because you really believe that, in some significant way, we are all the same, in spite of outer appearances. So you move toward people confident that you can find common ground because you have not just love on your side, but fairness, respect, courtesy, and the ability to truly listen. This is your arsenal, along with kindness and a natural way of relating to others. Sounds almost perfect, right? It is, if you are met with the same tolerance and interest.

You need others to be as fascinated by you as you are by them. People don't have to be the same as you; they just need to want to know you. However, if you are spurned or rejected in any way, you take deep offense and your heart turns to stone. Of course, it's not immediately obvious to others, because you maintain an outward appearance that all is well. After all, it's not okay to be rude or unkind. Your deeper motivation is protecting yourself and avoiding conflict, which is something that makes you deeply uncomfortable. So you choose not to deal with things directly and instead seek to balance the scales of justice passively and surreptitiously. This speaks to the deepest challenge you face: determining how to assert yourself. And that's a lot like climbing Mount Everest in high heels for you, because isn't asserting yourself impolite and, worst of all, isn't it just another word for being aggressive? Short answer? No. Being clear about who you are and what's important to you is healthy as long as you aren't shoving something down someone's throat.

Nice doesn't always work.

Relationships

This is your area of expertise. At least that's what you think. True, you do know a lot about making connections and forging the foundation of a relationship, and you are definitely socially gifted. However, when it comes down to the nitty-gritty of human interaction, you are often at a loss as to what to do. First, you really don't like disagreement of any kind. It always spins your world and causes you to retreat into yourself while you try to figure out exactly what to say or do. The key here is to recognize that love and approval are not the same thing. You can love or care about someone without liking everything they do, and vice versa. So if someone doesn't support a choice you've made, they are not telling you they don't like or love you. Second, you don't include yourself in your relationships. You are too busy seeing to the needs and desires of others, assuming that they will do the same in return. When they don't, you are shocked and resentful. Out comes your passive-aggressive side and the war is on. Oh, it doesn't look like war; you are far too nice for that. The solution to this issue is simple and it will lead to a far happier you: make your relationship with yourself your priority.

Career and Work

Quite often you take on a support role here, just as you do in other areas of your life. However, there's one thing you need to know: You have the capacity to be a great leader, if you could just see yourself that way. Of course, you tend to think the word *leader* is interchangeable with the word *boss*, but they really are two different animals. A leader brings out the best in others by trusting them and giving them the space to excel, while a boss oversees and manages what people do. This is an important message for you in 2019 because the forces at play in your life demand that you step up and be a leader in your own life so you can create more emotional satisfaction in your work life. So tap into all those skills you have in dealing with people and use them for yourself.

Money and Possessions

You can be quite acquisitive because you do enjoy having things, and that includes money. Why? Because it just feels good. Of course, the possessions you have must be aesthetically pleasing to you. No ugly or unattractive or odd things on display in your home or on your person. Stuff like that finds its way to the back of the closet, a box in the basement, or the recycle bin, no matter who gave it to you. Of course, you would never buy anything like that for yourself, with one proviso: If your mother gave you something, you probably put it out where she can see it when she visits. Therefore, your favorite present—and you do love those—is a gift card. You get what you want and you aren't insulted by people's lack of good taste as well as their lack of knowledge of you.

The Light Side of Life

Like everything else in your life, people are at the center of fun and enjoyment for you. Sometimes it's meeting a good friend for dinner and talking for hours about whatever crosses your mind. Sometimes it's snuggling up at home with your kids and playing a board game or watching TV. Sometimes it's a big party. Sometimes it's dancing. Sometimes it's going to a movie with your partner. In fact, you hate to do much of anything by yourself, because you really love to share your experiences with someone while they are happening. However, there are those rare moments when you soak in the tub or sit outside in the sun all by yourself. It's refreshing and fun to check in with yourself. You just don't tell anyone that.

Libra Keywords for 2019
Focus, liberate, shift

The Year Ahead for Libra

The one thing that you have in spades, the one thing that will see you through a year of internal and external challenges, is your optimism. Oh, and one other thing: your sense of humor. In fact, make sure you watch or read something that makes you laugh every day. It will help you maintain your equilibrium and keep your natural capacity to believe that everything turns out for the best from drying up. Hope is always your go-to position, and you'll definitely make use of it in 2019. Yes, it's going to be one of those years. Quite frankly, there are going to be days when you feel a little like a punching bag—not a pleasant prospect in the least for your peaceful sensibilities. But forewarned is forearmed. Not that this is going to be war. It's more a case where you feel that every aspect of your life is put under a microscope and found unacceptable, causing you deep turmoil.

The silver lining—and yes, there is one—is the knowledge that you are in charge of your destiny. And you end up discovering that you really are a force to be reckoned with, not the marshmallow you think you need to be in order to please others. Any discomfort you experience triggers a more warrior-like response than you are familiar with or comfortable with. Now, before you back away from that idea, remember that a warrior is someone who negotiates situations to avoid violence, not to initiate it. At heart, every Libra really knows this. You only go to war if there is no other way to avoid tyranny. So you may be entering into a dialogue with a part of yourself you've been told is not nice, but nice doesn't always work, nor does it serve you in any just way. And you know how you feel about injustice. Time to recognize that, in your commitment to being fair to others, you are often not fair to yourself. This is the imbalance that demands your attention this year through the ministrations of Saturn, Uranus, Neptune, and Pluto. There are going to be times when you'd like to make a hit list of planets, with those four at the very top of that list. However, all together they offer a singular opportunity to connect you to the length and breadth of who you are, rather than a somewhat one-dimensional version of yourself you believe you need to be. This promises to be a liberating experience, even if it is bumpy and even painful at times. Just know that what you are unearthing in yourself is worth every discouraging minute you endure. The treasure you discover is beyond value.

Saturn

There really is no way to escape what Saturn is asking of you in 2019. Oh, you can avoid his call to take off your blindfold (which can be used to be impartial or unaware) and see the truth, whatever that might be. This challenges your deeply imbedded habit of ignoring what isn't pleasing or pretty. Accept that this will not work in the next twelve months or maybe ever again. Saturn is only interested in what is, not in what it looks like, something that is difficult for you to swallow. Of course, it matters—in your world—what things look like. What Saturn is trying to show you, especially this year, is that the outer self needs to be congruent with the inner self, not camouflage the truth. If something looks nice but is rotten at the core, this is actually an insult to your sense of what is appropriate. However, you often forget that as you struggle to accept that not everything is good, beautiful, fine, awesome, etc. Time to let Saturn demonstrate to you that there are things more painful to your core self than unpleasantness or even ugliness. To do that, he's putting you on notice and introducing you to your deeper reality, whether you like it or not. Time, after all, is truly of the essence, and it's time to examine the foundation, the roots, of your life so you can remove any underpinnings that actually undermine you. This, of course, means looking at your family of origin and your early life experiences to determine what actually illuminates and fuels you on an inner level. The risk here is exposing things you have probably worked hard to leave buried deep within. However, the gift here is the kind of awareness that gives you the opportunity to get clear about your priorities, your boundaries, and your purpose, and get in touch with the very habitual patterns that always get in the way of your forward progress. What emerges is a more integrated, truthful, and beautiful you.

Uranus

As Uranus shifts gears on March 6, going from Aries into Taurus, he moves from getting in your face at every opportunity to subtly and quietly irritating you. You heave a sigh of relief and believe the worst is over. Just one small fly in the ointment: It's a lot easier to deal with something that's right out in front of you in the bright sunlight than it is to deal with something that perpetually comes out of left field, causing you great turmoil. So pesky Uranus is not done with you, not yet. For the next seven years, he shakes up your value system, your fear of being vulnerable, and your avoidance of revealing things about yourself and your life you consider to be unattractive or just plain bad. He is going to challenge your tendency to go out of your way to make sure there's nothing for anyone to dislike about you, nothing to besmirch your reputation. That's a lot of unnecessary work, as far as Uranus is concerned. What's more, it robs you of your basic essence, your humanness. Uranus is having none of that. So his intent is clear: Remove any masks that you hide behind. Because you are only hiding from yourself. And you shouldn't have to disconnect from who you are to be loved and accepted by others, because then you don't have a true connection with anyone. Uranus is asking you to embrace your authenticity. The results will astound you.

Neptune

There are days when you really have no clue just who you are or what you are doing here on this planet. This is more than a little disconcerting, because you feel Saturn's call to get practical, get down to business, and make some headway at the same time you feel you could disappear at any moment. Welcome to the standoff between Saturn and Neptune, which continues in 2019 even more intensely than in 2018. It's not unlike the eternal question of which came first, the chicken or the egg. In this case, it's whether structure (Saturn) or vision (Neptune) is first.

The best way to respond is to use the Neptune invitation to immerse yourself in the world of all possibilities so a new aspiration reveals itself, one you can manifest with Saturn's assistance. Your challenge is to recognize that you need a dream to pursue. And to do that, there has to be some space in your world so something magical can appear. Enter Neptune and that unexplainable emptiness that accompanies his appearance. It's his intent and his nature to make things foggy and murky in your outer world so you go inside to mine the gold that sits waiting in your unconscious mind. That's not always easy to embrace in a world where the message is that something tangible needs to occupy all the space in life. Perspiration over inspiration. Well, Neptune is asking you to rethink that. Everyone needs to be inspired, and no one more than you this year.

Pluto

The biggest challenge in dealing with Pluto in 2019 comes from his uneasy partnership with Saturn. Pluto really doesn't have anything new to tell you that he hasn't been whispering in your ear since 2008. Find the passion at the core of who you are by transforming the basic structure of your life. Locate the source of your true power. Then combine the two to rebirth yourself in a new, more meaningful way. This, of course, requires you to ask the obvious question: Who actually is in control of your life? You or the expectations you believe you need to meet? This becomes more difficult to answer as you grapple to interpret whether you can use Saturn's energy to begin to build that new structure you crave or whether you will fall back into doing what's easy for others instead of what's best for you. The choice is yours. The key is being willing to access the power and potency of Pluto to carve out a new reality. After all, that's the best way to make use of all that internal dissonance he's created in the last ten years.

How Will This Year's Eclipses Affect You?

Eclipses signal intense periods that highlight major growth opportunities for us in the process of creating our lives. They are linked to the lunar phases—specifically the New and Full Moon—and involve the relationship between the Sun and the Moon and the Earth. A Solar Eclipse is a magnified New Moon, while a Lunar Eclipse is a magnified Full Moon.

Eclipses unfold in cycles involving all twelve signs of the zodiac, and they occur in pairs, usually about two weeks apart.

In 2019 there are five eclipses, three solar (two in Capricorn and one in Cancer) and two lunar (one in Leo and one in Capricorn). The first Solar Eclipse arrives on January 5 in Capricorn, immediately challenging you to confront your tendency to take the line of least resistance and just do what is expected of you. What really is more important to you: never appearing to take a wrong step and always doing the right thing, or stepping outside outmoded behavior patterns to find a new strength in just being who you want to be rather than a version of yourself that is palatable and acceptable to others? This is definitely a life-altering year, because old patterns make themselves known again and again, not for the purpose of torturing you, but so you can clearly see how little space you often give yourself in your own life. On some deep level you know this. However, acknowledging it is difficult, because you may interpret this as an indictment of the way you have lived your life. It's not.

Intrinsic to being a Libra is the dance of who is more important, me or them. You can't escape that truth or that path. Just recognize that you are at a crossroads that allows you to redefine the steps to the dance, something that the Lunar Eclipse in Leo on January 21 can definitely help you do. Tap into the core principle of Leo, which is nobody is as important as I am. This is not the same as saying no one else is significant. It means your life springs from within you and if you don't honor and respect that, you diminish yourself. So love yourself. You deserve it. Embracing this approach gives you the internal fortitude to initiate healthier ways to nourish and nurture yourself. Self-directed ways. Self-determined ways. Self-affirming ways. In turn, this actually strengthens your relationships with others, and they become less of a performance of you being the nicest person you ever met and more a true sharing, creating the kind of connection you've always desired but weren't sure was possible.

Of course, the Solar Eclipse on July 2, the Lunar Eclipse on July 16, and the Solar Eclipse on December 26 continue to trigger this process of finding the best ways to change how you function in relationships. This requires you to release some of your cherished beliefs, including a good relationship is a balanced one, people who love each other don't disagree, and the purpose of relationships is to make others happy, to name just the top three. Placing yourself at the top of your list of priorities—which is your call to action in 2019—automatically shifts how you perceive relationships and what their purpose is.

Libra | January

Overall Theme

It feels like all the bogeymen in your closet—you know, the things you'd rather not acknowledge—come out to play all at once, which is not exactly the auspicious start to 2019 you hoped for. Rather than avoiding them or trying to shove them back where they came from, commit to working through the difficult feelings they bring up. Think of it as cleaning house. In this case, you are purging your emotional body. Just remember, be kind to yourself by taking your time.

Relationships

You begin to look at the people in your world with a higher degree of skepticism and mistrust than you may have ever experienced, or at least that you remember. You haven't gone over to the dark side. This is just a reality check, one that is necessary so you can release your expectation that it's your job and everyone else's to be nice *all* the time. Humans, including you, are more complex than that.

Career, Success, and Money

The push to find a new goal and a new purpose in your work life amplifies to the point that you find yourself being extremely unhappy with the current state of affairs. Something is gnawing at you from the inside, urging you to stop accepting less than what puts a smile on your face. Just because you've done something for a long time doesn't automatically make it valuable.

Pitfalls and Potential Problems

The desire to close your eyes and count to ten, hoping that when you are done everything returns to normal, is denial at its worst. Instead of indulging in this exercise, take a good look at what you think is normal. Ask yourself if that is acceptable to you. Yes, you. Not everyone else on the planet. Just you. Doesn't it feel good to say hello to yourself?

Rewarding Days

12, 13, 29, 30

Challenging Days

5, 6, 19, 20

Libra | February

Overall Theme

Be careful to recognize that there is more than one step to completely overhauling your relationship to your life. There's no payoff in trying to change everything all at once, even if it's appealing to believe that you can. In fact, that is likely to hijack the whole process. Step one was acknowledging that a change is necessary. Next step? Listening to yourself.

Relationships

You find yourself asking this basic question: Just what purpose do relationships actually serve in my life? This leads you in many directions you probably didn't anticipate, connecting you to a system of beliefs and attitudes that leave you a little stunned by how paradoxical they are. You do discover they have one thing in common, and that is the role you are meant to play: pleasing everybody all the time.

Career, Success, and Money

Don't worry if it seems like a good idea to mount a revolution in your workplace this month. You are tired of a series of unsettling events that have undermined everyone's morale, including your own. It boils down to a lack of good leadership, and you've had enough. Keep your counsel. The source of the problem is on the way out.

Pitfalls and Potential Problems

You definitely want to wrap up all the issues you unearthed last month into one huge ball, strap it to a rocket, and launch it into the universe. That would solve everything in one decisive action. However, when it comes to emotional detritus, that's not a viable solution. Instead, it requires honoring your experience, feeling the feelings, and being kind and compassionate to yourself. More time-consuming but also more satisfying.

Rewarding Days

3, 4, 24, 25

Challenging Days

9, 10, 21, 22

Libra | March

Overall Theme

Your head is suddenly full of all the practical ways you could put to use those weird and wacky ideas that have been flooding your consciousness for quite a while now. Before letting your excitement carry you away, take a deep breath and think them through one more time. That way you can choose the one with the most potential, so you don't find yourself running in several different directions simultaneously.

Relationships

Once again, you like people. Not that you ever really stopped. You just took a vacation from giving them all the space in your world. To you, that felt a lot like you disliked them. And, heaven forbid, you aren't allowed to do that. The rules say you are always supposed to find the good in others. Well, that doesn't preclude recognizing the rest of who they are, rather than turning yourself into a doormat to prove how wonderful they are.

Career, Success, and Money

It feels like the workplace stress never ends. That's because you are deeply sensitive to constant bickering and power struggles, and there has been a lot of both over the last year. Things finally come to a head. Maintain your objectivity, don't choose sides, and ride out the storm. You emerge unscathed and with the potential for either a new project or a promotion. Your hard work and dedication have not gone unnoticed.

Pitfalls and Potential Problems

It's not in your nature to confront people and situations directly. You are more likely to take a circuitous route, meaning that rather than saying or doing things in a direct manner, you are likely to be passive-aggressive. This month, it's better that you say and do things in an upfront manner. Otherwise the results are unpleasant.

Rewarding Days

5, 6, 27, 28

Challenging Days

15, 16, 21, 22

Libra | April

Overall Theme

Your imagination is taking you on quite the field trip, and you are content to go with the flow. After all, your joy and fun quota isn't being filled to your satisfaction, and you are tired of being out of sorts the majority of the time. Enjoy this lightening of your spirits. You deserve it. Leave the heavy lifting for another time.

Relationships

Understand that the first part of this month finds you feeling like a psychic sponge because you are slurping up everyone else's excess emotion. So build some downtime into your daily routine. Observe how you feel before and after you talk to the people in your world. Notice any change in your emotions. Otherwise, when Venus enters Aries on April 20, your circuits are so overloaded that you lose your temper.

Career, Success, and Money

Refrain from taking on any work that is not your direct responsibility, no matter what is promised in return. The reason is straightforward. There are definite changes afoot and you need to make sure there is no misunderstanding about what you are accountable for. Plus, enabling others only drains you.

Pitfalls and Potential Problems

This is the month in every year when the focus turns to the ongoing struggle you have between the needs of others and your own needs. This year, it is more intense and you are at your wits' end to figure out what to do. That's because it's not a case of either/or but both. Begin there. It's healthier and it offers a better chance of finding a solution.

Rewarding Days

13, 14, 26, 27

Challenging Days

4, 5, 15, 16

Libra | May

Overall Theme

Not normally rude or impolite, you'll need to cope with the impulse to say whatever comes into your head. It's a sign that every once in a great long while, the pressure to say what you really think builds to the point that the dam bursts. The root of this is your willingness to accept that other people have the right to say whatever they want to you. Tit for tat is not a healthy solution.

Relationships

As you struggle with what you can say to others and what you can't, take time to recognize what the real issue is. Do the choices you make require other people's approbation or permission? And is the reverse true? This is one of the biggest stumbling blocks to building healthy relationships. Does being close to someone give you the right to weigh in on everything they do? You're beginning to think the answer is no.

Career, Success, and Money

Watch your spending. As much as you might like to indulge in all things bright and beautiful, there may be some unexpected problems in practical areas that need attention and an infusion of cash. So conserve your resources and you'll be less stressed.

Pitfalls and Potential Problems

This year seems to be stuck on a theme. The reality of relationships doesn't match your wishful thinking. Resenting this awareness only prevents you from finding ways to create a happy and healthy relationship. It all begins with rethinking and reframing how to achieve an authentic and true bond. The answer, strangely enough, is in the fairy tales you adore, where all lovers undergo great trials and tribulations together to get to the happy ending. It doesn't happen automatically.

Rewarding Days

10, 11, 26, 27

Challenging Days

1, 2, 15, 16

Libra | June

Overall Theme

It's a great month to take a trip. You are tired of the routine of your life, because everywhere you look you feel that the sparkle of life is missing. Recognize that this is as much a reflection of you as anything else. That doesn't mean you shouldn't change it up. You do need a vacation to recharge you; it just won't solve everything weighing you down.

Relationships

Tired of dealing with your own inner turmoil, you are also not interested in anyone else's problems. Instead, you want to hang out, have a stimulating conversation about anything other than issues (and that includes politics), and feel that there is still joy in the world. Don't apologize for feeling this way. It's a sign you are honoring yourself.

Career, Success, and Money

You really don't want to think about any of these areas, or deal with them either. And that's hard for you to accept. Take this attitude in stride and don't worry. This is a passing phase. Remember, you don't have to like or approve of everything every minute of the day, week, month, or year of your life.

Pitfalls and Potential Problems

At some point your lack of interest in your life as it stands is going to raise internal alarm bells. Acknowledge the fear you feel. It's real. And it's something you are likely to feel as the depth and breadth of the shift you are making finally hits home. Know that you wouldn't have begun this process if you couldn't finish it.

Rewarding Days

9, 10, 22, 23

Challenging Days

4, 5, 11, 12

Libra | July

Overall Theme

Just when you think 2019 is going to be nothing but a tidal wave of dissatisfaction and overwhelm, the sun comes out and you feel brand-new again. Bask in these feelings, embrace the optimism percolating deep within, and know you are making headway. This gives you the necessary boost to grasp an opportunity coming your way and overcome any internal obstacles you try to put in the way.

Relationships

Your renewed buoyancy gets you thinking about what is likely to truly nourish you in your relationships right now. The answer is fun and play. The carefree spontaneity of just hanging out calls to you. No plans, no expectations, no demands. Just the chance to be in the moment and experience your innate pleasure in being alive.

Career, Success, and Money

Both the Solar Eclipse on July 2 and the Lunar Eclipse on July 16 invite you to go beyond your comfort zone and your old patterns to a new beginning—one that promises great growth and more emotional satisfaction, provided you acknowledge what isn't working for you. Sticking to the tried and true guarantees that you will continue to feel stuck.

Pitfalls and Potential Problems

As much as you might think it's unwise to throw caution to the wind, the risk that presents itself isn't the recipe for disaster you fear. The truth is, you've been preparing for this since the beginning of the year. There's no sense in choosing to back away from something you so deeply desire, which is releasing yourself from all the coulds, shoulds, and musts that keep you in chains. Seize the day.

Rewarding Days

20, 21, 25, 26

Challenging Days

2, 3, 15, 16

Libra | August

Overall Theme

Now that you realize disaster isn't going to strike, because you are totally prepared to remove anything or anyone keeping you from living your life to the fullest, you get a little pushy. It's all the unexpressed frustration you've felt over the years when your need to please others, coupled with their demands of you, held you back. This is a trap. Honor your past choices. Otherwise, you are dumping on yourself.

Relationships

It's time to redefine what love is to you, or at least begin that process. Stripping away how deeply responsible you believed you were for the well-being of others is not the same as knowing what kind of love you require. It's just getting rid of anything blocking the path to finding that out. So take that blank canvas and paint the picture in your heart.

Career, Success, and Money

Now that new doors are opening, you are getting a much clearer picture of the kind of change you need, so this part of your life brings out the best in you. This is a revelation, because for a very long time you believed that your lack of satisfaction was a sign of your ingratitude. No, it was a sign that you were capable of much more.

Pitfalls and Potential Problems

Finding fault in yourself for past choices and decisions interferes with your forward movement. It's highly tempting to analyze and measure everything you've ever done again and again, searching for what went wrong. This avoids the real purpose for looking at what you've done: knowing yourself and why you made the choices you did. That's healthy because it leads to change. Assigning blame isn't and doesn't.

Rewarding Days

4, 5, 19, 20

Challenging Days

16, 17, 30, 31

Libra | September

Overall Theme

Your forward momentum seems to come to a halt as you are suddenly confronted by deep fears that no matter how focused you are, how determined you are, or how confident you are, your insecurities always derail you. Only if you let them. It is, after all, a choice—your choice. Feed either your insecurities or your belief in yourself.

Relationships

Ignore that voice in the background telling you to abandon your intention to put yourself first and return to being the dutiful, obedient, people-pleasing person you are naturally inclined to be. Again, it's that fundamental fear of being all alone, with no one to care about you. This is old programming. Cherishing yourself doesn't equal failing to love others.

Career, Success, and Money

The Full Moon on September 14 brings to light unexpected criticism and hostility in your work world. You find yourself being forced to defend your actions against innuendo and, possibly, lies. Fortunately, your stellar reputation for hard work and keeping everyone in the loop saves the day. See the experience for what it is: someone taking potshots at you because they can.

Pitfalls and Potential Problems

Your socially adept exterior, brimming with confidence and kindness, really does hide the kind of insecurity and uncertainty you hide even from yourself. Acknowledging it gives it less power over you. Being human is essentially an exercise in dealing with insecurity. No matter how hard we try, there are no guarantees. Remember that and it alleviates a lot of the stress you are feeling.

Rewarding Days

7, 8, 28, 29

Challenging Days

12, 13, 22, 23

Libra | October

Overall Theme

Your equilibrium is restored, not by anything that the rest of the world has done for you but by you looking your fears and insecurities squarely in the eye. They aren't as scary or numbing or overwhelming when you acknowledge them. Fancy that! Some good does come from facing your demons. Celebrate. Throw yourself a party. The faith you've exhibited in yourself is exhilarating.

Relationships

Happy with what you see emerging in yourself, you are tempted to canvas everyone you know to get their approval. Fortunately, you see this inclination for what it is: a return to the familiar. The key is not to let it depress you. Pat yourself on the back for recognizing the trap you set for yourself. That's a real sign you are changing.

Career, Success, and Money

This is not a good month to partner with anyone, whether it's a project, a career move, or an expenditure. Your focus needs to be on valuing yourself enough to know what you truly desire, instead of being flattered into, pushed into, or guilted into doing something you know isn't what's best for you. And remember, you don't need to justify or explain your decision. A simple no is sufficient.

Pitfalls and Potential Problems

There's only one person who can cause you problems and it's actually you. The Sun is in Libra and that's your traditional stomping ground. This can be both comforting and counterproductive right now. It's okay to relax into enjoying all the finer parts of being a Libra, as long as you don't lull yourself into believing that the way things once were is the pot of gold at the end of the rainbow.

Rewarding Days

2, 3, 28, 29

Challenging Days

12, 13, 25, 26

Libra | November

Overall Theme

You are ready to take over the world. Your confidence and optimism are running high. And yet, you are off kilter. Something's percolating deep in your subconscious, disturbing the hard-won stability you worked so hard to establish. Resist the desire to figure this out. Let it go. Focus on what you can accomplish instead. It's a great time to make things happen.

Relationships

You are feeling truly magnanimous, which comes as such a relief to you and those you love. Shifting the way you build relationships takes its toll on everyone's patience, including yours. However, the transformation is liberating, bringing a newfound intimacy and joy to your life and your loves. It's okay to be satisfied with all you've done.

Career, Success, and Money

The transition in this area of your life hits a few bumps, simply because there are too many cooks in the kitchen. Expect some silly disagreement to temporarily make your work environment a little testy. The good thing is, you are simply an observer. As for your finances, don't take any unnecessary risks. The timing isn't good.

Pitfalls and Potential Problems

Use all that exhilaration and faith you have in yourself wisely. It's one thing to take the lead and initiate things, but it's quite another to think it's okay to push the process or other people, especially when the timing isn't right. Initiation is just the beginning. Enjoy the process. Let the rest unfold appropriately without you trying to control the whole enchilada.

Rewarding Days

3, 4, 28, 29

Challenging Days

11, 12, 26, 27

Libra | December

Overall Theme

Life takes you on a merry chase and you find yourself bouncing from one thing to another, distracted, with little ability to concentrate. Oh, you've still got lots of drive and desire, but just what are you accomplishing? It feels like nothing. The reality is, you are working to pull together a new way of being. That's a complex undertaking, and it's not always easy to discern if you are making any progress. Just know that you are.

Relationships

The old messages about who you are supposed to be in relationships resurface, both from within and from other people. This frustrates you because you wonder if you can escape this fear that you are only as valuable as what you do rather than who you are. Remember that it takes time to change attitudes, habits, and thinking. What you are experiencing is normal and to be expected.

Career, Success, and Money

Take a moment or two to review how this year has gone. That way you are able to set the tone for what's to come next. You can't see it just yet, but this area of your life is going to go through a tectonic change that brings an abundance of satisfaction and accomplishment as well as greater financial freedom.

Pitfalls and Potential Problems

As 2019 comes to a close, you realize how profoundly you want to be free of the need to be everything to everyone. You are unsure just how this is going to happen, because you still feel the necessity to take care of others before you nourish yourself. Stop backing yourself into a corner. The transformation isn't complete, but the desired change is gaining momentum and taking hold.

Rewarding Days

3, 4, 17, 18

Challenging Days

6, 7, 25, 26

Libra Action Table

These dates reflect the best—but not the only—times for success and ease in these activities, according to your Sun sign.

	JAN	FEB	MAR	APR	MAY	JUN	JUL	AUG	SEP	OCT	NOV	DEC
Move			27, 28							4, 5		6, 7
Start a class			10, 11	9, 10		2, 3			28, 29			
Seek coaching/ counseling							2, 3			11, 12		
Ask for a raise		4, 5				12, 13			2, 3			
Get professional advice	5, 6			11, 12				30, 31				
Get a loan		24, 25			17, 18					27, 28		
New romance	21, 25							4, 5			3, 4	
Vacation					2, 3		27, 28					11, 12

Scorpio

The Scorpion
October 23 to November 21

♏

Element: Water

Quality: Fixed

Polarity: Yin/feminine

Planetary Ruler: Pluto (Mars)

Meditation: I let go of the need to control

Gemstone: Topaz

Power Stones: Obsidian, garnet

Key Phrase: I create

Glyph: Scorpion's tail

Anatomy: Reproductive system

Colors: Burgundy, black

Animals: Reptiles, scorpions, birds of prey

Myths/Legends: The Phoenix, Hades and Persephone, Shiva

House: Eighth

Opposite Sign: Taurus

Flower: Chrysanthemum

Keyword: Intensity

The Scorpio Personality

Strengths, Spiritual Purpose, and Challenges

You are definitely one of the more complex souls rummaging around on the planet. The reason? You live life at the extremes. Here are a few examples: You are highly perceptive yet, at times, insensitive. You are profoundly aware of the complexities of being human, yet you see your own life as black and white. You are extremely trustworthy yet not very trusting. You are intensely involved yet oblivious. And those are just the highlights.

You definitely are a conundrum, even to yourself, although you aren't always as aware of yourself as you are of others. After all, you know better than anyone that it's not easy to navigate the subterranean waters that lie just below the surface. However, you are compelled to dig deep, because that is your spiritual purpose: to know life, with all its mysteries, paradoxes, and ambiguities, inside out. It's one of the reasons that you often ignore the obvious. There's nothing more to know, nothing that is mysterious, nothing to pique your interest. This puts you at odds with the rest of the world, who, to your amazement, are caught up in believing that what's on the surface is all there is. Meanwhile, your inner radar is loudly whispering in your ear, letting you know what's really going on. The result? A struggle to make sense of what you are told versus what you know is going on, creating an inner dissonance that affects you deeply, plaguing you constantly and leaving you unable to trust in yourself—at least until you learn to listen to yourself first and honor your own experience. Then you know your inner radar is rarely wrong and you are free to engage in life with all the passion that exists at your very core. No halfway measures or gray areas for you. Just one of two speeds: zero or 180. You are all in or missing in action. Yes or no. Simple as that. Is there any other way to live your life? Not if you are a Scorpio.

Relationships

You are fond of telling anyone who will listen that you don't need anyone. And that is the truth, because need is not what drives you. It's desire and sometimes fascination. They are much more likely to draw you into relationships. The irony is, it doesn't really matter what motivates you to connect to others. You always have to face your deepest fears: rejection, abandonment, and smothering. It's just that you believe that, if you need someone, they have the power and you are more vulnerable. The truth is that desire and fascination offer the same pitfalls; they are just more attractive to you because the initial feeling buoys your spirit rather than dragging you down.

By nature, you are curious—or is that suspicious? Either way, you love plumbing the depths of what makes people tick. This makes you an expert in what motivates others. There probably isn't a single thing anyone could do that would be a surprise or a shock to you. After all, you are well acquainted with both the most beautiful and the ugliest aspects of human nature. This is why people often reveal their deepest secrets to you. On the flip side, those around you often feel like they are under a microscope because you are always probing everyone's reality, whether you realize it or not. Not for any nefarious reasons but more so you know where people are coming from. That way you can protect yourself—which you absolutely believe you must do. Your biggest challenge is to embrace your vulnerability. This will make you stronger than you can imagine.

Career and Work

The worst thing you can experience is feeling like your work is a death warrant. No going through the motions for you. No hanging in there to get a paycheck and finding yourself doing that for thirty years. Whatever you choose to do, it must pass the litmus test: would you do this for free? That doesn't mean you want to do it without recompense. But the most important reward for you is doing something that stimulates you. Something that you feel deep in your soul is your calling. Something you feel is an imperative as much as a choice. Something that, if you didn't do it, you might wither away and disappear. Sounds extreme, but then that's the Scorpio way. The challenge is creating some wiggle room, because there are days when you are going to feel it's just a job. And that's okay. Your unparalleled commitment and your incomparable focus are your tools for slogging through any temporary swamp. As for success, once you've charted your course, there are few obstacles that can stop you. In fact, you view those as a sign that you need to keep going. So you redouble your efforts and, almost magically, things turn around in your favor.

Money and Possessions

You see money as an agent of transformation. It isn't necessarily something to be valued all by itself. If you can use it to relieve the pressures of life, giving you more space to be and do, then it is something to be cherished. Otherwise, you don't see it as a measure of who you are or how accomplished you are. It's a reward, not a reason for being. The same goes for possessions, with one proviso: if they are deeply meaningful, you hang on to them. Otherwise, whether you have them or you don't is not at the top of your list of priorities.

The Light Side of Life

Your intensity often convinces people that you and joy are not well acquainted. It really comes down to what you define as lighthearted. And for you, those things are obvious: anything that increases your passion, challenges your desire to break through obstacles, explains things you want to understand deeply, and gives you a break from the mundane. And last but not least: alone time on a daily basis. You are quite happy entertaining yourself.

Scorpio Keywords for 2019
Vulnerability, trust, imagination

The Year Ahead for Scorpio

The key to staying on top of life in 2019 is making sure you don't lull yourself into a false sense of security, which isn't your usual style. It's hard to take you by surprise, simply because your radar is almost always on high alert. However, after seven years of constantly being knocked off balance by Uranus in Aries, 2018 gave you a bit of a chance to regroup, as Saturn in Capricorn calmed things down considerably. You took full advantage and regained a sense of security that had disappeared almost completely. It's not that you weren't able to respond to the turmoil Uranus kept on introducing into your life, but just that you found yourself exhausted by the need to rise to life's constantly shifting landscape. Especially since Uranus seemed particularly able to avoid your radar, leaving you with no inkling anything was about to go sideways. So you spent much of 2018 recharging your batteries and thinking you were essentially out of the woods. That's fine. Everybody needs a break and you've had yours. Time to get back in the flow in 2019. Otherwise, your break turns into a choice to be complacent. And that only leads to a series of missed opportunities and the failure to sense the consequences of some surprising upheavals you won't see coming. Yes, Uranus is still going to be stirring the pot. The truth is he really never goes away. The only question is, what method is he going to use to turn things upside down?

So make sure that you take the messages from Saturn that all is well with a certain degree of skepticism. After all, he always thinks he's in charge, because his job in your life is to give you a sense of stability. However, it's you who is required to use what he offers to take charge of your own reality. There's absolutely no way he can guarantee anything, and part of you already knows that. Besides, you would be utterly bored if you thought everything was so secure that life was 100 percent predictable. Welcome to the paradox known as your life. You want both emotional safety and ongoing transformation.

In 2019 you get the opportunity to find a way to bridge what appear to be opposite requirements, and it promises to be a fruitful and mind-altering journey as long as you choose to fully engage. The biggest stumbling block is undoubtedly your fear of being vulnerable, which is the one thing that consistently hijacks your desire to plumb the depths of your soul. It's time to recognize that it's really okay to lay yourself bare to the one person you can absolutely trust: you. Nothing that you uncover has the power you fear it does, which is to extinguish your essence.

Saturn

Now that you are aware of Saturn's agenda—to make you believe that anything and everything he tells you is a bulwark against the insecurities of life—you can take advantage of what you know and use the best parts of his tool kit to solidify a deeper understanding of how you want to create your life going forward. All the inspiration in the world is of little or no use without some way to manifest it. That is Saturn's gift: turning dreams into reality, creating ways to put things into practice, making ideas accessible in physical form. This is not only powerful but necessary. And this year Saturn knocks on your door, ready to put all of this at your disposal. The key is to remember he is not the vision. He is the conduit to actualizing what you envisage—which is exactly what you need him to do in 2019 because there's a wealth of possibilities swimming around in your brain and they've been hanging out there for so much longer than you anticipated. Finally the timing is right to discover if any of them can actually become something more than just a wish. First, let go of the frustration you accumulated dealing with life's vicissitudes instead of following your passion. Saturn's message here is that delays are his way of letting you know it's not the time to proceed, which doesn't always suit your need to accelerate the process, not slow it down. Well, get ready. In 2019 you get to push the launch button.

Uranus

It may be difficult to imagine or, for that matter, believe, but Uranus moving into Taurus on March 6 is likely to make him easier to deal with. Not because he is going to be any less challenging or upsetting but because he will be right out in the open, where you can see him. While he was in Aries, he always stirred things up from a place where you couldn't see what was coming until it was on top of you. This left you in the position of mopping up messes, which, in your mind, didn't serve any useful purpose. However, his intention then was to stir things up so much that you'd have to make the kind of adjustments that fundamentally changed how you processed life internally. Now he is turning his attention to shaking up how you can apply that knowledge in your outer life, most specifically in how you relate and connect to other people. But before that shift happens, there are still some final hurdles to deal with as you complete your inner growth. Remember, you are clearing a path to a new beginning that promises to create the best of everything, provided you are willing to truly follow through and not just make the motions of change. Uranus never shows up in our lives to tell us we are wrong. He is far too detached for that. He simply wants us to recognize what no longer contributes to who we really desire to be.

Neptune

Here is the source of all those strange dreams, magical possibilities, and whimsical but seemingly impractical notions that have been occupying your consciousness since 2012. Sure, they are fascinating and entertaining, but are they nothing more than ephemeral torture? After a while, you begin to think that your dream state, whether awake or asleep, is just teasing you. After all, if there's no chance of actually creating what you visualize, you are left with only one outcome: extreme frustration. Why? Because, if your passion gets awakened by anything, you need to be able to do something about it. Well, 2019 promises to give you the opportunity to finally explore the potential of at least one of these imaginings in the real world as Saturn connects with Neptune to give it form. Go for the gusto and don't overthink it. The best things in the world come from following the stirrings of the imagination. So don't let your focus on what you are able to do on a practical level take up all the oxygen in your life. Keep on dreaming. It fuels your passion in more ways than you understand.

Pluto

Since 2008, the overhaul in what you think, how you think, and how you apply the conclusions that result has been so revelatory that you are astounded by how easily you once accepted what you were told was the truth. Under Pluto's guidance, you've pushed yourself to actually examine any and all ideas and perceptions that cross your conscious mind to see if they hold any value for you. In this process, you had to acknowledge how much you dislike two of the most-used phrases humans employ and how often, ironically, you've uttered them yourself: "Just because" and "That's the way things are." They always make you see red. First, they simply don't answer the most fundamental question in your world, which is *why*? Without that, what's the point? Second, they are mindless and evasive, both of which insult your intelligence. All this made you realize how often you collaborated in avoiding your own awareness and accepting the obvious, something that is counterproductive, not to mention damaging, to your very essence. In 2019 it is imperative that you not allow Saturn to override your newfound commitment to being truthful to yourself by dragging you backward into old thought patterns, triggering a bout of analysis paralysis. Instead, use his need for structure to apply this profound shift in your thinking in a practical way.

How Will This Year's Eclipses Affect You?

Eclipses signal intense periods that highlight major growth opportunities for us in the process of creating our lives. They are linked to the lunar phases—specifically the New and Full Moon—and involve the relationship between the Sun and the Moon and the Earth. A Solar Eclipse is a magnified New Moon, while a Lunar Eclipse is a magnified Full Moon. Eclipses unfold in cycles involving all twelve signs of the zodiac, and they occur in pairs, usually about two weeks apart.

In 2019 there are five eclipses, three solar (two in Capricorn and one in Cancer) and two lunar (one in Leo and one in Capricorn). The first Solar Eclipse arrives on January 5 in Capricorn, creating an immediate contretemps between what you say out loud and what you actually believe. The root of this issue is an old pattern resurfacing, and some things fall out of your mouth that surprise you. After all, you were sure you had dug out and destroyed those immature, rigid attitudes that really didn't and don't reflect who you are at the most fundamental level. Again, it's an opportunity for you to see how your subconscious hangs on to old perceptions and beliefs, no matter how much time and energy you've put into transforming them.

The purpose of this experience—and there is one—is to recognize that what is held in your subconscious never really disappears. It's always there. For example, if you believe you were rejected at birth, that belief is a profound part of your life experience and, as such, cannot be changed or erased. It's both a blessing and a curse, although, given your temperament, it may be hard for you to recognize the blessing part. The gift in it is the capacity to recognize difficult or even dangerous situations, because being rejected at birth is so complicated, painful, and very much a life-and-death experience. So the subconscious holds this belief in place, as it does many other perceptions, as a measure of self-protection. The key is to accept that, which will allow you to understand that transformation is not a form of eradication as much as a process of using all of who you are and your life experiences to shift how you respond to and what you do with what life dishes up. This creates a new way of being, fueled by awareness instead of reaction.

This, in turn, allows you to take the energy of the Lunar Eclipse on January 20 in Leo and continue your growth by embracing a level of vulnerability that still feels like foreign territory to you. This is necessary if you are to make use of the Solar Eclipse on July 2, the Lunar Eclipse on July 16, and the Solar Eclipse on December 26 to find a way to move beyond the rigid boundaries you've set for yourself in how you think and communicate so you can speak from your deep-feeling nature and your heart. There's no doubt this is scary. However, if you resist this process, you are choosing to shut yourself off rather than open yourself up. Time to trust yourself unequivocally.

Scorpio | January

Overall Theme

Every time you turn around there seems to be another obstacle in your path. This confuses you because you're sure your intuition told you there's no time like the present to get things started. So why aren't things going more smoothly? Welcome to the ongoing conundrum that you face throughout 2019: When is the right time to act?

Relationships

You aren't really sure why everyone misinterprets what you are saying. Perhaps it's because you aren't being as clear as you think you are, or perhaps you're leaving out pertinent details, assuming everyone knows what you know. As hard as it is to accept, you often think you've told someone a piece of information because you planned to. Find a way to keep track of what you've said and to whom. It saves a lot of time and angst.

Career, Success, and Money

The first Lunar Eclipse of 2019 shines a light on your career aspirations and sets the tone for what is going to be a year of unexpected accolades and success. The only thing standing in your way is timing. Instead of getting frustrated, get everything in order and wait for the green light. It will come.

Pitfalls and Potential Problems

Rather than being annoyed, irritated, and exasperated (and yes, you are all three), refocus all that pent-up energy flooding every cell of your body and find a new target for all that desire. Because you have more than one thing you intend to accomplish. You may not want to make this adjustment, but let it go. What's waiting in the wings has just as much potential, or maybe more, than your original goal.

Rewarding Days

4, 5, 21, 22

Challenging Days

12, 13, 27, 28

Scorpio | February

Overall Theme

Your natural inclination to retreat into yourself takes on special meaning, as you spend much of February focused inward, trying to figure out just what gives your life meaning and structure. It's a delayed response to last month's eclipses and it catches you off guard. Don't make the mistake of assuming this is an issue for your mind to resolve. It's all about your deeper feelings.

Relationships

Make sure to include those you love in your world. It will balance all the deep soul-searching you are doing and give you some much-needed perspective. Granted, you believe you can sort everything out on your own. However, you need to recognize your tendency to be so absorbed in your own reality that you find yourself going in circles. This leads to obsession rather than clarity.

Career, Success, and Money

You feel a lot like you are on autopilot. Nose to the grindstone and all that. The only challenge is taking time to check in with those around you for any updates. Otherwise, you miss some important information connected to what you are working on.

Pitfalls and Potential Problems

Your capacity for being able to block out the whole world and everyone in it when you are immersed in digging up and examining whatever is sticking in your craw is legendary. Sometimes it takes you so far off the beaten path that you completely disconnect from your life. That definitely could happen this month. The answers you seek aren't ready to reveal themselves yet.

Rewarding Days
11, 12, 23, 24

Challenging Days
8, 9, 21, 22

Scorpio | March

Overall Theme

Life takes on a lighter tone and you release yourself from the never-ending mental and emotional circles you couldn't quite avoid in February. Instead, you commit yourself completely to just having some fun and letting your imagination run away with you. The result is a much-needed vacation from contemplating all of existence.

Relationships

You feel obligated to apologize for being missing in action for a while. It's like you came out of a trance you weren't even aware you were in. Rather than apologizing, just spend time with all those you feel you may have disappointed. That's a far more effective way of connecting to people, because it's fun and it demonstrates that your commitment is real instead of perfunctory.

Career, Success, and Money

Things in the workplace remain steady and consistent. No major issues or challenges to deal with. But you'll need to keep on eye on your discretionary spending. No opportunity this month is worth adding more to your debt load than you can manage, no matter how good it looks or feels. There is definitely the potential to act in haste and repent at leisure.

Pitfalls and Potential Problems

While you are busy enjoying life, you feel some unsettling energy percolating just below the surface. Say hello to Uranus moving into Taurus. Don't worry about what that means or what's going to happen. All of that will be made clear at some point in the next seven years. For now, be in the moment and celebrate your life.

Rewarding Days

10, 11, 27, 28

Challenging Days

5, 6, 12, 13

Scorpio | April

Overall Theme

Exactly what is going bump in the night? You'd really like to know, but not because it frightens you. After all, you do love the dark. It's more that it's getting in the way of dealing with practical issues demanding your attention in the waking hours. You need sleep that is both restful and inspirational, not this really weird stuff that startles you awake. The solution? Do something to empty your mind before you go to sleep. Your consciousness is in overdrive.

Relationships

You need to be practical about your relationships. Why? You simply don't have a lot of extra energy right now, yet everybody is clamoring for your attention. Instead of tuning them out or grinding your teeth, make a schedule for brief consultations and stick to it. Yes, it sounds businesslike, but if you don't do it this way, you'll be exhausted and no one will be satisfied.

Career, Success, and Money

The demands in your work life grow exponentially in the blink of an eye. An important facet of a project you are working on is totally overlooked until the eleventh hour. And who gets the call to wave a magic wand and pull a rabbit out of a hat? You, of course. What's more, you succeed in saving the day.

Pitfalls and Potential Problems

It's not that you don't enjoy being the hero, the person who understands life's complexities, the person who always has time to listen to people's deepest fears, etc. You do. Until you don't. This in one of those times when you wish you were truly invisible. Do the next best thing: Think of the most unlikely place to go and head there. Peace and quiet await.

Rewarding Days

1, 2, 6, 7

Challenging Days

3, 4, 17, 18

Scorpio | May

Overall Theme

How many different ways can you be irritated? Well, you are about to find out. If it's not people talking endlessly and not getting anywhere, it's the turmoil of constantly changing plans. Doesn't anybody know which end is up? Usually you're the one who can see through the sea of complications and find a solution. This time, you bow out. It's that or scream, and not silently either.

Relationships

There's only one thing you require to be happy this month, and that's accountability—in others. You are aware that finding solutions for other people's life crises comes dangerously close to enabling them, if you aren't clear about your boundaries. Where to begin? Listen to them unburden themselves and then tell them you trust they know what to do.

Career, Success, and Money

The opportunity to meet new people with the potential to have a significant impact on this part of your life arrives unexpectedly, and just at the point where you wondered if May was going to be an ongoing train wreck. This boosts your spirits and gives you something delicious to get excited about.

Pitfalls and Potential Problems

Your equilibrium may be difficult to locate, but you need to do everything in your power to find it and maintain it. The number-one way to do this is to really listen to what your radar is telling you about the true nature of what's happening around you. You'll realize most of it doesn't constitute anything close to a crisis. If you stay centered on that, you'll weather the tempests in other people's teacups.

Rewarding Days

12, 13, 26, 27

Challenging Days

1, 2, 14, 15

Scorpio | June

Overall Theme
The first hint of summer uplifts you. Suddenly you feel alive again, instead of overwhelmed by the detritus of everyday life. It really is easy for you to get bogged down by stuff that feels meaningless to you. In order to nourish this emotional rebirth, go on holiday. It doesn't matter where you go, as long as it's a place that feeds your soul.

Relationships
Torn by desire. That's you in a nutshell. Even when you are able to identify what you desire, you often fight it or try to control it. Recognize it's what drives you and you'll be fine this month, whether you are hanging with all your favorite people or spending time in solitude. Or both. It really doesn't have to be one or the other. In fact, a bit of both is just what you need.

Career, Success, and Money
You feel a deep yearning or a calling. You aren't sure which, but you do know there's something pushing you toward a new beginning. By turns, you are exhilarated and stubbornly resistant. A fresh start would be wonderful. But why would you abandon everything you've already built? Understand that no decision is required right now. You are in a gestational phase.

Pitfalls and Potential Problems
This month provides some much-needed relief from feeling that life is always shoving you to and fro, with no visible signposts to guide you. Enjoy. Take it easy. And ignore the small stuff, and the big stuff too, for that matter. Anything that truly requires your input can wait.

Rewarding Days
13, 14, 22, 23

Challenging Days
11, 12, 25, 26

Scorpio | July

Overall Theme

You don't care if you have to push, pull, or drag the whole world with you. This month you are forging a new direction, complete in the knowledge that you are ready to shake things up. You may not have formulated just what that's going to look like, but that isn't as important as taking the risk. So fly by the seat of your pants and trust your instincts. You'll be amazed at the results.

Relationships

In your haste to move your life along, you find yourself exasperated by the demand that you slow down and explain yourself. Neither is your cup of tea when you are totally focused, which leads to some very tense moments. So count to ten and share the excitement you feel about what's ahead, rather than biting people's heads off at their ankles. The input you receive in return inspires you.

Career, Success, and Money

You really do feel like a kid in a candy store. There are so many directions you can go in, most of which you never really considered because you were totally absorbed in doing the stuff already on your plate. But you now realize it's getting a bit stale. Time for a complete change of pace. Start your engine.

Pitfalls and Potential Problems

You always have more than enough passion and drive to accomplish anything you put on your list of priorities. The challenge you face right now is an ongoing one: you get so single-minded that you ignore everything else in favor of the one thing that is currently charging your battery. Take time to consider all the ramifications of the shift you are going through. It saves you considerable time and energy.

Rewarding Days

10, 11, 25, 26

Challenging Days

2, 3, 16, 17

Scorpio | August

Overall Theme

Expect to experience the full range of your profound capacity to feel everything from complete joy to overwhelming terror, as you begin to comprehend just how big a change you are embarking on. You can see it all: the heights of accomplishment and the black hole of failure. None of this deters you. Ready, set, go!

Relationships

As you ride the rollercoaster of emotion, you aren't alone. All those closest to you come along for the ride, except they aren't as adept at dealing with extreme swings in mood and emotion as you are. You go from start to stop and back to start in the blink of an eye. It's natural to you but unsettling to others. Make sure to let them know when you return to equilibrium. You need their support. Yes, you do.

Career, Success, and Money

Nothing of long-term value ever comes to fruition on the back of passion and inspiration alone, or even determination. There needs to be a plan. And part of that plan is recognizing that you still need financial stability while you prepare for the future. Maintain your current source of income; you need the security to move forward.

Pitfalls and Potential Problems

The change you are planning is so monumental that you really can't do it alone. Of course, you absolutely and without reservation believe the opposite. Time to recognize that it's not a sign of incompetence, weakness, or stupidity to get input, support, or inspiration from others. Not only does it reduce the bumps in the road and create deeper connections, but it's also fun. You don't always have to do everything by yourself.

Rewarding Days

6, 7, 30, 31

Challenging Days

11, 12, 21, 22

Scorpio | September

Overall Theme

A critical part of your plan going forward falls into place out of the blue, providing a much-needed burst of enthusiasm at the exact moment you need it. It's not that things are difficult; they're just slow. Take heart. Everything starts to pick up speed toward the end of the month. The right time has finally arrived.

Relationships

You actually feel quite a bit more grounded and capable of engaging with other people now that the changes you intend to make are taking shape. Don't be surprised to discover that the people who matter most are a little cranky from a lack of attention. Rather than insisting you weren't ignoring them, make plans to do whatever they desire. And recognize that their perspective of what transpired is as valid as yours.

Career, Success, and Money

Now that you are firmly on your way in a brand-new direction, you find that many of the things about your job or career that were getting on your nerves no longer matter. It really doesn't surprise you. What astonishes you is how long you ignored the obvious and the reasons why. So you aren't always as aware of yourself as you think.

Pitfalls and Potential Problems

There is a strong need to exercise some restraint. Yes, things are moving ahead. Yes, the timing is right. Yes, you know what you are doing. The problem, as always, is that things never accelerate fast enough for you, causing deep frustration, not to mention unnecessary consequences. So trust the plan you set in motion, and stop watching to see when the kettle boils.

Rewarding Days

3, 4, 7, 8

Challenging Days

10, 11, 20, 21

Scorpio | October

Overall Theme

Put all those insecurities and fears bubbling just below the surface in the proper perspective. They signify the usual stuff you put yourself through just before you step across the threshold into the big shifts in your life. Consider it cleaning out the closet and getting rid of anything that doesn't fit anymore. And there's a lot inside you that doesn't mesh with where you are going.

Relationships

You are feeling mad love for all the people in your world who not only backed you up as you prepared yourself for a big unknown, but let you know how much they admire and respect you. Not used to all this adoration, even though you know it's warranted, you fake modesty. And it shows. Just say thank you. That's all that's required. Plus it's truly how you feel.

Career, Success, and Money

Not everyone in your world is excited by the opportunities you are creating for yourself, so be prepared to deal with some nastiness and insults disguised as compliments. Don't waste your time even acknowledging these immature outbursts. After all, these people aren't showing you anything you haven't seen before.

Pitfalls and Potential Problems

It never fails. You are always shocked when you stumble across the complexities of your own nature. That's because you prefer to believe that your world is black and white, with no gray areas. Well, the shift that's going on inside demands that you understand that complexities are not the same as complications. Accepting that frees you from a set of very rigid expectations you've trapped yourself in.

Rewarding Days

9, 10, 27, 28

Challenging Days

4, 5, 21, 22

Scorpio | November

Overall Theme

This is the happiest you've been in your own skin for such a long time, and the source is obvious: you've reignited your passion for life and you are seeing life in color again. Gone is that fear that the best of your life is behind you. No more dull, monochromatic days for you. No more feeling stuck and bored. Quite the opposite.

Relationships

It's that time of year when you struggle to balance what you desire with what other people want. And this quite often leaves you bewildered, because you never seem to get it right. What to do? First, take time to define what relationships mean to you. Then ask your partner and the rest of your posse the same thing. It's just a starting point, but it offers clues on how to create equilibrium.

Career, Success, and Money

So much is happening—and all of it good—you can barely keep up with it all. And you love it. Your dream became a purpose and then a plan, and now it's all coming to fruition. Each and every step is as much fun as the anticipated end result. Who knew you could be this delirious during every itty-bitty bit of this process?

Pitfalls and Potential Problems

Well, the problem this month is that there are no big hitches, nothing much to get in your way. This, in itself, is a challenge for you. Part of what makes you tick is anticipating problems so you can solve them. Relax. Enjoy the results of your intensity, creativity, and determination.

Rewarding Days

3, 4, 20, 21

Challenging Days

8, 9, 15, 16

Scorpio | December

Overall Theme

Navigating the last month of 2019 promises to be a bit of a rollercoaster ride, not because anything is going wrong in your external world but because the magnitude of all the changes you've made hits home. You are exhilarated and exhausted simultaneously, which is to be expected. What you've done is like moving a mountain. Celebrate this and then rest.

Relationships

You are busy processing all the feelings and insights that surfaced last month in examining both how you see relationships and how others see them. It's all been rather revelatory. You aren't sure exactly what the next step is. However, you feel freer and more able to create what will actually be satisfying. For that, you are grateful.

Career, Success, and Money

Expect a lot of internal dialogue about your financial situation as 2019 comes to a close. You are feeling particularly generous because things are going so well. However, resist the temptation to express yourself in ways that impact your bank account. What's required is moderation. Exhausting your financial resources drains all your resources—mental, emotional, spiritual, and physical.

Pitfalls and Potential Problems

The year comes to a close with a strong reminder that you've taken the first few steps toward moving beyond what is expected of you to what you truly desire. But they don't represent the whole journey. Celebrate what you've accomplished, secure in the knowledge that you have the courage to see this shift through to completion.

Rewarding Days
3, 4, 17, 18

Challenging Days
5, 6, 25, 26

Scorpio Action Table

These dates reflect the best–but not the only–times for success and ease in these activities, according to your Sun sign.

	JAN	FEB	MAR	APR	MAY	JUN	JUL	AUG	SEP	OCT	NOV	DEC
Move		3, 4					4, 5			27, 28		
Start a class	9, 10				12, 13							30, 31
Seek coaching/ counseling			21, 22				26, 27		28, 29			
Ask for a raise	14, 15							30, 31			28, 29	
Get professional advice		19, 20			1, 2					12, 13		
Get a loan			10, 11			15, 16						
New romance				1, 2				9, 10	3, 4			3, 4
Vacation				11, 12		4, 5					15, 16	

Sagittarius

The Archer
November 22 to December 21

Element: Fire

Glyph: Archer's arrow

Quality: Mutable

Anatomy: Hips, thighs, sciatic nerve

Polarity: Yang/masculine

Colors: Royal blue, purple

Planetary Ruler: Jupiter

Animals: Fleet-footed animals

Meditation: I can take time to explore my soul

Myths/Legends: Athena, Chiron

Gemstone: Turquoise

House: Ninth

Power Stones: Lapis lazuli, azurite, sodalite

Opposite Sign: Gemini

Flower: Narcissus

Key Phrase: I understand

Keyword: Optimism

The Sagittarius Personality

Strengths, Spiritual Purpose, and Challenges

Expansive and enthusiastic, you are open day or night for some kind of adventure, whether it's physical, intellectual, or spiritual. Not only because you are curious, but because it's only through searching that you can make sense of what life is all about. So your spiritual gift, quite obviously, is to seek meaning, and you go wherever that desire takes you. It can often appear to be just sheer impulse, but for you it is always a deeper quest than just having the experience. No, it's so much more than that, even if you don't really know exactly where you are going or what you are looking for. Your gift is to be open to whatever you discover, whatever crosses your path, whatever strikes a chord in you. No preconceived plans or ideas. Those get in the way of finding anything of true value to you. However, once something resonates, you can become quite dogmatic and self-righteous and lose sight of the reality that what is right for you may not be right for everyone. This makes you a paradox, because you unquestionably resist any attempt by others to force-feed you.

So you need to realize that choosing to align yourself with a thought, an idea, a person, a cause, or anything at all doesn't automatically make it absolute truth. It may be your truth and your truth alone. Not only do you need to be okay with that, but you need to offer the same honor and respect to others and their journeys as you expect for yourself. This is the only way you can be true to you and the guiding principle embedded in your core, which is that freedom is everyone's right, something you believe with every fiber of your being. For you, freedom isn't just a concept. It truly is a way of life. You simply can't imagine what the world would be like if that wasn't possible. And if, for any reason, you feel imprisoned physically, emotionally, intellectually, or spiritually, it's like turning out all the lights inside you, at least initially. You'll adapt, because you are good at doing that and finding a silver lining in any cloud. However, the toll it takes on you is immeasurable if you believe that the constraints on you can actually take away who and what you are. What's at your core can never be removed by anyone, not even you.

Relationships

Your approach to relationships begins with one basic requirement: no fences, no corrals, no ropes, no ties that bind. This applies to all your relationships. You view yourself as a bit of a maverick, free to roam wherever you want, doing whatever you want. This may not be true in your actual daily life, but it's still an internal vision you hold dear. The people who understand that about you always see the generous, open-hearted person you are at the core of your being, and they get your unreserved loyalty and love. However, if anyone tries to determine your reality for you, you are gone, emotionally and spiritually if not physically. Plus you find yourself acting out in ways designed to let anyone and everyone know that ain't nobody in charge of you. The difficulty with this is you often create more problems than you solve. You may think all you are doing is defining your boundaries when, in actual fact, you are just being defiant. The key here is not to demonstrate your displeasure by doing things you know irritate others. Instead, champion yourself and your needs by taking the time to talk things through calmly and responsively.

Career and Success

Life truly is a smorgasbord of knowledge just waiting for you to come along and devour whatever catches your fancy. The need to know is fundamental to you feeling and being alive, because it is the pathway to finding meaning, and from there purpose. So when it comes to this area of your life, you require more than just the satisfaction of doing a good job. Your work must fill some deep, often indefinable space inside you, whether it's the opportunity to call all your own shots, the opportunity to find out more about the world, or the opportunity to see a bigger picture. Otherwise, you feel constricted, constrained, and hobbled. However, if you feel that, at any given moment, there is always the possibility that things will expand, get bigger or always offer you an adventure, there are no limits to what you can contribute or accomplish.

Money and Possessions

You really don't have much attachment to either one. Money is simply a conduit to a better life, something to be used and something to be useful. As for possessions, you can take them or leave them, unless they hold special meaning for you—not from a sentimental point of view, but because they resonate with a deeper part of who you are, they symbolize something you truly value, or they remind you of an experience profoundly meaningful to you. There's one thing you are clear about: neither is the sole measure of you or your life.

The Light Side of Life

There's probably no one on the planet who knows how to have fun as much as you do. Period. You definitely enjoy trying new things and nothing is really off limits. One minute you can be outdoors on a long, treacherous hike, and the next you are attending a talk on the meaning of life. So obviously your interests range far and wide. It really is a case of the mood you are in, combined with what happens to be going on around you. But you are definitely never one to turn down an invitation or a challenge. After all, what fun would there be in saying no? That's not going to expand your reality.

Sagittarius Keywords for 2019
Clarity, optimism, realism

The Year Ahead for Sagittarius

Life is good, really good. At least that's what it feels like. Jupiter, your planetary avatar, aka the planet in charge of all things Sagittarius, has returned to his home in the sign of the Archer for almost all of 2019, bringing with him an abundance of your natural gifts: expansiveness, enthusiasm, faith, and joy. Could things get any better? Probably not, if you focus all your attention on this single facet of your astrological picture. And what's wrong with that, you ask? After all, Jupiter only comes home for a visit once every twelve years, so it would be rude to ignore him and detrimental not to make use of all that he offers. As much as that makes sense to you—and it really does—focusing solely on Jupiter leads to avoiding or putting off altogether important opportunities to redefine long-term hopes and wishes by indulging in a year of escapism, a year triggered by Jupiter's energetic relationship with Neptune. Their message? Things will take care of themselves. Don't worry. Be happy. Be in the moment. There's no harm in that. And that's true as long as the moments don't add up to the entire year, because this creates the potential of a lost year, one in which your vision of the future seems to vanish.

This may lead to consequences it takes a very long time to deal with, not the least of which is you feeling empty, out of sorts, and completely at a loss to find any meaning in what you did in 2019. Which is definitely not your cup of tea.

Of course, Jupiter and Neptune aren't all bad. They do offer positive, life-affirming energy. Jupiter's role is to lighten up the world and illuminate hope, while Neptune asks you to tune in to the deep well of your dreams. In order to access these gifts, you need to invite Saturn to the party. After all, because Saturn is in his home sign of Capricorn, he is going to remind you that reality must be served at all times, whether you like it or not. It's your choice. However, ignoring him means refusing to be accountable, and that simply won't do. Welcoming him, using his ability to create a supportive foundation, leads to a year of unparalleled success in whatever area you choose. The year 2019 can really be a fantastic confluence of abundant optimism, powerful imaginings, and purposeful structure.

Saturn

It's an understatement to say that Saturn represents some of your least-favorite aspects of life. He's the guy who insists on the mundane, serious, dull, heavy aspects of life. And you, quite frankly, don't really get why it has to be that way. But that is, in large part, because you view his efforts with a jaded eye. You are convinced that his only purpose is to get in your way. The truth is, no matter what you think, there's no avoiding his presence or his influence. He structures and contains the very reality you live in. Somebody has to take care of making sure there's something solid for you to stand on.

All Saturn asks is that you pay close attention to the consequences of the things you do. This isn't quite the inhibiting factor you perceive it to be. In fact, being accountable is the true path to freedom, because avoiding responsibility is a prison in and of itself. Accepting this is paramount in 2019 because Jupiter returns to Sagittarius, promising, as he always does, the sun, the moon, and the stars. It's always wonderful to feel that, but your reality will not support that if you fail to acknowledge the need to have a goal, a plan, a purpose, and the intention to work hard. Nothing is accomplished without a little elbow grease. Enter Saturn. That's his territory and his gift. Use him wisely. Take the exuberance of Jupiter in concert with Saturn, and not only will 2019 expand your horizons, but it will be fruitful and satisfying as well.

Uranus

It really has been a hoot hanging out with Uranus for the last seven years, discovering how creative you truly can be, pushing the limits of what freedom really means to you, and just generally clearing away anything getting in the way of you living a truly authentic life. As Uranus prepares to enter Taurus on March 6, there is a reckoning, as there always is when a planet changes signs. You may very well have been blowing down the walls you felt constricting you; however, you need to take an objective look at whether you have actually grown from the experience. It's not that hard to turn your life upside down. The more difficult part is actually using that experience to grow your life beyond where you were at. Freedom isn't just about tearing things down and walking away. It's about sticking around and building something in its place—in this case, a new way of being you. If you've done this, Uranus in Taurus gives you the chance to tinker and fine tune yourself moving forward. Otherwise, you'll be hit by a constant barrage of irritations and frustrations designed to let you know exactly what you left undone. Unpleasant, yes, but more importantly, you'll find yourself in an ongoing battle to shore up the self-confidence you so deeply rely on.

Neptune

If you're honest with yourself, you feel kind of floaty most days. Which, to your surprise, isn't very enjoyable. It's one thing to be free of limitations so you can pursue whatever catches your eye, but it's another not to know which end is up. And this is exactly what's happening. Some days you feel it physically, others emotionally, and still others mentally. It's quite disconcerting because it leaves you without any sense of how to take action, which simply won't do for a fire sign like Sagittarius. Action is what's required for you to be you. So, you might ask, why is Neptune causing this kind of disruption in your life? The truth is his purpose isn't always clear. He really is just asking you to go with the flow while he busies himself dissolving much of the foundation you've built your life on. And out of this murky, misty, shadowy process, a world of new possibilities emerges. Along the way, Neptune will give you hints—

in your dream life, in meditative experiences (anything that takes you out of your conscious mind), and in playing with your imagination. Neptune's greatest gift is inspiration. However, it cannot be delivered without the willingness to tune in to the unseen, the undetermined, the unknown. The solution for you? View this as another fantastic adventure and you'll be more than fine.

Pluto

For the better part of ten years (since 2008), Pluto has been asking you to delve deeper into the values that you demonstrate in your daily life. Do they truly represent who you are and what you stand for, or do they reflect the accommodations you've made to deal with the realities of the outside world? And do they match what you espouse? The purpose behind this is simple: to discover whether you are truly in touch with what is meaningful to you, not to question your honor or your integrity. Everyone, including you, can get caught up in doing what needs to be done and lose sight of what is really important to them. This process continues to be an opportunity to eliminate any thought, idea, or belief about what is valuable in your life and transform it. This includes your self-worth. In 2019, as Saturn and Pluto come close to joining forces, there's a powerful chance to ground the changes you are making so they serve you for a very long time. One word of caution: Continue to be open, and whatever you do, refrain from judging yourself.

How Will This Year's Eclipses Affect You?

Eclipses signal intense periods that highlight major growth opportunities for us in the process of creating our lives. They are linked to the lunar phases—specifically the New and Full Moon—and involve the relationship between the Sun and the Moon and the Earth. A Solar Eclipse is a magnified New Moon, while a Lunar Eclipse is a magnified Full Moon. Eclipses unfold in cycles involving all twelve signs of the zodiac, and they occur in pairs, usually about two weeks apart.

In 2019 there are five eclipses, three solar (two in Capricorn and one in Cancer) and two lunar (one in Leo and one in Capricorn). The first Solar Eclipse arrives on January 5 in Capricorn, catching you unawares and igniting an inner dilemma about whether your life holds meaning for you or not. As you look to your past, you find you've made a number of choices that tarnish your view of yourself and leave you wondering how that happened. Before you even answer that question, take a step back and remember that the ideals you hold dear haven't changed and that the choices you've made don't negate those ideals. Life is full of difficult decisions, and all you can do is be the best person you can be in any given moment. As long as any decision you made didn't sacrifice your basic honor, integrity, and decency, you need not judge yourself too harshly. Finding meaning in life comes from actually living it and navigating the challenges it represents, rather than from the perfect execution of any theoretical framework. Look at your life objectively and you'll find that there is much to be proud of, much to celebrate, and much to be grateful for. This is a better platform from which to determine what in your life is meaningful than soundly thrashing yourself emotionally, intellectually, and spiritually. Plus it's definitely more nourishing.

The year 2019 represents an opportunity to do some deep soul-searching in order to create a stronger foundation in your life, based on a realistic assessment of where you've been and where you might be going. This is enough of a challenge without adding an unnecessary layer of self-examination that is likely to lead you nowhere, especially if it's based on a rigid and intolerant set of expectations. Life is always about becoming, something you understand at your core, even if you aren't aware of it, and something you are naturally inclined and outfitted to do. Embrace that and you'll find the Lunar Eclipse on January 20 gives you a huge boost in rekindling your love of life and all the experiences yet to come. You realize that your journey is nowhere near being done and you choose to stop the negativity that is taking up so much oxygen in your life and return to your natural state of being: optimistic, hopeful, and full of trust.

With your natural buoyancy once again in top form, you are more than ready to meet the tests and the opportunities those tests provide created by the Solar Eclipse on July 2, the Lunar Eclipse on July 16, and the Solar Eclipse on December 26. One last word: Be kind and gentle to yourself in 2019. It provides the necessary uplift and support you need. And don't be afraid to share your inner doubts and questions about life. You don't always have to be the fun, joyful person or the one with all the answers. You can be human like everyone else.

Sagittarius | January

Overall Theme

Confused is probably the best way to describe your overall feeling about life as you start 2019. One minute you are upbeat and optimistic, and the next cranky and out of sorts. It's not in your nature to be moody, so you aren't really exactly sure what is going on. Recognize that this is about an inner feeling of being stuck. The upside is it's totally within your power to do something about it.

Relationships

You are a naturally friendly and sociable person who loves to meet new people. It's one of the ways you find out more about the world. People's differences, be they philosophical, cultural or religious, always intrigue you. So the beginning of 2019 finds you seeking new connections as a way of jump-starting your life.

Career, Success, and Money

Your work is definitely one area of your life that needs a breath of fresh air. The foundation of what you do still holds appeal; it's just that you feel bogged down in details, none of which support your current project, all because someone else chose to sidetrack you by sending you off on a wild goose chase. Oh, how you hate to waste your time on anything inconsequential.

Pitfalls and Potential Problems

Your biggest desire this month is to run away from home, or at the very least, take a vacation. That's fine, as long as your reason for doing it is a healthy one. Anything you do to avoid reality only comes back to haunt you. Anything you do to recharge your batteries brings unexpected dividends.

Rewarding Days

21, 22, 29, 30

Challenging Days

12, 13, 19, 20

Sagittarius | February

Overall Theme
You are in your glory. So much so that you are sure you are going to find the pot of gold at the end of the rainbow. Well, maybe not that, but you are sure life is going to bring you something pretty close to it—which may, among many other things, be finding your inner joy again.

Relationships
Your optimism and lightheartedness are infectious. Your charm is at its peak. Your ability to be in the moment is at an all-time high. So you find yourself needing to fight to get some space, some semblance of freedom, in your connections with others. It seems they can't get enough of you. Remember, it's not your job to lift up the whole world. Just yourself.

Career, Success, and Money
The wild goose chase taking up all your time in January disappears in what seems like a puff of smoke when someone higher up the food chain calls a halt to it. As relief sets in, you get a further surprise: a brand-new opportunity to take your career to the next level. You don't waste any time jumping on board.

Pitfalls and Potential Problems
It's imperative that you keep your feet planted firmly on the ground, not because anything is going to go drastically wrong but because you can let your optimism run away with you, so much so that you cross lines you shouldn't. For example, when your work situation shifts, make sure to keep your counsel. No need to comment on the stupidity of what you were doing. That's obvious. Mentioning it only leaves a bad impression, and you definitely don't need that.

Rewarding Days
3, 4, 19, 20

Challenging Days
8, 9, 21, 22

Sagittarius | March

Overall Theme

You feel a tremendous urge to retreat from the hustle and bustle of everything percolating in your life. And there is a lot going on. It's just a sign you need some downtime to reflect and consider where life is taking you. This probably isn't in your comfort zone, but it needs to be done. You can't be going full tilt all the time right now. It's isn't in your best interest.

Relationships

Patience is in short supply, not that you think you have a lot to begin with. But what surprises you most is that your tolerance isn't high either. This limits your capacity and probably your desire to spend time with too many people. It's a good month to spend as much time as possible with yourself and only those people with whom you can have an intelligent conversation.

Career, Success, and Money

Big change arrives and immediately you feel overwhelmed. It's not like you to experience this kind of uncertainty. Take a breath and you'll see just how much this chance means to you. Once you acknowledge the profound potential in the step you're taking, you'll calm down.

Pitfalls and Potential Problems

Make sure to nourish yourself in every possible way you can conjure up. Your life is shifting in some mind-altering, life-altering ways, some of which you just can't see right now. Taking time for yourself, eating properly, getting exercise, and sleeping well guarantees you are ready for whatever comes your way.

Rewarding Days

19, 20, 25, 26

Challenging Days

5, 6, 21, 22

Sagittarius | April

Overall Theme

How many different ways can you spell "standstill"? You find out again and again, as it seems like everything you are focused on grinds to a halt just as you are ready to return to full form and get things really moving. This isn't a conspiracy. It's life. Look around and it won't take long for you to find a new target for all that energy.

Relationships

This is a good month to practice listening to the worries and concerns of the people in your life without immediately offering them a list of things they can do to ameliorate their problems. First, they may just need to vent, and second, you have a habit of jumping to the conclusion that they actually need your help. Perhaps your presence is all they require.

Career, Success, and Money

Any delays you experience come down to one thing: you need to review the details connected to any plans, projects, or ideas that you have. Otherwise, things may not get off the ground. Time to acknowledge that broad strokes are not enough to get the job done.

Pitfalls and Potential Problems

One of your biggest challenges in life is believing that any time is the right time. That's because if you're ready, then so must the rest of the world as well. Welcome to your somewhat spotty relationship with time and what's going on around you. It's not a question of ignoring things; it's more about getting so caught up in your own enthusiasm and in your assumption that everyone is going to be as delighted by your plans as you are.

Rewarding Days

1, 2, 26, 27

Challenging Days

13, 14, 18, 19

Sagittarius | May

Overall Theme

Life is a little more than uncomfortable because you feel bogged down by a series of things you aren't in a position to take charge of. And you know how much you dislike not being able to do that. The key to weathering the storm is not to wind yourself up. Do what you can and let go of the rest. Live and let live. It's one of your strengths.

Relationships

No matter what unfolds in this part of your life, it's going to leave you scratching your head in disbelief. But, then, much of what goes on between people has that effect on you, because your basic nature is to be straightforward and, often, blunt. Your best course of action right now is simply to take a step back and not get involved.

Career, Success, and Money

Normally, you can rise to the occasion and handle whatever presents itself as a problem. In fact, you've never met a difficulty you didn't think you could take care of. Well, prepare to be tested. Not because the problems themselves are without solutions, but more because the people connected to them appear to have lost their minds.

Pitfalls and Potential Problems

This could, in fact, be your least favorite month of the year. It has nothing to do with the weather, people, work, play, or anything really tangible. The source of your dislike is connected to the disconcerting feeling that there's stuff going on inside you that you can't quite get a handle on. Your attitude is, if something's hidden, there's a reason, and maybe it should stay that way. This won't help you right now, because there are emotional issues trying to surface so you can release them and move on.

Rewarding Days

1, 2, 10, 11

Challenging Days

6, 7, 19, 20

Sagittarius | June

Overall Theme

You find yourself at odds with others more often than not, amplifying an internal battle you are having with yourself about what you value. Do you stick to the tried and true or do you seek to overhaul many of the beliefs you've based your life on? The key is to understand that beliefs are not the same as principles. Reconnect with your core principles and things become much clearer.

Relationships

You'd like to close your eyes, put your hands over your ears, and sing loudly, all because it appears everyone has something to say about your life, your beliefs, your intentions, and anything else they can conjure up. This leaves you feeling shocked and backed into a corner. No point in responding, or entering the fray. Politely ask them to stop, or better yet, just walk away.

Career, Success, and Money

Everything you consider a resource comes under intense scrutiny, with most of the focus on money and your overall financial picture. It's a good month to take an overall inventory of where you are and whether you'd like to make any changes. Be wary of making any hasty decisions, or any decisions at all. You haven't got all the facts.

Pitfalls and Potential Problems

Of course, you like to ponder the meaning of life, but when it comes to dealing with daily life, you are less likely to spend much time over-analyzing what you need to do. Make a decision and be done with it. Well, this month it's vital that you take your time, because your circuits are overloaded and you may not be seeing things as clearly as you think.

Rewarding Days

9, 10, 22, 23

Challenging Days

4, 5, 25, 26

Sagittarius | July

Overall Theme

The internal pressure that's been lurking under the surface since January threatens to do more than boil over. Not that anger is problematic for you, but this feels like so much more. It is. Either you are going to explode or you are going to implode. Those are the only two choices you think you have. There's another. Relieve the pressure by acknowledging it and then dig deep to find its root cause.

Relationships

You are not one to spend a lot of time delving into your emotional reality, much less share what you find with anyone. The reality is that you are, at your core, deeply sensitive, even if it's not obvious to you. With all the emotions pushing themselves into your conscious mind, it's time to find someone to open up to. You don't always have to do everything all by yourself.

Career, Success, and Money

Refrain from the desire to spend money in order to alleviate your fear that you are losing control over your life. You aren't, unless you believe that what is emerging from deep within is, somehow, about someone other than you. The truth is, what is being revealed to you strengthens your life going forward.

Pitfalls and Potential Problems

In an attempt to escape how you are feeling, you turn to overworking your physical reality because it's the only place you believe you can exert your will. Time to recognize that this isn't always the solution. Consider that confronting deeply held perceptions about you and your life is something that you can master. All you have to do is choose to see it as another adventure that will expand your life and offer remarkable rewards.

Rewarding Days

4, 5, 20, 21

Challenging Days

2, 3, 15, 16

Sagittarius | August

Overall Theme

Finally, the clouds part and the sun shines in your life again. At least that's the way you feel, even if you aren't sure it's real. It is. So celebrate. Take a vacation. Pat yourself on the back. Do something that makes your heart sing. You deserve it. After all, you've proven once again that nothing can ever keep you down.

Relationships

You really are irrepressible, no matter what area of life you are bouncing around in. And relationships are no exception. Especially this month as you find yourself in love with love again. And life, for that matter. So are you ready to do your best Pied Piper of Hamelin imitation and find a whole bunch of people to join you in an adventure? Of course, no one can resist you when you are full of fun. Mission accomplished.

Career, Success, and Money

Your motto is pretty simple: What's work got to do with it? And by it, you mean life. This doesn't mean you aren't ready to get things done. However, you are not interested in dithering about or making things more complicated. That's work. What you are prepared to do is achieve something.

Pitfalls and Potential Problems

The only thing to be concerned about is spreading yourself too thin, something you are naturally inclined to do when you are high on life. Which you are. That often leads to exhaustion because you suddenly don't have an off switch. Save some of that joie de vivre for next month and the month after that. You'll be happy you did.

Rewarding Days
4, 5, 30, 31

Challenging Days
11, 12, 23, 24

Sagittarius | September

Overall Theme

The direction and overall purpose of your life are under the microscope and you put them there. That's because some major but very different opportunities present themselves in your work world. Time to decide whether the path you are on is going to sustain you for much longer or whether it's time to completely change gears.

Relationships

The only relationships getting a lot of traction are those directly connected to your career, not because that's necessarily your choice, but because colleagues old and new seek you out with information and possibilities. Listen carefully and be grateful. The seeds of something fantastic are being planted.

Career, Success, and Money

You are definitely on cloud nine as the month unfolds. The kind of success that truly feeds you is within reach. Take time to clarify for yourself exactly what that looks like so you can plan accordingly. This isn't one of those times when flying by the seat of your pants reaps the rewards you deserve.

Pitfalls and Potential Problems

Be careful to check with your instincts about any and all offers you receive. If you feel a sudden lurch in your solar plexus—you know that slight sinking sensation—it's both your body and your intuition telling you something isn't quite as marvelous as it sounds. Also be aware that lies could be told about someone important to you.

Rewarding Days

5, 6, 28, 29

Challenging Days

10, 11, 22, 23

Sagittarius | October

Overall Theme

A certain playfulness takes over and you live life at full tilt. That is until events going on around you bring you to a jaw-dropping, bewildering stop. You are stuck trying to answer these age-old questions: How could that happen? And what were they thinking? Bottom line? If events hit close to home, don't get involved.

Relationships

Don't be surprised if friends seek you out looking for someone they can confide in. At least one of them is facing serious challenges and needs a sounding board. You are fine with that until you hear what it is they have to tell you. It's a big secret that impacts someone you know and love. Keep your counsel. Listen. Refrain from making a judgment. And remember, this is none of your business. That relieves you of any responsibility to do anything.

Career, Success, and Money

Some underhanded stuff going on in your work environment comes to light, surprising everyone, including you, and damaging the reputation of someone in a leadership position. The ramifications are serious for the entire organization, making it a good time to remain silent.

Pitfalls and Potential Problems

You are not someone easily shocked by the idiosyncracies of human behavior, but even you find some of the things going on in your immediate circle to be beyond the pale. It's nothing salacious. Rather, what's happening is more hypocritical, dishonest, and without honor. You are always struck by how easily people abandon the principles they espouse.

Rewarding Days
9, 10, 29, 30

Challenging Days
12, 13, 27, 28

Sagittarius | November

Overall Theme

Things in general settle down and normalcy is restored, not that it matters to you as much as it does to other people. However, in this instance, you are quite happy to relax into a routine, grateful that a semblance of common sense is the order of the day. You like adventure, not drama, and last month provided more than enough of the latter.

Relationships

You find yourself softer, kinder, and more than a little romantic. You want to court and be courted. It's a way of soothing your fear that the closer you get to someone, the more likely they are to hurt you. This is hard for you because you believe people always take the high road. Accept that the only person you can ask that of is yourself.

Career, Success, and Money

The amount of work that confronts you is crazy. Yet somehow you manage to complete everything, whether it's the challenges you love or the details that tend to annoy you. Happiness this month is giving your all to the tasks at hand, and your new approach is acknowledged.

Pitfalls and Potential Problems

Don't go looking for trouble, and by that I mean something to stir the pot. It really is okay for you to enjoy the routine of putting one foot in front of the other day after day. Of course, the imp in you finds that boring and may start whispering in your ear, encouraging you to do something a little outrageous. Not too much, mind you. Just enough to alleviate the boredom. Oh, wait. You aren't bored. You are content. Enjoy the respite before things shift into high gear next month.

Rewarding Days

3, 4, 26, 27

Challenging Days

8, 9, 18, 19

Sagittarius | December

Overall Theme

You've barely drawn a breath in December before a big change is upon you. Jupiter, your planetary avatar, moves from his home in Sagittarius into Capricorn on December 2. But before that happens, take a moment or two to review how much you've grown in 2019 while dealing with all manner of life challenges. Gather the wisdom you've gained. It offers you the support you need to move into 2020.

Relationships

Your attention is focused firmly on the future, so you probably aren't going to notice issues brewing between you and one or two of the more significant people in your life, at least not until you're confronted. It's not as serious as it sounds at first, unless, of course, you choose to find somewhere else to be until the problem blows over. Sit down and listen. You discover that all that's needed is an ongoing commitment to doing just that.

Career, Success, and Money

The Solar Eclipse on December 26 gives you a clear heads up about where your priorities need to be in the coming year—focused firmly on drawing on your unique resources to make things happen. To do this, you must organize your world to avoid looking for ways to distract yourself—which is one of the things you do to prove you are free to do what you want.

Pitfalls and Potential Problems

As a new chapter in your journey opens—as it does every year when Jupiter changes signs—it's imperative that you understand you have a once-in-a-lifetime chance to accomplish something of real magnitude in your life in 2020. The choice is definitely yours. Just know that the tools you'll have at your disposal are unparalleled and taking this leap of faith is definitely worth it.

Rewarding Days

2, 4, 17, 18

Challenging Days

5, 6, 21, 22

Sagittarius Action Table

These dates reflect the best—but not the only—times for success and ease in these activities, according to your Sun sign.

	JAN	FEB	MAR	APR	MAY	JUN	JUL	AUG	SEP	OCT	NOV	DEC
Move				1, 2		16, 17			5, 6			
Start a class	1, 2			21, 22							3, 4	
Seek coaching/ counseling					17, 18		1, 2			27, 28		
Ask for a raise		19, 20						30, 31				17, 18
Get professional advice			5, 6				15, 16				12, 13	
Get a loan					12, 13	22, 23				4, 5		
New romance	21, 22		25, 26						28, 29			
Vacation		3, 4						4, 5				23, 24

Capricorn

The Goat
December 22 to January 19

Element: Earth

Quality: Cardinal

Polarity: Yin/feminine

Planetary Ruler: Saturn

Meditation: I know the strength of my soul

Gemstone: Garnet

Power Stones: Peridot, onyx diamond, quartz, black obsidian

Key Phrase: I use

Glyph: Head of goat

Anatomy: Skeleton, knees, skin

Colors: Black, forest green

Animals: Goats, thick-shelled animals

Myths/Legends: Chronos, Vesta, Pan

House: Tenth

Opposite Sign: Cancer

Flower: Carnation

Keyword: Ambitious

The Capricorn Personality

Strengths, Spiritual Purpose, and Challenges

It's a tough job. Somebody's got to do it. Therein lies Capricorn's view of life. Others may cringe at that, but for you it's a call to action, one that you cannot and will not ignore. Because tough is okay with you. In fact, the tougher the better. That way you know you've actually done something. What are you here for if not to accomplish something, to make things happen, and to strive for the best? After all, no one ever managed to achieve anything sitting around waiting or thinking or staring at their navel. You only have so much time and there's so much to be done. This clearly illuminates your spiritual purpose, which is to manifest. That's why you are always considering all your options and what will come of any choice you make. You are a consequence-driven person, seeking to know and understand what the end results will be. It's not that the steps along the way are unimportant. It's obvious that they are necessary to achieving the goal. But the goal remains the most important thing because accomplishing it is a true measure of your capabilities and your integrity.

If you say you are going to do something, it is done, in your mind. Otherwise, how can you be trusted if you don't do what you promised you would? That applies as much to your commitment to yourself as it does to your commitment to others. No one is ever likely to be as disappointed in you as you are in yourself if you fail to achieve the challenge set for you. This leads to the two biggest self-imposed beliefs that consistently get in your way, forcing you to adopt almost superhuman skills to feel successful. The first is to know that you don't have to struggle to succeed. Yes, you can work hard, but life doesn't have to feel like climbing Mount Everest in high heels. If it does, you know you are trying to meet impossible expectations. The second is to know that control is an illusion. Sure, you can take charge of your life—something you really are a master at—but control it? Not so much. Consider this. Control is based on fear and fear is a task master that no one can ever satisfy, not even you. It's healthier and more realistic to celebrate your tremendous capacity to build foundations and structures that stand the test of time.

Relationships

Like everything else in your life, you approach relationships with a high degree of pragmatism, which isn't always greeted with the approval and openness you expect. This knocks you more than a little sideways because you aren't really sure what the problem is. After all, isn't common sense desirable? It is. However, this is the arena where the focus is 99 per cent emotional, probably because it is the only place where emotions seem to have any place at all. This automatically puts you at a disadvantage, at least initially. Until you realize the best thing you can do is listen and not try to solve problems, and the rest of the world recognizes that you are not really hard and unfeeling. Then you can find common ground and begin to build a connection that has as its foundation the one thing you require as much as love: respect. And remember, it is a two-way street, something you have a tendency to forget. For you, the path to building good relationships is to see them as vehicles for growth, expansion, and emotional satisfaction, not as a series of duties and obligations. You don't always have to be useful to love and be loved.

Career and Work

You are naturally built to make your mark in the world, so finding a career, aka purpose, is deeply important to you. Without it, life lacks a pathway to success. The key here is to recognize that before you start down the road, you need to take time to define what success is to you. Is it the template provided by your parents, the world at large, or any other authority in your life? Or does it spring from your own consciousness? You often put more stock in the opinions and input of others than in what you know and feel about yourself. Following all the rules doesn't necessarily guarantee the rewards you seek if you never take the time to define what really is going to be the source of the most satisfaction for you. There's no doubt though, that no matter what you choose, you devote all of your skills and energy to seeing things get done properly. Just remember, you don't need to keep upping the ante to prove yourself worthy.

Money and Possessions

There are not enough words in any language to describe how important both of these are to you. They are proof positive that you are a valuable, capable, hardworking person. This is the true status that you seek—not an ostentatious, over-the-top demonstration of the power of accumulation but a reflection of what you truly cherish. You have the capacity to overcome any challenge to build a legacy that stands the test of time. If, along the way, you create a lot of abundance, you choose to manage it wisely, carefully, and without a lot of fanfare. In fact, you don't really like to draw attention to what you have, because for you it isn't the sole arbiter of your worth. It's a one-dimensional measurement that doesn't take into account all the moving parts of who you are and what you've done.

The Light Side of Life

There's no getting around it: You are serious. Life is serious. But that doesn't mean you lack the capacity to laugh, to enjoy, to have fun. In fact, you can take that as seriously as work, which means when it's time to let your hair down, you set everything else aside and go for the gusto. However, it isn't always easy to persuade yourself that it's just as healthy to play as it is to work. You can require a lot of convincing. But remember, play is useful. It releases endorphins into your body and often helps solve problems, to name just two potential benefits. Besides, how can it be wrong to feel good?

Capricorn Keywords for 2019
Recognize, refuel, refresh

The Year Ahead for Capricorn

What an interesting confluence of energies await you in 2019! First, Saturn, your planetary avatar, continues his journey through his home sign of Capricorn, giving you that sense of security and strength that only he can provide. This, of course, is the most important part of your yearly astrological equation, and everything else pales in comparison. In many ways, you are correct. However, because you are a realist, you need to remind yourself that although Saturn might be the king of your castle right now, there are other energetic players still knocking about the place and demanding your attention, and if you don't acknowledge them, they are likely to again disturb that solid ground you are sure you're going to stand on forever now that Saturn has come home to put things in their proper place.

Part of your desire to ignore these other influences, aka Uranus, Neptune, and Pluto, is directly connected to the impact they've been making on all facets of your life—Uranus since 2011, Neptune since 2012, and Pluto since 2008. So, of course, Saturn's return to your sign in December of 2017 was a welcome respite from all the nonsense those other three hooligans (and yes, you are probably tempted to call them that) have been up to. The reality is not as simple as that. As much as you might like to turn back the clock, you can't. And all that nonsense was just life unfolding, though perhaps not in the way you planned or organized. But then life is like that, largely because it is too big a thing for any of us to control in any consistent and systematic way, something you don't like being reminded of at all.

However, in order to make the best use of the energies present at this time, you need to be able to apply Saturn's capacity for creating structure, justly and fairly, to the newfound realities resulting from Uranus's demand that you step outside any ideas about yourself that you believed were written in stone, Neptune's call to dissolve structures that no longer serve you, and Pluto's plea to look deep into your soul to find your true source of power. No doubt you feel everything about your world has been rearranged without the courtesy of a consultation. Actually, it goes deeper than that. Your world really doesn't look like it once did. Accept that and you can use Saturn to build yourself a new, better version of yourself and your world. After all, you never met a mountain you didn't want to conquer.

Saturn

Of course, when Saturn crossed the threshold into Capricorn, his first question was, exactly what happened to the place—that being you—while he was gone? Well, quite a lot. And that's always the way it is. After all, it takes Saturn a very long time—twenty-eight to thirty years, to be exact—to go around the zodiac and return to the sign he rules, the place he calls home, your Sun sign. His natural instinct when he gets there is to review what's happened in his absence. In other words, he asks you to look back at what has transpired during the last twenty-eight to thirty years, assess what you've accomplished, and determine how satisfied you are with your life. In reality, it's a life review, one whose purpose is to get you ready for a new set of goals and priorities. It's not a report card, although you are inclined to view it as such. For Saturn, the purpose of measuring things is to determine the next, best course of action, not to indulge in an endless analysis of failure. For him, there's no practical use in that.

It's a waste of precious time. Saturn knows that success comes from not giving up, rather than sheer luck, which is something you believe at your very core.

So here you are, partway through this process, probably ready to create that new plan for the future. But before you do so, recognize the dialogue that needs to take place before you are able to do that—the one between Saturn and Pluto, between the part of you that just wants to get on with the job and the part of you that is busy recreating yourself from the inside out. Which is more important? Well, both are. Saturn, because this is his home, appears to have the upper hand, but do not underestimate the intensity of Pluto and the pressure he can bring to bear on your psyche. Integrate the two, using Saturn to give you a foundation that supports all that power Pluto has helped you discover buried under all the duty and obligation you built your life on. You'll end up feeling that anything is possible.

Uranus

What a thorn in your side Uranus has been for the last seven years, expecting you to change the very safe and reliable definition you had of yourself, demanding that you take steps to knock down structures that you spent quite a lot of time building, and asking that you be realistic enough to realize that being rigid isn't the same thing as being strong. Well, you discovered, much to your surprise, that he did you a favor. And not only did you rise to the various challenges he presented, but you reinvented yourself in some astonishing ways, stripping away things no longer essential to your sense of self or your well-being. It became clear that it's very difficult to maintain contact with your authentic self when your insides and outsides get cluttered with things you are just holding on to. You realized the external world is not what defines you. Anything you create or build comes from inside you. All this was totally eye-opening and exciting. And now, as Uranus enters Taurus on March 6, you are completely ready to make use of all this new awareness to build the next phase of your life, one that relies on your creativity and your capacity to manifest as your guiding principles. Of course, there are still some bumps in the road to deal with. But they are tiny and they are directly connected to a further refinement of how to apply what *you* truly value.

Neptune

Now here's an energy you find totally perplexing, because you really never know what to do with anything of an ephemeral nature. You always relate better to what is third-dimensional, what is quantifiable, what is connected to the five senses. Yet Neptune has been working hard to shift your perceptual framework by playing an interesting game of now you see it, now you don't. His purpose is to get you to release the rigid belief that nothing is real unless it's in physical form—not so he can scare you or dissolve your reality, but so you can understand that inspiration is as important to the process of life as perspiration, that your imagination plays as vital a role in what you accomplish as action, and that reality is a constantly shifting target that largely depends on how you see things. This is definitely not your comfort zone. You would prefer to believe that everything is finite, because that makes it more manageable. However, Neptune's message, from his own sign of Pisces, is to be open and realize that what makes up the human experience is as mysterious and magical as how the Universe was created. That way you are able to release yourself from rigid expectations that hobble you, dry up your capacity to dream, and disconnect you from the world of all possibilities.

Pluto

Pluto's tenure in your Sun sign continues to be uncomfortable and truly distressing. It's as if his mission is to undermine the very fabric of who you are. After all, he's mucking about, disturbing stuff that you chose to set aside because you couldn't see any practical purpose in spending more time on something that you couldn't possibly change. The truth is, your tendency, no matter what happens, is to just pull yourself up by your bootstraps and carry on. No good comes from dithering about, trying to fix something that is clearly broken. The challenge here is your perspective. Digging deeper into yourself and your life isn't about fixing anything. It's about letting go of the heaviness that repression leaves you with. It's about lightening up your inner self so you have more energy to get things done. It's about recognizing the strength and determination it takes to carry on in the face of adversity. In doing so, you free yourself and find the source of power that truly sustains you. And it's not anything you've done or accomplished. (Those are symbols of the power, but they are not the power.) It's your own essence. So remember this if, at any time in 2019, the face-off between Saturn and Pluto feels like a choice between maintaining the status quo and birthing a shinier, more confident, more deeply connected you. Consider this instead. You can always create a new status quo. You've done it your whole life. So do it again.

How Will This Year's Eclipses Affect You?

Eclipses signal intense periods that highlight major growth opportunities for us in the process of creating our lives. They are linked to the lunar phases—specifically the New and Full Moon—and involve the relationship between the Sun and the Moon and the Earth. A Solar Eclipse is a magnified New Moon, while a Lunar Eclipse is a magnified Full Moon. Eclipses unfold in cycles involving all twelve signs of the zodiac, and they occur in pairs, usually about two weeks apart.

In 2019 there are five eclipses, three solar (two in Capricorn and one in Cancer) and two lunar (one in Leo and one in Capricorn). The first Solar Eclipse arrives on January 5 in Capricorn, triggering deep fear about what the future holds. Your inclination is to scrap any change you've been contemplating in an attempt to return to the known, the familiar, the status quo. After all, those are tried and true, and you know exactly what you are going to get if you stick with what already works. This is you sticking your head in the sand, and it won't work, no matter how much you wish it would. Time to remember the symbol for your Sun sign. And it's not an ostrich. It's the mountain goat. He is sure-footed, knows his own strength, and trusts his capacity to navigate and overcome any obstacle. Sounds like you, right?

So rather than giving in to your fear, understand that the reason for your reluctance may be as simple as the need to find new ways to nourish yourself, to refuel yourself emotionally. Consider it a new challenge, a new mountain to climb, instead of a sign of weakness or failure. It's time to stop sucking it up and always doing what needs to be done without any consideration for the toll it takes on your overall well-being. Exhaustion and depletion are not medals of honor. They are signs you are pushing yourself to extremes. Time to let go of the need to be all things in all circumstances to all people. Seek support from others. Let someone take care of you. Not babysit you. Not run your life. Just love you, cherish you, and do things for you. That is the message of this year's eclipses.

Once the fear generated by the January 5 Solar Eclipse subsides—and it will—the Lunar Eclipse on January 21 in Leo gives you a huge opportunity to begin this process. So have a party and invite only the people you know are always in your corner. Let everyone know this is a celebration of you. Yes, you'll feel more than a little squirmy, but you need to offer yourself and the Universe a clear, external symbol of your intentions for 2019. After all, you are a Capricorn, and, if it's not in the physical realm, it's not real. This—or something like it—sets the tone for the rest of the year and gives you a growing capacity to handle the challenges presented by the Solar Eclipse on July 2, the Lunar Eclipse on July 16, and the Solar Eclipse on December 26. Stepping outside the ways you've chosen to define your life during the last nine to seventeen years might seem like something even Hercules couldn't manage. Since when has that ever stopped you?

Capricorn | January

Overall Theme

This is your time of year, right? So why do you feel so physically queasy and just plain off? Well, if you are looking for an external cause, you can blame it on the Solar Eclipse set to land on January 5, or you could recognize that your body is giving you a clear signal that it's not going to support you in maintaining unhealthy patterns.

Relationships

If you find you are unable to truly understand or process exactly what people are asking of you, take a deep breath and consider this: perhaps they are just touching base and checking in to make sure you're okay. The truth is you don't labor or live in obscurity as much as you think you do. So welcome the contact and embrace the support.

Career, Success, and Money

As much as your brain is prodding you to get moving, your physical energy comes and goes, leaving you frustrated. How can you get anything done if you can't count on your body to cooperate? Accept that it is being consistently inconsistent. That makes it easy to work to your potential when you are energized and take a break when you aren't. Otherwise, you are exhausted, with little to show for your effort.

Pitfalls and Potential Problems

Just because everything on your list of priorities doesn't come together quite the way you planned is not a sign of any incompetence on your part. It's a sign that either you have too much on your plate or your expectations are unrealistic, or both. This isn't news. It's the way you do life. Except it's time to see that perhaps this way of living is costing you too much.

Rewarding Days

10, 11, 25, 26

Challenging Days

5, 6, 20, 21

Capricorn | February

Overall Theme

Things feel less like the bottom of a dirty, ugly swamp, and normal order is restored. Good thing, too. You'd almost reached the end of your patience and perseverance, which is a true measure of how out of sorts you were. Time to push forward with all the plans and ideas you had to delay. No more waiting. Strike while the iron is hot.

Relationships

You are feeling particularly benevolent toward the entire world. That's what happens when you are finally able to follow your bliss and get things done. Be aware that feeling kindly toward people isn't the same as actually spending time with them, so make sure you nourish the people in your life with the same intensity and commitment you demonstrate toward your goals.

Career, Success, and Money

You jump into the deep end of your work with a mixture of joy and relief, happy to be hard at it again and grateful to be rid of the guilt haunting you. It really gnaws at you when it looks like nothing is getting accomplished. Well, that's not a problem this month. You return to such fine form that every day is full of satisfaction.

Pitfalls and Potential Problems

Now that your worry, uncertainty, and insecurity are fading in the rearview mirror, take time to recognize the underlying purpose of these feelings. The year 2019 is truly a search for a new way to structure yourself and your life, and those feelings are a reminder of that. So when they return, and they will, use them as an avenue of exploration.

Rewarding Days

19, 20, 23, 24

Challenging Days

8, 9, 17, 18

Capricorn | March

Overall Theme

You really hate retracing any step in your life, because for you, it's going backward. But that's definitely on your agenda right now, not because of any failure on your part, but because a sudden inspiration offers you the chance to shift a project from good to remarkable.

Relationships

For you, what's imperative to healthy relationships this month is directness and clarity. Forget vagueness or any kind of camouflaging of the truth. Both waste your time and create unnecessary interference and difficulties in working through some communication issues that crop up.

Career, Success, and Money

It's a good time to reevaluate how much you are worth and revamp exactly what you expect in remuneration. This is a lengthier process than you might think because it requires a full assessment of what you contribute to your job. Make sure you acknowledge everything you do, not just for the sake of asking for a raise, but so you can recognize all that you bring to the table. Then hold your fire. The timing is not quite right to ask for what you desire.

Pitfalls and Potential Problems

Communication is simply not going to be easy in March, with many problems likely to crop up. Understand that this is not a conspiracy, but just a sign that no one really knows which end is up. That way you can keep your impatience in check, knowing this is a temporary aberration.

Rewarding Days

10, 11, 27, 28

Challenging Days

8, 9, 17, 18

Capricorn | April

Overall Theme

How to deal with a revving engine stuck in park? That is the question that stymies you for much of April. So far, 2019 is turning into a year full of the promise of action and the reality of waiting and waiting and waiting. Normally, you'd find a way to adapt by working around the challenges this paradox creates. Instead, you just want to push through and forget the consequences. Don't. You'll understand why later.

Relationships

You are so consumed by the obstacles holding you back that you inadvertently take out your frustrations on those around you. Take a good look. The people in your life aren't the problem. And perhaps, if you turned your attention to improving this area of your life, you'd feel better about yourself and your life.

Career, Success, and Money

With the inventory of your accomplishments complete, you begin watching and waiting for the opportunity to improve your financial remuneration. And just when you thought your patience would run out, you get an unanticipated promotion. While you are busy smiling from ear to ear, make sure you clarify the salary situation. The promotion needs to improve not only your standing but your wallet, too.

Pitfalls and Potential Problems

It's going to be a challenge to maintain a calm and grounded perspective, but it's necessary. Yes, a lot of things stall out for no apparent reason, something that just drives you crazy, but giving in to a feeling of frustration only creates more stress. Sometimes you have no choice but to wait until the tide turns.

Rewarding Days

1, 2, 15, 16

Challenging Days

4, 5, 13, 14

Capricorn | May

Overall Theme

You are back in your happy place, not because things have shifted dramatically but because you choose to be. You decided it was high time you put what's going on in your life through the most important litmus test of all: How much does this really matter? The result? A list of priorities that relieves your stress considerably.

Relationships

All the things you generally have to talk yourself into making time for jump to the top of your list of priorities: fun, play, love, romance—all of which require a little help from your partner, friends, family, and anyone else who's available. It's a welcome break from feeling like the only thing happening in your life involves you spinning your wheels.

Career, Success, and Money

Yes, you are hard at work, but with a renewed focus and a more realistic approach to what can actually be accomplished. It's been a tough slog since the beginning of the year because you've been bombarded on an inner level by this insistent feeling that no matter what you do, it's not enough. Time to let yourself off the hook.

Pitfalls and Potential Problems

Ignore that tiny voice in the back of your mind that constantly calls into question every step you take. This is the part of you that keeps you chained to the belief that if you are doing things right, everything should turn out just the way you planned it. What truly matters is your dedication, your commitment to excellence, and your integrity. If those three things are in play, you've done your best, which is all you can ask.

Rewarding Days

12, 13, 26, 27

Challenging Days

1, 2, 21, 22

Capricorn | June

Overall Theme

Life may not be going according to any plan you set for yourself, but there's one thing that this year and this month continually demonstrate to you: your tool kit is full of all that's necessary to succeed in solving the problems confronting you. It's important to remember that finding solutions is what really drives you, not trying to control every little thing.

Relationships

You feel a little under the gun when it comes to the people in your life, and you aren't really sure why. Much of it is connected to the ongoing internal anxiety overwhelming you when you look at the constantly shifting picture of your life. Just remember not to project it onto others by initiating unnecessary disagreements.

Career, Success, and Money

The number-one thing on your list is to get clarity about whether the direction being taken to bring an important goal to fruition is actually effective. You can see a number of problems with the current strategy, but you are having a difficult time being heard. Be consistent, not argumentative, and put your words on paper. It works better than talking and gets the results you seek.

Pitfalls and Potential Problems

You really want to be right about everything, without exception. But before you turn your whole life into a do-or-die scenario, ask yourself what purpose it serves to be right in any given situation. If it's to make sure a project is working to its optimum, that's appropriate. If it's to prove that you know the exact location of a certain restaurant, well, that's a waste of your time. Recognize that this need is based in shaky self-confidence.

Rewarding Days

13, 14, 27, 28

Challenging Days

4, 5, 25, 26

Capricorn | July

Overall Theme

The outward expression of your emotions catches you completely off balance as you experience one of the weepiest, most sensitive months of your whole life. You aren't sure whether you are fascinated or repulsed. How about both? Of course, this is outside what you consider to be normal and appropriate. Nevertheless, it's happening and it does have a purpose: to integrate parts of who you are that you suppress and/or ignore.

Relationships

The trigger for all that never-ending emotion flowing out of you from the very core of your being is people, the ones close to you and the ones you barely know. It gets to the point where you are afraid to look anyone in the eye because you might start crying or complaining or arguing or being pushy. You just don't know what your reaction is likely to be. Choose to let your feelings surface in spaces and places where you feel safe. That way you won't be ambushed.

Career, Success, and Money

You may be tempted to bury yourself in your work to avoid all that volcanic emotional stuff that keeps crashing into your life. Well, that won't solve the problem, nor will spending money. The first exhausts you, and the second drains your bank account.

Pitfalls and Potential Problems

Above all, be kind to yourself. And recognize that all the emotion seeping out of every cell in your body is largely old stuff you've held on to for a long time. All it's seeking is to be released, not to take over your life. So create healthy ways to let go of it.

Rewarding Days

10, 11, 25, 26

Challenging Days

2, 3, 15, 16

Capricorn | August

Overall Theme

Your sense of self-worth rebounds with such speed that it takes you by surprise. After all, you thought you were doomed to spend a much longer time in the emotional dungeon that shook you to the core last month. The upside? Now you are seeing the purpose and reward in dealing with all aspects of your life, not just the ones you are comfortable with.

Relationships

Part of you thinks it's a good idea to hide out after all the weird encounters that took place in July. Of course, that won't work. Plus it seems you are the only one harboring any fear or anxiety. What you consider abnormal, ill-mannered, or unforgivable is just being human in everyone else's mind. Accept that and you'll find your relationships in a really good place.

Career, Success, and Money

Shared resources of all kinds, but most specifically money, take center stage. Before taking on any new financial commitments involving other people's needs, ideas, or projects, it's time to do a thorough analysis of your current financial status. This gives you the chance to update yourself as well as the space to carefully consider any proposal.

Pitfalls and Potential Problems

Because you are hard-wired to think in pragmatic terms, being able to assess the impact of emotional changes isn't that easy for two reasons. One is the actual subject matter. The other is the belief that you can't measure feelings in any tangible way. No, but you can trust that you feel lighter, more in touch with yourself, and more hopeful.

Rewarding Days

6, 7, 30, 31

Challenging Days

11, 12, 23, 24

Capricorn | September

Overall Theme

Everything finally is in the correct working order, so you intensify your efforts to get as close to the finish line as you can. Only then can you actually believe that this year isn't just an accumulation of everything that drives you crazy. Being challenged is one thing, but being tortured is another. Even though you may not be able to see it, you are takings steps that promise long-term rewards.

Relationships

Because you are in work mode, which is one of your very favorite places to be, your head is down and you aren't paying much attention to what's going on around you. You assume, incorrectly, that if anyone really needs you, they'll tell you. First, everything isn't always about need. Second, no one wants to feel like a task. So include time to spend with those you love, and, irony of ironies, you realize you need it.

Career, Success, and Money

The volume of what you accomplish is going to astound you. It lets you know that even though you felt nothing was actually getting accomplished for much of this year, you did so much of the preparation that it was easy to finish the process. This gives you a new appreciation for the full scope of your capabilities. Too often you see things only through the lens of completion, instead of the whole picture.

Pitfalls and Potential Problems

If you are truly taking steps to transform your life from the ground up, this is a month when that is put to the test. With all the projects, plans, and jobs that you finally get to complete, it's easy to fall back into old habits and focus solely on them and forget your commitment to yourself. Remember, you are not your work and your work is not you.

Rewarding Days

3, 4, 17, 18

Challenging Days

15, 16, 22, 23

Capricorn | October

Overall Theme

The chickens are coming home to roost, and oh, what chickens they are! Everywhere you look you are being treated with such appreciation and respect. In fact, it feels like you've won a popularity contest. Put aside your innate skepticism and enjoy. That way you're ready for the gargantuan opportunity that comes out of left field.

Relationships

Your usual measured response to people gives way to an intensity and a passion that leave you wondering just who you are. Well, this is a sign that you are changing your approach to everything in your life. You realize that always trying to contain yourself doesn't guarantee safety or security. All it does is limit your capacity to connect and build real intimacy.

Career, Success, and Money

There's an idea or a project you've been toying with for quite a while. Recognize how good it is. It's not reluctance that has stopped you from proposing it, but timing. You may not give a lot of credence to your instincts, but when it comes to sensing the right time to do things, you are a master. So listen when your gut tells you *now* is the right time to put this idea forward. Go for it.

Pitfalls and Potential Problems

Life isn't always about tidying things up, including yourself. Too often, you find yourself presenting what you think is the socially correct, most acceptable version of yourself. After all, you must maintain your reputation, your standing, your respect. But what if doing this robs you of actually being the length and breadth of who you are? And what if you find you don't admire and respect the sacrifices you've made to sustain the image?

Rewarding Days

14, 15, 23, 24

Challenging Days

4, 5, 12, 13

Capricorn | November

Overall Theme

Your inner fire is still burning hot, so take a deep breath and stop trying to make everything happen in a single day. Otherwise you and frustration renew your close connection. Refrain from being so single-minded and shift your focus around a little. If one thing can't be kick-started, turn your attention to something else. You'll be happier and you never know what you'll find sitting on a back burner.

Relationships

You are gripped by a desire to delve into the deeper waters of your own sensitivity, which leads you, of course, to think about the sensitivity of others—not just from a place of acknowledging it, but from a place of truly understanding what it is and how it's experienced. The result? Very meaningful conversations that lead to an openness, a vulnerability, that strengthens you.

Career, Success, and Money

Ignore anyone who decides it's their mission to get in your way. Instead, focus your attention on continuing to rebrand yourself, not just as a person who works hard and solves problems but as one who is creative and full of vision. See this as part of a strategy to broaden awareness of who you are and what you are able to do.

Pitfalls and Potential Problems

It's often a challenge to navigate the parts of you asking for two different things. It may seem that your drive to accomplish and your desire to be more open to your deeply buried sensitivity are diametrically opposed. Using that sensitivity that processes unspoken communication helps you know exactly where to focus all that drive.

Rewarding Days

20, 21, 29, 30

Challenging Days

11, 12, 22, 23

Capricorn | December

Overall Theme

No one is more aware of time than you are. So when December rolls around, you automatically begin to evaluate all that's happened since January 1. Actually, it was probably a Capricorn who invented the year-end review. But before you begin, you need to toss out your old ways of analyzing what has transpired and substitute methods that focus on growth and change, not just accomplishment.

Relationships

This year has definitely been an eye-opener for you, both in terms of your relationships with others and your relationship with yourself. Being more aware of the need to take care of yourself has created better, more satisfying relationships with the people closest to you—something you definitely didn't see coming, and something that has opened you up.

Career, Success, and Money

You take stock of all that 2019 turned out to be in this department and you are pleasantly surprised. This just fuels your drive and determination for 2020. Make sure to keep tabs on what still needs to be done. Something you believed would carry over to next year is suddenly being fast-tracked for completion *now*.

Pitfalls and Potential Problems

A year-end review isn't just natural to you, it's a life-affirming process, but only if done in the spirit of supporting yourself instead of trying to figure out where you may have failed. That doesn't mean you gloss over problems, nor does it imply ignoring reality. It means examining the big picture—the context and the content together—instead of going category by isolated category.

Rewarding Days

17, 18, 30, 31

Challenging Days

5, 6, 25, 26

Capricorn Action Table

These dates reflect the best—but not the only—times for success and ease in these activities, according to your Sun sign.

	JAN	FEB	MAR	APR	MAY	JUN	JUL	AUG	SEP	OCT	NOV	DEC
Move					1, 2				3, 4	12, 13		
Start a class			5, 6	1, 2							3, 4	
Seek coaching/ counseling	21, 22					15, 16					26, 27	
Ask for a raise	4, 5					13, 14			28, 29			
Get professional advice			20, 21		26, 27		1, 2					
Get a loan		3, 4						4, 5				3, 4
New romance				6, 7			25, 26			27, 28		
Vacation		19, 20						30, 31				30, 31

Aquarius

The Water Bearer
January 20 to February 19

Element: Air

Quality: Fixed

Polarity: Yang/masculine

Planetary Ruler: Uranus

Meditation: I am a
wellspring of creativity

Gemstone: Amethyst

Power Stones: Aquamarine,
black pearl, chrysocolla

Key Phrase: I know

Glyph: Currents of energy

Anatomy: Ankles, circulatory
system

Colors: Iridescent blues, violet

Animals: Exotic birds

Myths/Legends: Ninhursag,
John the Baptist, Deucalion

House: Eleventh

Opposite Sign: Leo

Flower: Orchid

Keyword: Unconventional

The Aquarius Personality

Strengths, Spiritual Purpose, and Challenges

At the very heart of who you are lies the one thing that drives you to live your life: being authentic, being true to who you are, being the best version of you that is possible. And in order to do that, you are okay with breaking down the walls, the limitations, and the rules that get in the way of making that happen. Of course, this sets you on a course for a direct confrontation with judgment from the very world you live in. While it feels like everyone else is trying to find a way to fit in, you are resisting any and all attempts to conform, for one simple reason: If you conform, how will you know who you truly are, and how will you be able to live a life that symbolizes the very fabric you are made of?

The only way to answer that is to carve out a path that you and you alone choose. In doing so, you demonstrate your spiritual purpose, which is to be a catalyst—to challenge those around you to look beyond the known, the predictable, and the obvious to find what sets them apart, what makes them singular; not for the purpose of separating from others but for the purpose of being totally present for oneself. So any attempt to dissuade you from following your heart or to force you to kowtow is met with resistance. Your challenge is recognizing what is a request rather than a threat, what is an insight versus a judgment, what is support versus a criticism. You can't always tell the difference because your automatic reaction is to resist, no questions asked. Then you are confronted with a choice: Do you stick stubbornly to the resistance, even if you end up shooting yourself in the foot, or do you call on your innate objectivity to sort things out?

Relationships

Ah, relationships. So complicated for you when all you seek is simplicity—straight talk, no games, and definitely no attempts by anyone to control you ever. However, in practice, in the real world, this approach creates a lot of challenges in everything from basic social interaction to the closest, most intimate relationships. You just don't get why it's such a big deal to call things the way you see them, to ask others to put their cards on the table, and to make it clear you don't need to be told what to do. So you end up shaking your head in disbelief when everyone thinks you have a problem. And what's more, they accuse you of being cold and aloof when really you are ill equipped to deal with the subterfuge and duplicity that others accept as not just normal but perfectly okay. Of course, in the end you learn to adapt, but it can leave you with a bitter taste in your mouth while, at the same time, you still seek authentic connection. The true gift you offer others is complete openness to who they are, what they believe, what they desire, and what they choose to do. Because you feel so outside the box yourself, you have no expectations that people should be like you, or anyone else, for that matter. In fact, how boring would life be if everyone was exactly the same?

Career and Work

You fare best in an environment where you can exhibit a large degree of independence. So, of course, you don't like to be micromanaged. That's your definition of a nightmare, because it means that your boss thinks you aren't smart enough to do the job without supervision, and that just won't do. So the cornerstone of success for you begins with the ability to explore your own talents and abilities without interference. This is often interpreted by others as rebellion, when all you are doing is following your inner call to be yourself, even when you are not always clear what that means. For you, being yourself is a work in progress, not a finite equation, so it's foolhardy to think you need to have all the answers before you participate in living, or creating a career, or aiming for success. And what works one day, one week, one month, one year, or one decade may not turn out to be the career that sustains you for a week, never mind your whole life. That reality isn't as hard for you to comprehend as it might be for others, nor does it disturb your equilibrium. You welcome experimentation. It's that little push that helps you clarify where you want to go and what you want to do.

Money and Possessions

Your attitude to both of these is often quite fluid, so it's completely normal for you to waver back and forth between periods of holding on to every penny you have and periods of spending every penny you have. The same is true for things. You can use the same spatula for forty years but insist on getting a new pair of boots every winter. The irony is, this isn't a problem for you, largely because you simply don't see life as an either-or proposition. Again, decisions are made in the moment, based on incoming data. After all, a forty-year-old spatula sits in a drawer and is used sparingly, while boots in a winter climate are used every day for a minimum of three months of the year. Therefore, it's logical to need a new pair of boots every fall. Welcome to the Aquarian mind, with its infinite capacity to make sense of its own decisions. The bottom line is that you are not overly attached to either money or possessions. You like them. They're nice. But they're not as important as being able to be yourself, do what you want, and go where you want.

The Light Side of Life

Quite a lot in life amuses you. To start with, there's people, the things they do, and the things they say. In your mind, this isn't laughing at anyone or anything as much as it is being delighted and entertained by how creative humans truly are, and how as much as we all want to be different—and you know you do—there's something that is essentially common to us all. We're human. And we're all living life. This truth fuels all the other things that bring joy to your life: thinking, reading, talking, friendship, or anything that stretches your mind or takes you places you've never been.

Aquarius Keywords for 2019
Courage, willingness, heart

The Year Ahead for Aquarius

It's going to be a banner year. The only question is, what will the banner say? The answer to that won't come until 2019 is over, which is both exhilarating and annoying at the same time. You are famous for believing that you never met a change you didn't like. But the truth is you only like change if you thought of it. Then you are willing to go through the ups and downs, the ins and outs, of the unpredictability that accompanies any change. However, and that's a big however, you are just as resistant to change as anyone else if you didn't actively choose it.

Well, get ready to dig in your heels, because Uranus, your planetary avatar, is about to change signs, moving from Aries to Taurus on March 6. Last year he gave you a taste of what that's going to look like, but now it's time for full immersion. Are you ready to switch gears from seven years of pushing your need for freedom and complete self-expression to seven years of using that knowledge to shake up both the foundation of your life and the values it's sitting on? To your surprise, you find that not everything in your life is as new and up-to-date as you've idealized and idolized, that quite often you opt to stick to things that no longer reflect where you are or what you desire. It's time for a complete makeover so that what you say and what you do are more congruent. The truth is, what's required is an objective look at how you were raised, what you were taught, and how you unwittingly hang on to an ideal or a belief or a value because it was once so close to your heart. Resist the temptation to find fault with any inconsistencies you find. They are nothing more than that, and are not a sign that you are actually a hypocrite.

Living life is an art, not a science with a single, absolute pathway to follow. And you know this. Yet the idealist in you expects that everything you do needs to be a shining moment for humanity. That's not possible or even desirable. You are human, like everyone else, even if you do feel like you don't belong on Planet Earth, at least some of the time. And humans are full of interesting nooks and crannies, where stuff gets left behind or forgotten until the spotlight is turned on them. Welcome to seven years of Uranus in Taurus, a time for digging up all those outworn and outdated perceptions about what's important, dusting them off, taking one last look at them, and then letting them go.

Saturn

Well, enough is enough. Really. Can't this guy (Saturn) stop rattling around in your unconscious mind, conjuring up all manner of fears and insecurities? Except he's not conjuring them up, even if it feels that way. The reality is that Saturn is connecting you to what you have stored there and asking you to clean out this particular storage space. You know, the one where you've stockpiled and kept hidden anything and everything that dredges up anxiety, panic, or trepidation. Of course, you know you are human and you can't erase the feelings of rejection, judgment, and insecurity you've actually experienced, no matter how much you use your innate objectivity and detachment. However, you can avoid them. And you do. Until you are given no choice but to tackle them. Enter Saturn. There's nothing he likes better than to demand you take care of business—which, in this case, is to get rid of all that junk, no matter what it takes. However, it's not that simple. What he is pushing you to do runs counter to what Pluto has been asking you to do since 2008. Saturn doesn't view what you've stored as useful in any concrete way, while Pluto sees it as fuel for transformation. The truth is, you need to find a way to respect and honor what Saturn is challenging you to do.

No more hiding from the painful, the ugly, the difficult. Acknowledge it and you find just how strong you really are, because it takes a lot of energy to carry what you've hidden from your conscious mind. Once you've done that, you can turn the rest of the process over to Pluto.

Uranus

You feel a deep kinship to Uranus, even if you don't like his methods. His job is to take you outside your comfort zone so you can expand your view of life, so you can get rid of any limitations that keep you from growing, and so you can discover your own strength. All admirable goals, and yet it could be argued that he quite simply likes to stir the pot. Well, after March 6, it's going to initially feel a lot like the latter as he leaves behind all those exhilarating opportunities he gave you to actually glimpse and embrace a healthy ego and instead challenges you to put your growth into practice in a real and tangible way. Until then, you have one last chance to review the trajectory of your life since 2011 and see whether you have truly applied the insights of Uranus in Aries to find your voice and to express your authenticity from deep within. If you have, then his move into Taurus will open up a multitude of ways for you to demonstrate how true to yourself you really are. Of course, because it's Uranus, this process is not predictable or without challenges and difficulties. Such is his way: to always keep things just beyond your capacity to anticipate. Therein lies the gift. Just when you surrender to the knowledge that you just don't have a clue comes that aha moment, that lightning bolt that shifts your whole life, that exhilarating awareness that life can and will be different. This is your life's blood. You welcome chaos, not because you like it but because it's better than the alternative: a life of inertia.

Neptune

You are definitely fascinated by the fluidity that is Neptune—until it just goes on and on and on. Then you are just plain irritated and maybe a little frightened. Not that you need everything in life to be nailed to the floor. You don't. In fact, you welcome the unknown. However, when you are consistently at a loss to find any sense of direction because everything feels like oblivion, it challenges you at your very core. After all, you are an air sign and you like to make immediate sense of things, even if it's only that things are in upheaval and they are changing. With Neptune that is impossible. The kind of consciousness he represents is limitless and indefinable. You simply have to go with the flow and accept that there are no signposts to guide you, either inside you or outside you. This is scary stuff for you, especially when it affects your sense of self-worth, your understanding of what you value, and the well-being of your resources, the ongoing challenge facing you since 2012. This year promises to bring firmer ground to stand on and more stability as you put to use some of what Neptune has revealed to you. All that wispy, dreamy, and extremely symbolic stuff that often felt nonsensical begins to coalesce into a vision that clarifies just how much the changes you are making demand a new set of values—ones that reflect a blend of idealism and practicality.

Pluto

In Pluto's world, nothing is to be wasted. Everything has the potential to be transformed—reused, recycled, reanimated. So in 2008, when he entered the space in your life you use to set aside any life experiences you simply aren't sure what to do with, he awakened a deep resistance you didn't know you were capable of. Not because you fear change, at least not the kind that is intellectually driven, but because he demanded you dive deep into the underground caverns of your life and dig up stuff you thought was better left undisturbed—stuff that is impervious to any application of logical analysis or thinking, stuff built of pure emotional response, stuff definitely outside your comfort zone. Gradually you let go of your resistance and began to see value in processing that material, if for no other reason than it freed you from carrying around a whole bunch of negative experiences in their raw state, something you weren't aware you were doing.

This year, things intensify to a degree of discomfort you didn't think possible as Saturn questions the need for all this poking around, forcing you to take a step back and revisit your commitment to transforming the detritus you accumulated in the recesses of your unconscious. Just remember, it may be time to recalibrate, but it's definitely not a time to stop or try to turn back. You can't undo what you've already done. And Pluto asks, why would that even appeal to you when you have taken the difficult and turned it into a deeper, more passionate, wiser you?

How Will This Year's Eclipses Affect You?

Eclipses signal intense periods that highlight major growth opportunities for us in the process of creating our lives. They are linked to the lunar phases—specifically the New and Full Moon—and involve the relationship between the Sun and the Moon and the Earth. A Solar Eclipse is a magnified New Moon, while a Lunar Eclipse is a magnified Full Moon. Eclipses unfold in cycles involving all twelve signs of the zodiac, and they occur in pairs, usually about two weeks apart.

In 2019 there are five eclipses, three solar (two in Capricorn and one in Cancer) and two lunar (one in Leo and one in Capricorn). The first Solar Eclipse arrives on January 5 in Capricorn, triggering a major bout of apprehension over whether or not you can ever move past some of the most difficult aspects of your life. You are suddenly confronted—yet again—with how depressing life has often been for one simple reason: you are always just a little out of step with the rest of the world, not necessarily by design but by just being yourself. Somehow others find this unacceptable or unwarranted or undesirable, which leads to judgment, rejection, or even punishment. All this is like a knife in your heart and totally incomprehensible. Isn't everyone different? Probably, but they choose to keep it hidden and you don't. It's just not in your DNA. So you adapt by doing your best to detach yourself from the impact of such attitudes and responses, believing you've dealt with them, when, in actual fact, you've simply walled them off.

The Solar Eclipse on January 5 is a cyclical reminder that life's experiences cannot be erased just because you didn't know what to do with them at the time. It's also an invitation to find a way to heal the wounds you experienced by acknowledging the damage done and using the wisdom gained to celebrate your strength, your fortitude, and your resilience. That way you are prepared to open your heart to the possibility of more loving, fun relationships with others promised by the Lunar Eclipse on January 21. You really do need an open heart as much as an open mind in order to follow your prime directive: to be true to yourself and to live your life as authentically as possible.

All the eclipses in 2019, including the Solar Eclipse on July 2, the Lunar Eclipse on July 16, and the Solar Eclipse on December 26, give you the chance to clear away any shadows and limitations currently standing in the way of you growing into the fullness of all that you can be. To do this, you can't shy away from confronting whatever surfaces, no matter what it looks like or feels like. It's the only way you can uncover the hidden treasure. What happened to you isn't as important as what you did with it. There's nothing buried deep within you that you don't have the will and the capacity to transform.

Aquarius | January

Overall Theme

The best use of your time and energy isn't in fighting what you feel is an overwhelming tide of discontent with your life. This is just old stuff surfacing so it can be released. Be aware of that and you refrain from creating unnecessary complications. Plus you give yourself the chance to be free of old pain and old disappointments, a win-win for all parts of you.

Relationships

On the surface you appear to be your usual friendly self, but the truth is you really aren't in the mood for people, at least not in close proximity. It's not because you suddenly want to disassociate yourself from the entire human race, but because right now you feel like the walking wounded and you aren't sure you really want to talk to anyone about it.

Career, Success, and Money

On a heart level, you feel you are missing in action from this part of your life. That doesn't mean you aren't working hard and keeping your eye on when is the best time to make some changes you've had in mind for some time. You can always count on your brain to keep you going in the appropriate direction while you wait for satisfaction and desire to make a comeback.

Pitfalls and Potential Problems

There is a deep sense that somehow you are running out of time. Well, it's true, but only in one context. On balance, your life is truly good and whatever you are feeling is the recognition that an avenue of change and growth is closing. This always leads to some anxiety on your part that you haven't taken full advantage of any and all opportunities offered. Relax. You've still got a couple of months to address that.

Rewarding Days

12, 13, 25, 26

Challenging Days

5, 6, 21, 22

Aquarius | February

Overall Theme

If it were possible for you to smile all the time, you would. Life is humming along, the shadows are gone, and you are truly ready to take on anything and everything. In fact, you are in no mood for any kind of interference or resistance. Just remember to exercise a little caution and a little restraint. Not everyone and everything operates at the same hyper speed you do.

Relationships

Be careful that you don't wear out your welcome with some of the people in your life. In your haste to cast away the dark clouds you experienced last month, you begin to act like everything is all about you all of the time. It's compensation for feeling overwhelmed by fear and insecurity and the need to reassure yourself that you are fine.

Career, Success, and Money

Keep a careful watch on a couple of things: what you spend and what you say in your workplace. Both could create ongoing problems because you are in touch with external reality only on an intermittent basis. You are being driven solely by a need to do what you want.

Pitfalls and Potential Problems

You are so sure it's imperative that you grab this one last opportunity to define your individuality and make your mark that you are in danger of undermining yourself. Welcome to Uranus on the last leg of his journey through Aries. You might think you'll never get another chance to stand in the spotlight, but you are wrong. This is a beginning, not an ending.

Rewarding Days

3, 4, 23, 24

Challenging Days

1, 2, 17, 18

Aquarius | March

Overall Theme

The gloves come off, figuratively speaking, as Uranus enters Taurus on March 6. Internally, you aren't the least bit impressed with the push to shift into a new seven-year rollercoaster ride, so you predictably do what you do: Dig in your heels, on sheer principle. Well, resist away. It's your way of telling yourself you have a choice. In this case, the choice to be made is when to stop fighting the inevitable.

Relationships

Prepare to meet some interesting new people who offer you a glimpse of the positive potential of this new beginning, as well as the promise of at least one significant friendship. This buoys your spirits and leaves you more open to the whisperings of your inner voice, alerting you to the reality that some of your relationships are definitely due for a much-needed overhaul.

Career, Success, and Money

You find yourself having to answer questions about what you said and did last month that leave you extremely uncomfortable. There's no sense trying to avoid this reckoning. All it takes is an honest acknowledgment that you weren't at your best—along with solutions to any problems you created. It's not like you are unaware. And fixing things is much better than offering endless apologies.

Pitfalls and Potential Problems

The truth is, you hate the initial entry of Uranus into a new Sun sign, no matter how many times you've experienced it or how well you understand the process. It always leaves you breathless and off kilter, which, if you are honest with yourself, is as invigorating as it is upsetting, often at the very same time. But isn't this what makes life what you need it to be—unpredictable and illuminating?

Rewarding Days

2, 3, 19, 20

Challenging Days

12, 13, 17, 18

Aquarius | April

Overall Theme

How is it possible to navigate a world that simultaneously feels wispy and heavy? Good question, and one that is likely to challenge your formidable skill in understanding things that are diametrically opposed to each other—not because your brain is missing in action, but because your circuits are on overload adjusting to the new state of your life: upside down.

Relationships

Expect some intense and even heated discussions about life, what's important, and why. This catches you unawares and strangely unable to make even a modicum of sense out of what comes out of your mouth. That's because you are already in the midst of a deep assessment about what holds value for you. This leaves you at a loss to say anything with any certainty. Don't worry. You'll figure it out.

Career, Success, and Money

So, just at the point where you think you might truly lose your mind, work comes to the rescue with a couple of potential new projects or pathways guaranteed to charge your batteries and give you something to put your stamp on. It's precisely what you need: something new and something tangible.

Pitfalls and Potential Problems

You are definitely irritable, which is a sure sign that you are waging an internal battle between resisting the change you know is coming, whether you like it or not, and embracing the possibility of new growth in your life. This is likely to continue until you once again realize that what makes you tick is the fresh, the innovative, and the different. And that simply doesn't happen without a little topsy-turvy.

Rewarding Days
11, 12, 26, 27

Challenging Days
13, 14, 24, 25

Aquarius | May

Overall Theme

It's not that you are unhappy or even discontent. You are just plain tired. So you find yourself looking for a hole to crawl into, anywhere where you can rest, recalibrate, and avoid even a hint of change. You can probably accomplish the first two by taking refuge at home, but dodging the inevitable is only going to amplify your stress.

Relationships

Your internal response to people in general is likely to be "Go away. Leave me alone." However, instead of telling people you need some downtime, you are likely to be a bit curmudgeonly, which translates to extremely unsympathetic and more than brutally blunt. Try the first option. It avoids the kind of fallout you don't like dealing with: hurt feelings and anger on their side and guilt on yours.

Career, Success, and Money

You generally don't tolerate anything that amounts to willful stupidity, which is someone choosing to do something knowing it is likely to fail. What you forget is that not everyone is as perceptive and sharp as you are at seeing the big picture. Remember this when you are confronted with just such a situation at work. There's no sense in creating enemies or drama.

Pitfalls and Potential Problems

Everything is getting on your nerves. Normally it's just the little things that go sideways that earn your disapproval, but this month it seems to be everything. It's because you feel so out of sorts and out of energy that your usual tolerance is replaced by the attitude that there is nothing in the whole wide world even remotely pleasing. Take a break and don't talk to anyone, including yourself.

Rewarding Days
1, 2, 26, 27

Challenging Days
8, 9, 21, 22

Aquarius | June

Overall Theme

Enter a rejuvenated, happier Aquarius. Taking a timeout worked wonders, and you return to the world full of your usual optimism and hope. One of the true joys of being you is the capacity to vault yourself out of any swamp you choose to dive into. The only difficulty you face is recognizing that not everyone understands how quickly you shift gears.

Relationships

Time for some play and some fun. Now all you need to do is find someone to do that with. The question is, where did everyone go? The truth is they sought refuge until the storm that was you passed. So it's up to you to let them know it's safe to come out and hang with you. Perhaps an apology or two is needed, along with a polite and welcoming invitation.

Career, Success, and Money

The opportunity to fast-track a favorite idea or project tops the agenda, but with one proviso: be prepared for some stalling at the higher levels and the potential for complete opposition from someone you thought you could count on. Be patient, even though it's not your strong suit. Everything works out in the end, as long as you don't push.

Pitfalls and Potential Problems

It is rare when the space you are in is the same as the one everyone else is inhabiting. Which is fine. What still confounds you and knocks you off balance is the demand that you must conform to the prevailing human condition. So if everyone else is sad, so must you be, and vice versa. Time to disengage from this game. It's okay for you to be happy and hopeful, even if everyone else is not.

Rewarding Days

9, 10, 22, 23

Challenging Days

4, 5, 17, 18

Aquarius | July

Overall Theme

Your capacity for objectivity and detachment disappears and you find yourself unable to resist the temptation to react immediately and defensively to the slightest shift in life. Recognize that there's a push from deep inside you to expel a number of fears and insecurities that limit you. Then explore ways to ease this process and find peace. It's preferable to feeling bad about yourself.

Relationships

Out of the blue, many of the most important people in your life show up to offer you support in dealing with all the negative and unflattering things you believe about yourself. You thought you'd hidden them well. You did, but only from yourself. This surprising turn of events lightens your load and creates new trust in your relationships.

Career, Success, and Money

You feel like you are peddling as fast as you can while going nowhere. It's a hangover from last month's difficulties in getting anything moving in what you consider the right direction. Keep focused on what's truly important and accept that there are days when it looks like no one has a clue. In the end, your clarity of vision succeeds.

Pitfalls and Potential Problems

It's clear that this isn't an easy month, but hold fast to what you know to be true about yourself. Understand that you absorbed other people's stories about who you are and what you are about and then buried it all because you just didn't know what to do with it. Bringing it out into the open is necessary so you can actually see that what was said is not your truth but another's opinion or judgment.

Rewarding Days

8, 9, 25, 26

Challenging Days

2, 3, 15, 16

Aquarius | August

Overall Theme
August begins and ends with light, love, laughter, and genuine excitement about what is just around the corner. Not only are you unbowed by facing the demons you skillfully hid from yourself, but you are proud of your innate capacity to use your life's experiences to grow and expand. In fact, you see everything in life as a catalyst of one kind or another.

Relationships
You are truly filled with deep appreciation for the strength and depth of the most important relationships in your life—and surprised as well. Because you are not quite like other people, you tend to see yourself as completely on your own. However, it's becoming clear that is simply not true. This awareness makes love real and authentic rather than illusory and sentimental.

Career, Success, and Money
You find yourself the center of attention and gratitude. Your foresight and willingness to stay true to what you know is the appropriate course of action keeps a very important company project from compete implosion. This creates an opening for potential advancement—and not just with your current employer.

Pitfalls and Potential Problems
The only challenge you face is trusting that it's okay to embrace the good things that keep finding their way into your life. You really can trust that they will sustain you and not disappear in a puff of smoke. In fact, they are signs that what is happening now is the foundation of the future, while the anxiety you have is connected to the past.

Rewarding Days
9, 10, 19, 20

Challenging Days
11, 12, 30, 31

Aquarius | September

Overall Theme

Much gets accomplished in every area of your life, in part because your belief in yourself reaches a new high. This amplifies your confidence and you set about taking care of business. It's time to get things in order so you are able to use the energy of change when it starts to shake things up. You know you can't predict what's going to happen, but you can make sure you are ready to respond.

Relationships

Your need for deep connection continues to intensify, and you respond by trying to back away. This confuses you, because you really desire the kind of bond that comes from revealing who you are. What's startled you is how much you actually camouflage about yourself out of fear that you will be judged or criticized. It's time to trust yourself and let your guard down.

Career, Success, and Money

In the middle of all the effort you willingly put into your career comes a sudden but compelling desire to take a holiday, which leads to a long-overdue look at your finances. To your surprise, things are a lot better than you expected. And as if by magic, a space in your work life opens up so you can take time off. Vacation, here you come!

Pitfalls and Potential Problems

There's not a lot going on that's likely to create any significant issues in either your outer world or your inner world. You are standing strong and sure, dealing with any hiccup or thorn in your side with awareness and determination. Embrace this experience and this feeling. You deserve it.

Rewarding Days

5, 6, 28, 29

Challenging Days

10, 11, 22, 23

Aquarius | October

Overall Theme

Life is a little hectic, as you are confronted almost daily with a litany of things big and small demanding your attention. It's not that you don't have any solutions. The reality is that there are only so many hours in the day and you'd rather focus on the big things and let the smaller things slide. A better strategy is to ask for help. That way nothing gets ignored or comes back to haunt you.

Relationships

Networking isn't always that appealing to you because it feels forced and required, and you know how you feel about that. Well, this month offers some once-in-a-lifetime opportunities to meet the kind of people who could change your professional trajectory in ways you only dream about. So set aside your resistance and accept any and all invitations to mingle.

Career, Success, and Money

It feels like the only thing in your life is your career, and yet you are not unhappy about that in spite of the long hours and the increased number of responsibilities. You love nothing better than being able to put all your skills, talents, and abilities to the test and meet the challenge. Nothing satisfies quite as much as that.

Pitfalls and Potential Problems

You can get so singularly focused on one thing that you forget to take care of the other things you value: big-picture things like your health, your personal relationships, keeping promises you've made, your finances, etc. The best way to ensure that doesn't happen is to schedule those things when you aren't as busy are you are this month. Otherwise, life catches up to you in ways you don't appreciate.

Rewarding Days

10, 11, 28, 29

Challenging Days

12, 13, 21, 22

Aquarius | November

Overall Theme

There's a face-off brewing between home and family versus career and professional development, and it has the potential to boil over, especially if you don't take steps to address the issue. It's not a case of choosing one over the other. It's recognizing that you've put your personal life on the back burner because work is so mesmerizing right now.

Relationships

You are stretching your personal relationships to the limit by expecting those closest to you to continually accept the commitments you make to your work. Take a good look at your attitude and recognize that the people who love you don't object to what you want to do. They just need you to include them in the decision-making process.

Career, Success, and Money

Stop telling yourself that the only reason you are working so hard is to ensure your financial security. That's a justification that you think sounds good. Well, it is plausible, but it's not the main motivation. You truly love what you are doing right now so much that it's taking up all the oxygen in your life. That's not healthy or necessary.

Pitfalls and Potential Problems

Sometimes you are blind to what really matters to you because you get so engrossed in things that are novel or off the beaten path. This leads to a failure to see where you may be sacrificing the very things that sustain you in order to avoid boredom or to prove that you can do what you want when you want. Ask yourself whether there isn't a bit of that going on right now.

Rewarding Days

3, 4, 8, 9

Challenging Days

13, 14, 28, 29

Aquarius | December

Overall Theme

It's really not in your nature to look backward. However, as 2019 comes to an end, take time to review what you've experienced, not so you can cobble together any kind of report, but so you can gather the insights revealed to you. They will form the platform for how to handle the next year of your life, as well as give you a true appreciation for what you have accomplished.

Relationships

The simple act of remembering how much you desire and need friendship in all your important relationships smooths over any difficulties that surfaced in November. Why? Because you take time to let everyone know how much their support has always meant to you, how much you appreciate their insights and directness, and how much their presence in your world brings a smile to your face.

Career, Success, and Money

It's been a hectic year and you haven't had much time to assess all that you've contributed or whether it's being valued beyond the acknowledgment that you did a great job. You are beginning to realize that it isn't enough to be the person who can always pull a rabbit out of a hat. What you need is more remuneration.

Pitfalls and Potential Problems

You can't help but look ahead and wonder what next year's challenges are going to look like. It's one way to distract yourself from acknowledging any missteps you made in 2019. And therein lies your problem. As much as you insist you are okay with your choices, you often find fault with what you've done. Instead, be kind to yourself. Accept that choices often have consequences you hadn't planned on. Then you can celebrate how you handled the unexpected.

Rewarding Days

5, 6, 28, 29

Challenging Days

13, 14, 25, 26

Aquarius Action Table

These dates reflect the best—but not the only—times for success and ease in these activities, according to your Sun sign.

	JAN	FEB	MAR	APR	MAY	JUN	JUL	AUG	SEP	OCT	NOV	DEC
Move				26, 27					2, 3		11, 12	
Start a class		3, 4			1, 2				28, 29			
Seek coaching/counseling	5, 6					3, 4		30, 31				
Ask for a raise			10, 11	9, 10		22, 23				28, 29		
Get professional advice							1, 2					15, 16
Get a loan		19, 20					20, 21				19, 20	
New romance	21, 22				23, 24							23, 24
Vacation			25, 26					9, 10		15, 16		

Pisces

The Fish
February 20 to March 20

Element: Water

Glyph: Two fish swimming in opposite directions

Quality: Mutable

Anatomy: Feet, lymphatic system

Polarity: Yin/feminine

Colors: Sea green, violet

Planetary Ruler: Neptune

Animals: Fish, sea mammals

Meditation: I successfully navigate my emotions

Myths/Legends: Aphrodite, Buddha, Jesus of Nazareth

Gemstone: Aquamarine

House: Twelfth

Power Stones: Amethyst, bloodstone, tourmaline

Opposite Sign: Virgo

Flower: Water lily

Key Phrase: I believe

Keyword: Transcendence

The Pisces Personality

Strengths, Spiritual Purpose, and Challenges

You dream. And then you dream some more. Awake. Asleep. Big. Small. There isn't a crevice of the Universe that you haven't visited in one form or another. That's because you are tuned in to a frequency that no one else is even aware of, and you spend much of your life trying to translate that experience into something tangible and understandable, even to you. Just because you live in a world of all possibilities doesn't mean it's an easy thing. In fact, it's downright confusing, because trying to make sense of the infinite is a job for the Divine, right? Possibly, but that's not what you are trying to do. You are simply seeking awareness and illumination.

You are fundamentally wired to always be in search of the indefinable, which often finds you at cross-purposes with what being on planet Earth is all about—third-dimensional stuff. It's not that you are unable to navigate the whys and wherefores of daily living. But if you are to honor your spiritual purpose, which is to envision, you must be tuned in to all the levels of your consciousness. And you know from personal experience that there are quite a few of those. They are your playground, sustaining you and opening up all kinds of potential. What others often don't understand is it's not necessary for you to physically manifest all the things you imagine. The joy comes in the visualization, in the dreaming, and in the fantasizing. But that is only the partial truth. Deep in your heart, you know it's imperative that you make something tangible out of all that possibility. And you have a boundless amount of inspiration, creativity, optimism, and faith with which to accomplish anything you desire. Live your dreams. Of course, they won't be as perfect as they are in your imagination, but the act of creating what you envision opens the door to more. Having dreams is the spark. Using them is lighting the fire.

Relationships

This isn't possible for any other sign of the zodiac but you: Within seconds or minutes of meeting someone, you can find a way to create a bond, a connection, or a relationship with them. The reason for this? Well, actually there are a few. First, you are compassionate and you believe everyone deserves a bit of kindness and acceptance. Second, you really don't have any boundaries, because you believe that everything is one with everything else—which may be true on another frequency but not on Planet Earth, where everything is about the very opposite: duality. Third, you are deeply intuitive and sensitive, so you can feel exactly what others are feeling, so much so that you get totally absorbed in their reality without being aware of it. All these qualities are both a blessing and a challenge. How do you stay true to your essential self without giving yourself away completely? To begin with, recognize that having boundaries is not the same as building walls. Next, understand that you have the right to choose with whom you share your gifts. Develop discernment by using your innate talent for connecting to others to see the third-dimensional reality of who they are now rather than who they possess the potential to be. That way you honor yourself and others, which is essential to a healthy relationship, whether it's the one you have with yourself or someone else.

Career and Work
The standard definition of success only works for you if what you do to achieve it is meaningful to you. The challenge here is defining exactly what that is. This often takes you on quite the journey, in and out and around, before you focus your attention on any one thing. And even then, you remain open to the notion (or is it a dream?) that something else is just around the corner. This speaks directly to this feeling deep down in your soul that you need to find your calling. Because whether or not you are aware of it, you seek to find a career or job that nourishes your body, soul, and spirit. This is such a powerful intention, yet it often feels like chasing butterflies. That might deter a more pragmatic or impatient soul, but not you. Reaching out for what's just beyond your knowing gives you a sense of purpose and ignites a passion for living.

Money and Possessions
Are you acquisitive in the obvious sense? Definitely not! However, if, in the course of following your dream, your passion, or your mission, you end up accumulating either one, you welcome them as a symbol of what you've accomplished. With one requirement: It must either be beautiful (in the case of belongings) or contribute to making things better (in the case of money). How things find their way into your life is usually serendipitous. You know. You found this little shop and you walked in

the door and there it was—a piece of art or jewelry or a chair, etc. These treasures reflect something about who you are and resonate deeply with something in your heart and your psyche. Anything that doesn't has no place in your life.

The Light Side of Life

What brings you the most joy in life are the things that warm your spirit: a beautiful sunset, smiles from the people you love, an inspirational story, sitting in the sun, walking by the ocean, a powerful meditation, and the list goes on. It's not easy to give a complete inventory, because you are so open to what life serves up that what speaks to you now might not next year. You are truly someone wishing to experience anything that takes you one step closer to your soul.

Pisces Keywords for 2019
Honor, manifest, act

The Year Ahead for Pisces

Because of your profound sensitivity, you already know there's a big change coming in the energetic fabric of your life. It's leaving you a little queasy, just when things settled down in 2018 as Saturn gave you the opportunity to feel less like you were about to float off into space and more like you were still on the planet. At first it came as a shock to you to discover that you actually needed to feel grounded, because the density of the third dimension is a challenge to the little fairy that lives inside you. You like to flit, not sit. However, after Neptune, your planetary avatar, entered Pisces in 2012, he introduced you to a whole new definition of what it means to be out of body, one that truly discombobulated you and left you appreciating the capacity to keep your feet firmly planted. Sure, you've had some wild dreams and powerful perceptions, but this whole, newfound foggy bottom blurred your already less-than-clear sense of who you are. It's fine to lose yourself in your dreams, but in your waking life, it's been difficult to know what to do with the feeling that you might disappear at any moment. So when Saturn came to the rescue, he reconnected you to your body and helped you begin getting clear and organized. Plus you got a sense of just how you could use some of those wonderful imaginings Neptune provided to create something lasting and substantial.

Now you feel the ground under your feet starting to tremble oh-so slightly and you know a shift is coming. And it is. Uranus enters Taurus on March 6, offering you the chance to further solidify your future in ways that are definitely not predictable. So refrain from trying to anticipate anything. Rather, take time to meditate on what change you'd like to see in your life. Your tendency is to think of yourself as an empty vessel, but the reality is your consciousness is home to a lot of psychic garbage that needs cleaning out. Let Uranus help you with that. He won't disturb anything that doesn't need to be disturbed. Remember that, and 2019 will be a year you never forget because of the surprising yet brilliant strides you make in being you. After all, how could it be otherwise when the planetary forces represented by Saturn, Uranus, Neptune, and Pluto are working in harmony with you to do just that?

Saturn

As far as Saturn is concerned, the task of supporting you in getting your whole life in order isn't done, which is great news. The progress you made in 2018 in getting your life on a firmer footing is still taking root, and you don't want to see all the work done and all the potential yet to be fulfilled go to waste. It won't if you realize you are the only one who can sabotage this. The key to continued success is acknowledging the very real fears and insecurities you have about your ability to see things through. First, define what success is to you. You can't accomplish a goal if you don't know what it is. Sometimes you avoid doing this because if there's no clear aim, then you can't fail. Well, that's truly a case of doublespeak, and you know this.

Second, don't try to compensate for the feeling that you've been missing in action by taking on too much. Keep it simple. Recognize that time is on your side. That way you can use it to your advantage without sacrificing your intent or wasting the resources you have at your disposal. It's a complex dance you need to choreograph: taking your powerful imagination and vision and marrying it to the reality of time and space. See this process as creating a wonderful container for all your dreams. It's far more practical, hopeful, and satisfying than believing that keeping your dreams in their pure state—in your imagination—protects them from destruction. It's the opposite. Refusing to give them physical form is a sure-fire guarantee that they will wither and die. So take that leap of faith and make the physical world work for you. You won't regret it.

Uranus

You may not have consciously noticed Uranus much during the last seven years as he traversed Aries. His messages got lost or were hard to comprehend, because Neptune was busy dominating the energetic conversation going on in your consciousness. Oh, there was the odd occasion when Uranus broke through; for example, when a crisis occurred connected to your resources, whether personal and financial, or when you felt completely disconnected from the values you placed at the center of your life. But it wasn't easy to understand what those experiences were all about because you felt clueless much of the time.

Well, when Uranus enters Taurus on March 6, what he has to say is loud, clear, and unequivocal. It's likely to be a shock to your system, precisely because there is no interference. Although he has moved into a new sign, he will insist on making sure you understand what he shifted in your life while he was in Aries. How will he do that, you wonder? It won't happen in any way that you are conscious of until you open your mouth and say something that totally astounds you, not because it's terrible or mean or unkind but because it's not congruent with what you believed was important. That's when you realize he overhauled much of what you value when you weren't looking. And it's okay. This makes you feel better about the next step of your Uranian journey: shifting how you think, how you communicate, and how you use your knowledge. Let the change begin.

Neptune

Although still insistently present in your life, Neptune's influence is less wispy and more clarifying. You still experience moments of feeling invisible not only to the rest of the world but to yourself as well. That's in part because you and your ego haven't always been that well acquainted so it's never been easy to know yourself with any certainty. And Neptune's entry into Pisces in 2012 more than amplified this issue. He sent it into the stratosphere and beyond, which is where you think you've been living—not particularly helpful when it comes to living life on Planet Earth. Your already soupy sense of yourself vaporized into the mists and now you are struggling to figure out how to make sense of this, how to deal with this, and, most certainly, how to find meaning in the process.

Well, 2019 promises to give you plenty of opportunities to answer all these questions, once you release the notion that having no ego at all is an admirable and noble thing. You cannot live your own life if you don't include yourself in it. And that requires a healthy self, which is actually a healthy ego. Neptune's intent is to dissolve any of the icky sticky notes pasted onto you (either by you or by others) that are thought to be an accurate description of you. That way you are free to create a more authentic image from the inside out. Time to remember that you are not the sum total of anyone else's projections, including your own. Time to be energetically open to yourself, first and foremost. Time to trust that you deserve to treat yourself with the same sensitivity and compassion you offer others. Then you can reach for the stars, knowing what you are truly made of.

Pluto

You tend to resist Pluto, not because you are afraid of immersing yourself in deep waters but because what he's asking you to look at isn't very pretty. And you know how much you like your rose-colored glasses. They come in really handy when life is, well, not very attractive. Of course, Pluto doesn't care about that at all, which offends you. And so the two of you have been at loggerheads for more than ten years. You resist and he persists. The irony is that you misunderstand his intentions. Pluto isn't interested in sticking your face in the muck and suffocating you. True, he is asking you to face some profoundly painful, ugly, and horrid experiences, but solely for the purpose of finding a way to transmute and transform your life, using the very energy those situations created. This is alchemy: the capacity to take all experiences (including the most difficult) and find the treasure within, and use this awareness to transform the deepest parts of your psyche, which ultimately shifts your whole life. Recognize that the next two years offer an optimum time to immerse yourself in this process as Saturn approaches contact with Pluto, giving you the chance to harness all that power with purpose and focus. What emerges is pure you on all levels—physical, emotional, intellectual, and spiritual.

How Will This Year's Eclipses Affect You?

Eclipses signal intense periods that highlight major growth opportunities for us in the process of creating our lives. They are linked to the lunar phases—specifically the New and Full Moon—and involve the relationship between the Sun and the Moon and the Earth. A Solar Eclipse is a magnified New Moon, while a Lunar Eclipse is a magnified Full Moon. Eclipses unfold in cycles involving all twelve signs of the zodiac, and they occur in pairs, usually about two weeks apart.

In 2019 there are five eclipses, three solar (two in Capricorn and one in Cancer) and two lunar (one in Leo and one in Capricorn). The first Solar Eclipse arrives on January 5 in Capricorn, stirring up some old fears about how capable you are of navigating this new path you are on. The commitment still feels so new to you that you are sure it's going to disappear in a puff of smoke if you look away for even a second. See the fear for what it is: reconnecting to old judgments about how you live your life. Once you recognize that, ask yourself where these judgments came from. Are they self-imposed or are they projections? Probably a bit of both, but knowing their source helps illuminate how deeply they still impact your life. The purpose of this eclipse is to let you know the time has come to set all of this aside because it's toxic. The temptation, though, is to do the opposite and hang on to the fears, the insecurities, and the judgments as the absolute truth of who you are, relieving you of the need to change the script of your life.

The key here is to know that viewing your life through a filter of right and wrong is limiting and diminishing. Instead, use the energy of the Lunar Eclipse on January 21 to love yourself as unconditionally as you do everyone else. Take that wellspring of optimism and faith deep inside you and nourish yourself, and accept that what makes you original and special is your ability to see beyond the physical, to dream larger than life, to hold the vision of what is ideal, and to hope against all odds. Of course, these qualities do and always have put you at odds with prevailing attitudes and beliefs about what life is meant to be. However, deep in your core, you can't really align yourself with the status quo because you know there's so much more to being. Your direct connection to all that is divine tells you that every day. Honor that. Follow your innate awareness. And you will get where you want to go. Just not in a linear way. But then, straight lines are not really your cup of tea.

This year constantly offers you the chance to emerge from the need to be like everyone else. Tune in to the energies of the Solar Eclipse on July 2, the Lunar Eclipse on July 16, and the Solar Eclipse on December 26 as they illuminate just how to celebrate yourself by truly taking care of you, so that, as 2019 comes to a close, your faith and confidence in yourself reaches an all-time high.

Pisces | January

Overall Theme

The doubts constantly cropping up on all levels of your consciousness are not a sign of impending doom. They are simply a wake-up call designed to let you know you it's time to bring them out into the open so they don't sabotage you as you get ready to make important, life-changing decisions in 2019. Anything you ignore is far more dangerous than anything you shine a light on.

Relationships

Life always feels easier when you know exactly what people expect from you. That approach comes under scrutiny when the Solar Eclipse on January 5 triggers a huge amount of resentment as you realize just how often you do precisely what others want without considering your feelings or your desires. The solution to this begins with you putting yourself at the top of your list of priorities.

Career, Success, and Money

Be prepared to deal with some last-minute difficulties with an important project that you thought was all set to go. Rather than reacting negatively to what you consider unnecessary changes, just get the job done, and recognize that this is a tempest in a teapot, not a criticism of what you originally did. Someone needed to throw their weight around.

Pitfalls and Potential Problems

Don't be knocked off balance by some extreme shifts in how you feel about, well, everything. You are in the midst of a huge restructuring of the very fabric of who you are, what you value, and how you intend to live your life. That's a lot, and it's bound to create some inner turmoil. No matter how intense things get, remember that this is transitory.

Rewarding Days

10, 11, 14, 15

Challenging Days

5, 6, 21, 22

Pisces | February

Overall Theme
You experience a period of heightened sensitivity so intense that you feel like you are going to crawl out of your skin. It's not because you are confronting any difficulty in your own life. In fact, things are moving along rather nicely. Nevertheless, you are on high alert. Recognize that your sensitivity is directly connected to your ability to tune in to everyone else's free-floating anxiety.

Relationships
You get a multitude of opportunities to test your newly minted determination to make sure your relationships hold space for you. Of course, this causes some consternation for the people in your life who wonder what happened to the old you, the one who was always so accommodating and understanding. Remind yourself that being compassionate isn't the same as being a doormat.

Career, Success, and Money
The desire to keep a low profile dominates your work life, and it's because you are fairly certain it's necessary so you can stay out of the line of fire. Something is happening behind closed doors. You can feel it. Just know it's not about you. But that doesn't mean you shouldn't follow your instincts.

Pitfalls and Potential Problems
Wow, if you could just bottle your nighttime dreams and your daydreams, you'd find life so much easier to navigate. No matter how complex, odd, weird, or wonderful they are, they illuminate your life in ways you can't explain. However, this month you need to be cautious about using them as an escape from all the sensitivity overwhelming you. You could end up overlooking something important.

Rewarding Days
11, 12, 23, 24

Challenging Days
15, 16, 21, 22

Pisces | March

Overall Theme

Your conscious mind feels like it's left town without you, making you wonder if you can get anything accomplished. Rather than chasing after it, turn to your inimitable intuition to guide you through a period of reframing, recalibrating, and refreshing the plans you were working on. This leads to a major breakthrough in solving an issue before it rears its ugly little head.

Relationships

You can see people talking. After all, their mouths are moving. But you haven't got a clue what they are saying. It's as if your capacity to comprehend words no longer functions. The irony is that you are bombarded by images that tell you what you need to know. Strange but true. The challenge comes in how to respond. Best to tell everyone your brain is short-circuiting and you'll get back to them later.

Career, Success, and Money

The only thing that really interests you is playing around in your head, following all those fascinating intuitive bread crumbs that keep popping up. Of course, this is a natural state of affairs for you, so it doesn't keep you from doing your job. It just means your body is present but not your consciousness.

Pitfalls and Potential Problems

Make sure you put in place the necessary checks and balances that ensure you take care of the practical details of daily life. Your imagination is on fire and the outer world feels like a bit of a drag. Some of this is directly connected to your fear that life is about to get a little too real as Uranus moves into Taurus, asking you to change your relationship to the physical world.

Rewarding Days

10, 11, 27, 28

Challenging Days

5, 6, 17, 18

Pisces | April

Overall Theme

Not sure which inner promptings you should follow, you find yourself at something of an impasse. Which is different from indecision. Do you shore up your own sense of self-worth by taking practical steps to manifest a long-term dream, or do you give your time and energy to support joint endeavors? Well, you can certainly find a way to do both. Just remember that your number-one priority is *your* dream.

Relationships

Don't worry if it feels like you're slipping back into old patterns because you want to tend to the needs of others. You can't expect to change life-long default positions overnight. See this as an opportunity to take the next step in your growth by letting others know you need their support while being there to give them some much-needed inspiration.

Career, Success, and Money

You find yourself on the brink of taking a huge risk, so you start looking for ways to distract yourself. Enter your work environment, where there's more than enough drama to do that, including a coworker who tries to persuade you to help them at the expense of doing your own job. Just say no. It's intensely liberating and it clears the way to take that risk.

Pitfalls and Potential Problems

This is definitely a year for taking your dreams outside of your imagination and moving them into the physical realm. And it is so scary, largely because you've been told again and again that what's done is better than what's imagined. One is real, and the other fantasy. It's time to recognize that everything begins as a spark of inspiration so you can take at least one of yours to the next level.

Rewarding Days

1, 2, 6, 7

Challenging Days

9, 10, 17, 18

Pisces | May

Overall Theme

Much to your surprise, you are not as willing to negotiate with others as usual. You want what you want when you want it. Rather than chastising yourself, understand it's time for you to stick to your desires, your plans, your needs. Hence the unexpected lack of interest in anything not directly connected to your own well-being.

Relationships

If anyone dares to suggest that you are being selfish, ignore the comment. It's the best course of action, because there's no way to persuade them they are wrong, nor do you need to explain your choices or how you live your life. What they are doing is attempting to control you, pure and simple. By not engaging, you leave space for a different conversation to take place.

Career, Success, and Money

The timing is good to put your plans and propositions in front of people who can help you take the next steps toward successfully manifesting them. You are finally prepared to answer any and all questions because you've thought of every eventuality. But before you schedule those meetings, practice your presentation a couple of times. That way you are completely prepared.

Pitfalls and Potential Problems

Your imagination is continually pouring out possibilities of every variety. And, of course, you know which ones are actually viable. The issue for you is that you always get so caught up in everyone else's responses and opinions that you lose sight of your original vision. This results in you dismissing your own creative impulses, which can be quite damaging to your self-worth. Time to honor yourself first.

Rewarding Days
17, 18, 26, 27

Challenging Days
6, 7, 14, 15

Pisces | June

Overall Theme

You are the epitome of confidence—in yourself, in your ideas, in your plans. All systems are a go and you are so excited. You feel this is your moment, the one you've been dreaming about for a very long time. And then the obstacles start cropping up. Don't panic. Take a deep breath. Find solutions. It's all just a question of a little tinkering and timing, nothing else.

Relationships

Your optimism and exuberance spill over into your relationships, bringing a whole new group of people into your life as well as refreshing your connections with those closest to you. Suddenly you are in high demand and your social life is booming. Enjoy it. Have fun. You really deserve to be the center of attention.

Career, Success, and Money

There will be many times in June when you wonder if all your efforts to make your dreams come true are a waste of time. Fortunately, you have enough sense not to prolong the uncertainty or amplify the fear. You realize you are not being stymied, just challenged. And you are definitely ready for that.

Pitfalls and Potential Problems

The biggest hurdle this month is confronting your willingness to walk away from your dreams if the going gets a little tough. It's happened many times, and not because you lack faith, optimism, or desire, but because you are not always very adept at handling the external world and because your circuits get overloaded so easily. After all, you are so very psychically sensitive. This combination is almost lethal in its capacity to unnerve you and completely knock you off course. But something shifts inside and you stand your ground.

Rewarding Days

13, 14, 22, 23

Challenging Days

11, 12, 25, 26

Pisces | July

Overall Theme

This is an intensely emotional month for the entire planet, so you need to take steps to protect yourself emotionally and psychically, whether it's through meditation, sitting under a tree, taking a vacation, finding new and different ways to have fun, listening to music, etc. It's the best way to keep your focus on nourishing yourself and refraining from turning yourself into a psychic garbage dumpster.

Relationships

Be very picky about who you hang out with for the following reasons. First, you are cranky and you don't have much patience for listening to anyone complain about anything. Second, you are moving mountains inside you and it doesn't leave you with much energy to support anyone else. Third, you just want to relax and enjoy life. Life doesn't always have to be about heavy lifting.

Career, Success, and Money

Forget frugality or denying yourself what you want. Spend money on something that truly brings you joy. You definitely need a whole lot of that after several months of navigating work issues, pushing yourself to take risks, and redefining what success really is for you.

Pitfalls and Potential Problems

It feels like everything happening on the planet is making a pit stop in your consciousness. You are not amused, nor should you be. The time has come to learn how to either shut off your intake valve or create ways to let things pass through you. This requires you to acknowledge that you actively choose to play this role. Once you do that, it won't be difficult to give up feeling responsible for the whole planet and everyone on it.

Rewarding Days

6, 7, 20, 21

Challenging Days

4, 5, 17, 18

Pisces | August

Overall Theme

It's like someone turned the light on in the attic of your consciousness and you simply can't ignore all the dusty, archaic things you've stored there. At first it's fun poking around, but then you energetically stumble across memories and feelings that are deeply painful and difficult. Refrain from diving headlong into this quagmire. Honor what you feel and let it go.

Relationships

Loving people can be such a challenge sometimes, and this is one of those times. Someone you adore deeply asks you to support them in something that violates your principles. So you politely decline to help them and they turn on you. You are at a loss about what to do next. That's because you think you need to fix this—but you don't. Just love them with your heart and soul as you always do and carry on.

Career, Success, and Money

Work is insane. Truly. That would be fine if what you were doing brought you any sense of accomplishment, but what's on your plate is completely and utterly mundane. Welcome to the nitty-gritty of making your dreams come true. It is necessary, and right now there's no one else to do it but you. Recognize how important it is for you to lay this groundwork, and that will inspire you.

Pitfalls and Potential Problems

How can you make peace with the reality that you always feel at odds with what the rest of the world considers to be normal? That's the question at the heart of all the issues that present themselves throughout August. Perhaps you don't have to. Perhaps you need to embrace being you without worrying about whether or not you are in sync. That's just a red herring. Being you isn't about what's usual.

Rewarding Days

6, 7, 30, 31

Challenging Days

1, 2, 23, 24

Pisces | September

Overall Theme

Be prepared to receive a lot of unsolicited advice. It's as if no one else has anything better to do than weigh in on whatever aspect of your life catches their attention. What to do? There is no one-size-fits-all solution. First and foremost, listen to your intuition. If you feel it's an exercise in criticism, shut it down politely. If you feel it's a real attempt to support you, listen.

Relationships

You find yourself asking what you want from your relationships, which creates something of an internal shock wave. Why? Recognize that just asking the question constitutes a huge shift in how you live your life, which means finding the answer or answers might take a while because it's complex and there's a lot to sift and sort through first. In the end, it's definitely worth it.

Career, Success, and Money

It's business as usual, with no major challenges or ups and downs, in the usual day-to-day world of work. However, you are busy mulling over whether there isn't something else you could be doing to further your career aspirations. The answer is likely to be no. You've done quite a lot in the last few months to create more success. Now it's just a waiting game.

Pitfalls and Potential Problems

Be careful not to exhaust yourself with a constant internal litany of what-ifs. Of course, there's always something you could have done differently in any given situation, including the current major changes you are making to your life. Respect your decisions. Trust that you can handle the consequences of those decisions. That's really the only thing you can do unless you want to make yourself crazy.

Rewarding Days

3, 4, 7, 8

Challenging Days

16, 17, 24, 25

Pisces | October

Overall Theme

You really do need to get away from it all, and probably by yourself. There's been so much activity in your life since the beginning of the year, and you just need some time to breathe, plus some space to do it in. So don't go anywhere crowded. A spa or somewhere quiet by water will do the trick.

Relationships

It might look to others like you are in something of a funk. Not true. You aren't in the mood for companionship, whether it's casual hanging out or deep soul-searching conversations. You are taking a vacation from people. No talking, no interacting, no socializing. Just the pleasure of your own company so you can regenerate and rejuvenate.

Career, Success, and Money

Things continue to intensify in this area of your life because your focus is split between the daily requirements of your job and your dream project. The latter hits a critical stage of its development, causing you to panic ever so slightly. You're certain this is the point at which it's going to vaporize. Stay true to your vision and all is well.

Pitfalls and Potential Problems

You aren't sure how you ended up feeling like a two-ton truck ran you down. Every fiber of your being is deeply fatigued but excited at the same time. Well, that combination is bound to overstimulate you because both your body and your consciousness aren't exactly sure how to deal with what appears to be a paradox. Don't waste your time analyzing the situation. Go on a retreat.

Rewarding Days

9, 10, 23, 24

Challenging Days

17, 18, 30, 31

Pisces | November

Overall Theme

Well rested and reinvigorated, you put all your energy into making even deeper changes to the way you live your life. This results in a full-scale review of not just where you've been but where you're going. Much to your surprise, this turns out to be a truly satisfying experience. You emerge with a lot of appreciation and gratitude for the path that led you to this moment in time.

Relationships

The steps you initiated earlier in the year to redefine who you are in your relationships lead you to issue a personal declaration of independence to those closest to you. In a quiet, loving, yet firm manner, you let them know how hard it's been to feel you must always acquiesce to what others want. Because you only talk about your experience rather than interpreting what their intentions were, you are heard.

Career, Success, and Money

Good things happen on all fronts. Your daily responsibilities are reduced because the powers that be are truly impressed with the way your dream project is progressing and they want to be sure it gets the attention it deserves. Plus they want to know if you have any other brilliant ideas. You do. But keep them to yourself for now. That way you can focus on this stage of your dream project.

Pitfalls and Potential Problems

Temptation comes in two forms. First, now that you are rested, you think it's fine to repeat the very behavior that exhausted you. It's time to realize that you don't need to be on high alert to make sure things work out. Second, the choice to share your feelings about your relationships triggers the desire to play the blame game. Being a victim isn't a healthy way to make a new start.

Rewarding Days

6, 7, 20, 21

Challenging Days

13, 14, 26, 27

Pisces | December

Overall Theme

Your connection to time is, well, a little bent, so it tends to speed by without you really noticing. However, when you look up and realize it's almost the end of 2019, it truly knocks you off balance—not because you don't know what you did, but because you've accomplished more than you thought possible yet you still need more time.

Relationships

Overcome by both sentimentality and gratitude, you seek out everyone who means anything to you. This fills you with joy and them with a feeling that you do appreciate them. Of course, it never occurred to you that they might be baffled by the changes you decided to make. Now, it's clear that you are still that unconditionally-loving, tender-hearted person they can count on. You just have a new set of boundaries.

Career, Success, and Money

Not content to rest on the strength of what you initiated this year, you are busy planning your next success. Relax. Let things percolate for a bit. Besides, all you have now is an inspiration, rather than a full-blown concept. Play with it rather than trying to manifest this vision before its time.

Pitfalls and Potential Problems

As 2019 comes to a close, do an inventory of the things you intended to do but didn't have time for this year. Then take care of them so they aren't hanging over your head as you begin the new year. You need a clean slate, because life isn't going to slow down in the least in 2020 and things left undone tend to be a drain and a drag, which you definitely don't need.

Rewarding Days

3, 4, 17, 18

Challenging Days

13, 14, 25, 26

Pisces Action Table

These dates reflect the best—but not the only—times for success and ease in these activities, according to your Sun sign.

	JAN	FEB	MAR	APR	MAY	JUN	JUL	AUG	SEP	OCT	NOV	DEC
Move				1, 2		16, 17						3, 4
Start a class		3, 4	12, 13		12, 13						11, 12	
Seek coaching/ counseling								4, 5		9, 10		
Ask for a raise	10, 11							30, 31			28, 29	
Get professional advice		19, 20					27, 28					17, 18
Get a loan	13, 14				1, 2				28, 29			
New romance				10, 11		22, 23			3, 4			
Vacation			6, 7				11, 12			27, 28		

GET MORE AT LLEWELLYN.COM

Visit us online to browse hundreds of our books and decks, plus sign up to receive our e-newsletters and exclusive online offers.

- • Free tarot readings • Spell-a-Day • Moon phases
- • Recipes, spells, and tips • Blogs • Encyclopedia
- • Author interviews, articles, and upcoming events

GET SOCIAL WITH LLEWELLYN

Find us on  🐦 @LlewellynBooks

www.Facebook.com/LlewellynBooks

GET BOOKS AT LLEWELLYN

LLEWELLYN ORDERING INFORMATION

Order online: Visit our website at www.llewellyn.com to select your books and place an order on our secure server.

Order by phone:
- • Call toll free within the US at 1-877-NEW-WRLD (1-877-639-9753)
- • We accept VISA, MasterCard, American Express, and Discover.
- • Canadian customers must use credit cards.

Order by mail:
Send the full price of your order (MN residents add 6.875% sales tax) in US funds plus postage and handling to: Llewellyn Worldwide, 2143 Wooddale Drive, Woodbury, MN 55125-2989

POSTAGE AND HANDLING
STANDARD (US):
(Please allow 12 business days)
$30.00 and under, add $6.00.
$30.01 and over, FREE SHIPPING.

INTERNATIONAL ORDERS,
INCLUDING CANADA:
$16.00 for one book, plus $3.00 for each additional book.

Visit us online for more shipping options. Prices subject to change.

FREE CATALOG!

To order, call
1-877-
NEW-WRLD
ext. 8236
or visit our
website

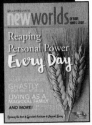